Women in Industry

A Study in American Economic History

Edith Abbott

VERNON PRESS

First published in 1909 by D. Appleton and Company. This
edition Copyright © 2013 by Vernon Art and Science Inc. 1000 N
West Street, Suite 1200, Wilmington, Delaware 19801, United
States

www.vernonpress.com
Vernon Press is an imprint of Vernon Art & Science Inc.

ISBN 978-1-62273-000-1

Printed in Spain.

Contents

List of Tables

Introductory Note

The work of women for wages under a competitive organization of industry presents a problem of compelling interest. Women have, of course, always worked. The invention of the processes essential to orderly and secure group life was the contribution of primitive[1] women. Under the organization of labor developed by the Greeks and Romans;[2] in the workshops of the monasteries and convents of the Middle Ages;[3] as members of the crafts in which they took an honorable position,[4] governed by the regulations as to hours, wages, fines, apprentices, and promotion, identical with those under which men worked; in the English "factories" of the fourteenth century;[5] in the domestic or cottage system of industry which prevailed largely in England prior to the industrial revolution;[6] in the work of household production in America during the colonial and early republican period; under every industrial system, women have had a recognized position.

The dignity and honor of their relation to their work have varied with the dignity and honor with which they have been gener-

---

[1] Bücher, "Industrial Evolution," Chaps. I, II; Thomas, "Sex and Society," p. 126; Pearson, "Chances of Death," ii, 49. "The civilization of woman handed down a mass of useful custom and knowledge; it was for after generations to accept that and eradicate the rest. When I watch today the peasant women of Southern Germany and of Norway toiling in the house and field, while the male looks on, I do not think the one a downtrodden slave of the other. She appears to me the bearer of a civilization to which he has not yet attained. She may be the fossil of the mother age, but he is a fossil of a still lower stratum — barbarism pure and simple."

[2] Leroy-Beaulieu, "Le travail des femmes au dix-neuvieme siecle," p. 5.

[3] Eckenstein, "Woman Under Monasticism," Chap. VII.

[4] For example, in Paris, see Dixon, "Craftswomen in the Livre des Metiers," *Economic Journal*, v, 209.

[5] Taylor, "The Modern Factory System," p. 53.

[6] Taylor, pp. 57, 68; Toynbee, "Industrial Revolution," p. 63.

ally regarded. When they were slaves their occupation assumed a servile character; and it may be that the dishonor often apparently attaching to labor grows out of the fact that production was first exclusively in the hands of women.[7] On the other hand, under some systems the position of women in relation to their work has been one of real power In such a system as characterized American life during the earliest period described in the following study, when goods were made in and for the household from raw materials furnished by the household, the woman determined what should be made and how the product should be distributed. In fact the extent to which the spending function is conceded her by the family group today when the family has become simply a center of consumption, is a survival of the control which was hers when the family was still a producing unit.

Women have not, however, always worked for wages. Without dwelling upon the fact that, under simple forms of organization, the return for labor is often combined with payment for the use of tools and for materials, it might be noted that in the period just preceding the introduction of the factory system both in England and America, production was often so carried on as to allow the return for the labor of the entire family to be collected by the head of the family who had the legal right to the time and earnings both of his wife and of his minor children.[8] The family wage was common then, and it was determined in part by the standard of the group, and in part by the bargaining power of the man who collected it. Today there is a group wage in so far as various classes are paid "supplementary wages", but these are determined not by the bargaining power of the man, but often by the helplessness of the woman and of the minor children who have become the apparent collectors of their own wages.

Objections are, therefore, raised and difficulties encountered, due not to any novel industrial activity on the part of women, but to the disturbance created by their participation in the bargaining function. For they have been on the whole poor bargainers. They have found great difficulty in adjusting themselves to the attitude of modern business. They have never accepted the ideal of giving as little and

---

[7]Veblen, "Barbarian Status of Women," *American Journal of Sociology*, iv, 501.

[8]See in a later discussion, for illustrations of the way in which the man collected the wage for the group well into the nineteenth century and even after the members of the group had followed their work to the factory.

getting as much as they can. They respond as slightly to the appeal
to sell their labor as dearly as possible as they do to the exhortation
to spend their wages in buying as cheaply as they can.[9]

From this helplessness which characterizes women workers in bargaining spring many difficult problems. There is the question of their
inability to secure right conditions under which to do their work, to
limit the amount and duration of their work so as to maintain their
own health and that of their children. From this weakness arises
the necessity on the part of the community of assuming control over
the wage contract so as to protect women wage earners from un-
due exploitation and to safeguard its own future. The length of the
working day, the prohibition of night work, the provision of certain
decencies in working conditions, the relation of marriage to work, the
relation of the work of mothers to the life of children, the payment
of like wages for like work, these become questions of vital concern
to the community, the subject of widespread interest and of popular
agitation.

But although problems involving interests of such importance
deserve thoughtful discussion on the basis of complete information,
such treatment as the subject of women's work has hitherto received
in this country has been for the most part either emotional and prej-
udiced or a presentation in official reports of elaborately compiled
but unexplained statistical data. But facts as to present conditions
are of little service unless supplemented by careful and accurate analysis and by a correct understanding of the historical development of
which present conditions are the sequence.

Of first importance is the effect of the factory system on the opportunities of women in connection with the work they have always
shared. Since, serious as is the situation in which the day's work
is too long, or is done by night when women should sleep, instead
of by day which was meant for work, is done under bad conditions,
or is excessive in the light of the fact that the worker is a mother;
more serious still is that in which there is no work at all. For women
must work. They must work, because to be deprived of the right to
exercise "lordship over things" is to be denied a satisfaction essential

---

[9]It is a fact of interest that women wish to pay a "fair price", and they will,
for example, often buy a more expensive garment in the belief that it has been
made under fairer conditions than one which is cheap. This is frequently the
only means by which they are able to console themselves for their helplessness
as buyers or quiet their conscience for not assuming control over the productive
process.

to full human life. And they must work for wages. There is today no other access possible for the self-respecting woman to that flow of wealth which is at once the product of the labor and the source of satisfaction for all members of the community. The following study is, therefore, offered in the belief that it has real significance for those concerned with the problem of wage-earning women.

It has, however, a wider interest than this. A field in American economic history hitherto substantially untouched is here disclosed. Moreover, with the history of the growth of our great manufacturing industries for the most part still unwritten, the difficulties in the way of such an inquiry as the present are very great. But there is for the same reason greater value in the contribution which is made by this study to our knowledge of early economic conditions and relationships, of the technical development of the industries discussed, of early governmental policy relating to industry, as well as to our correct understanding of the industrial opportunity of the working woman of an earlier time and the progress which she has made up to the present day.

S.P. BRECKINRIDGE.

The University of Chicago

Preface

The following investigation was begun in 1905 when I published jointly with Dr. S. P. Breckinridge, of the University of Chicago, with whom I was then studying; an analysis of recent census statistics dealing with the employment of women. The result of our statistical inquiry was to show that, while the present tendency was toward an increase in gainful employment among women, that increase had been only normal, considering the rate of increase in the population, in the group of industrial occupations designated in the census as "manufacturing and mechanical pursuits" while there had been a disproportionately large increase only in the occupational group "trade and transportation." With nearly a million and a half women in our manufacturing industries and no recent influx into the occupations in this group, it was evident that the presence of women in our mills and factories was not a new phenomenon; and it became a matter of interest to discover just how long and how far women had been an industrial factor of importance.

The employment of women, therefore, became a problem in economic history, and although we realized that, at a time when so many questions concerning the working woman were pressing for immediate solution, it might well seem academic and impractical to deal only with her past, we believed that a truthful account of that past might throw some light on present-day problems.

This volume is, therefore, an attempt to carry on the investigation from the point at which it was left four years ago. The continuation of the study was made possible in the first instance through the assistance of the Carnegie Institution of Washington, and to the late Carroll D. Wright, then at the head of the Department of Economics and Sociology, grateful acknowledgment must be made.

I have already said that Dr. Breckinridge and I began this study as a joint investigation, and although my absence from Chicago for three years made it impossible for us to continue the work together, I have throughout that time worked under her general direction and I have had always the benefit of her generous and sympathetic counsel. It has been my privilege during the past year to be again closely associated with her, so that in the work of revision and in preparation for the press, these chapters have been constantly submitted to her for criticism. It is not possible for me to say just what or how much the book owes to her, but without her assistance it would never have been written.

It is a pleasure also to acknowledge the debt which I owe to two other friends, to Miss Clara B. Collet, M.A. Honorary Fellow of University College, London, and senior investigator of women's industries in the Board of Trade (Labour Department), and to Dr. Frances Gardiner Davenport of the Department of Historical Research in the Carnegie Institution of Washington.

To Miss Collet I am indebted, not for direct help in connection with the preparation of these chapters, but, in common with all students of the history and statistics of women's employment, for the invaluable work which she has done in this field. Four years ago, in our first published study, Dr. Breckinridge and I made public acknowledgment of the stimulus and help we had received from a study of Miss Collet's reports to the Board of Trade on the "Employment of Women and Girls." Not only for these but for her reports on the same subject prepared for the Royal Commission on Labour as well as for her earlier investigations in connection with the preparation of Booth's "Life and Labour of the People," and for her other brilliant and suggestive studies of women's work, all later students of the subject are under obligation to her.

The debt to Miss Davenport is of quite another sort, for her own studies have been in a more remote field of history. But it has been my privilege, at different times, to submit several of these chapters to her for criticism, and the book does, therefore, embody some of her suggestions. It has, moreover, been a constant source of reassurance, during the four years in which this volume has been in preparation to know that she believed the subject worthy of investigation as a neglected chapter in our economic history. A large part of the material presented in this book has appeared from time to time since 1906 in the form of a series of articles in the Journal of Political

Economy, and acknowledgment should be made to the editors for their courtesy in placing this material again at my disposal. While it has been in large part revised and rewritten, chapters VII and VIII are reprinted substantially as they appeared. I have also to thank the editors of the American Journal of Sociology and of the Publications of the Association of Collegiate Alumnae for kindly allowing me to use again some of the material published in their magazines.

E.A., Hull House, Chicago,

October 1, 1909.

Chapter I - Introduction

Public opinion in this country has been recently concerned with
the increase in gainful employment among women, and misappre-
hension has arisen from a failure to understand the complexity of
the problem; for the employment of women presents not one question but many questions. There is, for example, the familiar problem of domestic service which is, numerically, the most important
women's occupation. Quite different problems appear in connection
with agriculture and the other extractive occupations such as mining and smelting. In the professions there are still to face the old
questions of restriction of opportunity, of equal work for unequal
pay, as well as the new and larger question of the way in which new
power acquired by women through the removal of educational and
social barriers may be most easily turned to social ends.

In the group of occupations, including stenography, typewriting,
bookkeeping, and salesmanship, which are connected not with the
industrial but with the business organization of the day, there is a
long series of problems of which perhaps the most pressing is the
effect of the pin-money worker who makes of her occupation a "par-
asitic trade" And finally, there is the question of the employment of
women in industrial occupations, about which there is some prejudice and a good deal of misunderstanding.

An increase, therefore, in gainful employment among women becomes a distinct question for each of these several groups. "While it
is true that the public mind does, unconsciously perhaps, differen-
tiate them, this is done for the most part illogically and unscientifi-
cally. With regard to the number of women entering two of the five

1

occupational groups, agriculture, in which the women employed are chiefly the negro women of the South, and domestic service, public opinion has little concern. There is no fear of a disproportionate increase in either of them. But it is, on the other hand, generally assumed that the number of gainfully employed women has increased alike in the professions, in "trade and transportation," and in manufacturing industries. The professional woman and the woman commercially employed are, however, almost exclusively characteristic of the present day, while the woman in industry is older than the factory system itself. In the first half of the nineteenth century, at a time when educated and uneducated women alike worked in mills and factories, the employment of women in the professions or in clerical positions was comparatively rare. As late as 1855, for example, the employment of women as clerks was unusual. An article in *Hunt's Merchant's Magazine* for that year called attention to the "employment of ladies as clerks in stores" as an item of special interest, and a contemporary newspaper commented as follows: "The New York *Times* is earnestly advocating the employment of females as clerks in stores — particularly all retail dry goods stores. It is an employment for which they are well fitted, and would properly enlarge their sphere of action and occupation and it is a business that they can do better than men. ... It would give employment to a great many young ladies, and would be degrading no one willing to earn a living."

Between the year 1870, when the census first presented statistical data on the subject, and the year 1900, the percentage which women formed of the total number of persons employed in "professional service" had increased from 1.6 per cent to 10.5 per cent, in "trade and transportation" from 24.8 per cent to 43.2 per cent, in the manufactures group from 13 per cent to 19 per cent.[10] Census statistics for the last decade of the nineteenth century make more clear, perhaps, the fact that in recent years the increase in gainful employment among women has not been in the industrial group. A study of the two tables given below will make this point more clear. The tables show the number of women and the number of

---

[10]This is the increase according to the Census of Occupations. According to the Census of Manufactures it would be from 16 per cent to 19 per cent. The former percentages are used here for the sake of uniformity since those for the other occupational groups can be obtained only from Census of Occupations. But those from the Census of Manufactures are believed to be more reliable. On this point, however, see Appendix B.

men employed in the five large occupational groups of the census classification in 1890 and in 1900. The tables also make possible a comparison not of absolute numbers and percentages alone, but of the number of persons in each ten thousand of the total number of persons over ten years of age who were employed in these different groups of occupations in 1900 and 1890, and the resulting increases or decreases.

From these two tables it appears,[11] (1) that the most striking increases both for men and women are in the group "trade and transportation," (2) that for women three of the other groups — "professional service," "manufacturing and mechanical pursuits," "domestic and personal service" — show fairly equal gains and the group "agriculture" is not far behind; (3) that the increase in the number of men who are going into "manufacturing and mechanical pursuits" is greater than the increase in the number of women entering the same group; that is, 19 more women and 34 more men out of every ten thousand of each sex in the population went into the manufacturing group in 1900 than had entered in 1890. It should be pointed out that the percentage increase would be slightly larger for women than men, 27.7 against 24.1, but such percentages cannot, of course, be properly compared, for a comparatively small increase in a small number will show a larger percentage of increase than a much larger increase in a large number. For women, then, trade and transportation alone shows a disproportionate increase; it is into this group of occupations that the new recruits to the ranks of gainfully employed women have largely gone; and whatever the problem of women in industry may be, it is clearly not a new one within the last ten, or even the last thirty, years.

The point of departure today in most discussions regarding women in industry is the home. It is assumed that the presence of women in industrial life is a new phenomenon and one to be viewed with alarm. The employment of women, it is feared, will mean greater competition and ultimately the displacement of men. Because the labor of women is cheaper, the woman, it is said, will usurp the place of the breadwinner; and the home will be ruined. Much attention has been given in late years to the employment of women in our manufacturing establishments of the present day, to questions con-

---

[11]For a more elaborate discussion of this table, see an article on the "Employment of Women," Twelfth Census Statistics, by Sophonisba P. Breckinridge and Edith Abbott in the *Journal of Political Economy*, Vol. xiv, pp. 14-41.

Table 1: WOMEN ACROSS OCCUPATIONS, 1890-1900

CLASSES OF	WOMEN.		MEN.	
OCCUPATIONS	1900.	1890.	1900.	1890.
AGRICULTURE	977,336	769,845	9,404,429	8,378,603
PROFESSIONAL SERVICE	430,597	311,687	827,941	632,646
DOMESTIC AND				
PERSONAL SERVICE	2,095.449	1,667,651	3,485,298	2,553,161
TRADE AND				
TRANSPORTATION	503,347	228,421	4,263,617	3,097,701
MANUFACTURING AND				
MECHANICAL PURSUITS	1,312,668	1,027,928	5,772.641	4,650,540
ALL OCCUPATIONS	5,319,397	4,005,532	23,753,836	19,312,651
POPULATION OVER				
TEN YEARS	28,246,384	23,060,900	29,703,440	24,352,659

cerning the physical and moral surroundings under which they work, their wages, the length of the working day. But no attempt has as yet been made to deal with the historic background out of which these questions emerge; and upon the student of economic history, therefore, devolves the task of tracing out from the records of our industrial development, such an account of the working woman's past as may throw light on the problems of today.

The present study is, therefore, not an investigation into present conditions of women's work and wages, but an inquiry into the history and statistics of the employment of women in America. Without such a study it is impossible to examine properly certain fundamental questions relating to women's work. How far is the gainful employment of women, either in the home or away from it, peculiarly characteristic of the nineteenth century? Has the growth of our manufacturing industries provided a new field for the employment of women? Or has there only been an increase in the opportunity for work in those employments which have long existed? And has the result of it all been that what was formerly "men's work" has passed into the hands of women?

It is believed that an inquiry into the history of women's work and a consideration of the early attitude toward such work, together with a study of the statistics of their employment during the last century, may be worthwhile, not only as a contribution toward the history of an important subject, but because of the practical bearing

4

Table 2: EMPLOYMENT OF WOMEN ACROSS OCCUPATIONS, 1890-1990

CLASSES OF OCCUPATIONS	NUMBER OF WOMEN EMPLOYED PER 10,000 WOMEN OF AND ABOVE 10 YEARS OF AGE			NUMBER OF MEN EMPLOYED PER 10,000 MEN OF AND ABOVE 10 YEARS OF AGE			
	1900	1890	INCREASE	1900	1890	INCREASE	DECREASE
AGRICULTURE	346.0	333.8	2.2	3166.1	3440.5	...	274.4
PROFESSIONAL SERVICE	152.4	135.1	17.3	278.7	259.7	19.0	
DOMESTIC AND PERSONAL SERVICE	741.8	723.1	18.7	1173.3	1048.4	124.9	
TRADE AND TRANSPORTATION	178.1	99.0	79.1	1435.3	1272.0	163.3	
MANUFACTURING AND MECHANICAL PURSUITS	464.7	445.7	19.0	1943.4	1909.6	33.8	
ALL OCCUPATIONS	1883.2	1736.9	146.3	7997.0	7930.3	66.7	

5

it may have upon the problems connected with the employment of women today. Women's work is often considered too exclusively in its theoretical aspects. Statistics for the first half of the century are not brought into their proper relation with those of the latter half. The early attitude toward the employment of women is not only outgrown but forgotten. Moreover, attempts to discover how far women have taken the places of men as factory employees by a study of census statistics for the last few decades have been, and must necessarily be, futile; for that is merely touching in a superficial way a problem that is as old as the factory system itself.

It will appear that it is essential to any profitable discussion of women's work that a line of delimitation be drawn between questions concerning the employment of professional women and those relating to the employment of women in industry. While the problems of all gainfully employed women, whether professionally trained and educated or untrained and unskilled, are fundamentally interdependent, yet for many purposes they must be considered separate questions; and the working woman has undoubtedly been wronged in the past because of the pseudo-democratic refusal to recognize class distinctions in discussions of the woman question. Moreover, a failure to see important points of unlikeness has led, at times, to confusion in theory and to unfortunate practical results. It is, for example, a part of the history of the struggle for factory legislation in England that an unwillingness to grant that the working woman had peculiar grievances delayed the progress of very necessary reforms.[12]

It has, finally, been too often assumed that the conspicuous broadening of the field of opportunities and activities for educated women during the latter half of the nineteenth century has been a progress without class distinctions in which all women have shared alike. But the history of the employment of women in professional and industrial life has been radically different, and the fruits of that long struggle of the last century for what is perhaps nebulously described as "women's rights" have gone, almost exclusively, to the women of the professional group.

---

[12]See the chapter on "The Women's Rights Opposition," Hutchins and Harrison, "History of Factory Legislation," pp. 183, 184.

Chapter II - The Colonial Period

A STUDY of the relation of the woman wage earner to the factory system in this country involves some preliminary inquiry regarding her share in the work done under more primitive methods of production. Industrially we were a backward nation and, for a considerable time after our political independence had been secured, we remained economically dependent upon England. At the close of the first decade of the nineteenth century development of our manufacturing industries had scarcely begun.

A detailed survey of the field of employment for women during this earlier period is impossible because of the scarcity of records. Moreover, such a study would be on the whole unprofitable. It has, however, seemed justifiable to present the following body of material dealing with the employment of women during the seventeenth and eighteenth centuries, because though somewhat fragmentary, covering a considerable period of time dealing with a large and miscellaneous group of occupations, and confined chiefly to a single section of the country, it is believed to contribute to an understanding of the relation of women to the later industrial system.

Our primary interests during this early period were agriculture and commerce, and there was very little field for the industrial employment either of I men or women. Such manufactures as were carried on in these early centuries were chiefly household industries and the work was necessarily done in the main by women. Indeed, it would not be far wrong to say that, during the colonial period, agriculture was in the hands of men, and manufacturing, for the most part, in the hands of women. Men were, to be sure, some-times weavers, shoemakers, or tailors; and here and there women of notable executive ability, such as the famous Eliza Lucas of South Carolina,[13] managed farms and plantations.

It is of interest to note, too, in this connection that in the case of land allotments in early New England, women who were heads of families received their proportion of planting land; and in Salem, Plymouth, and the Cape Cod towns women could not get enough land. Although spinsters did not fare so well, it is a matter of record that in Salem even unmarried women were at first given a small allotment. The custom of granting "maid's lotts," however, was soon discontinued in order to avoid "all presedents and evil events of graunting lotts unto single maidens not disposed of."[14] In accordance with this ungallant decision, the "Salem Town Records" show one "Deborah Holmes refused Land being a maid but hath four bushels of corn granted her . . . and would be a bad presedent to keep house alone." In 1665, in Pennsylvania, 75 acres of land were promised to every female over fourteen years of age, and while this does not mean that the management of the lands was necessarily in their hands in many cases this must have happened.

But although daughters and wives often helped at home with what was rather rough work, cutting wood, milking, and the like, and the girl in service did similar "chores," it was not customary to employ women to any large extent for regular farm work. This was, of course, in contrast to the practice in England and on the Con-tinent, where women, at this time, were regularly hired as reapers, mowers, and haymakers. An early account of Virginia says with regard to this point that "the women are not, as is reported, put into the ground to worke but occupie such domestique employments as in England. . . . Yet some wenches that are not fit to be so employed are put into the ground."[15] It seems, therefore, clear that, with the exception of such cases as have been reported, the work on the farms was done by men.

Women on the other hand, were, for the most part engaged in the domestic cares of the household, which included at that time the

---

[13] See Harriott Ravenel, "Life of Eliza Pinckney."

[14] These details are found in Professor Herbert B. Adam's interesting study in the "Johns Hopkins University Studies," First Series, vols, is-x, "Allotments of Land in Salem to Men, Women and Maids," pp. 34, 35.

[15] Hammond, "Leah and Rachel" (London, 1656). Reprinted in Force, *Tracts*, iii.

manufacture within the home of a large proportion of the articles needed for household use. And besides the occupations of a domestic kind, there were, in the seventeenth and eighteenth centuries, various other employments open to them which it may be worth while to notice without attempting to apply the classification growing out of the more complex organization of the present day. An attempt will be made, therefore, to give a brief account of all gainful occupations in which women were engaged without attempting to classify them.

One of the oldest of these was the keeping of taverns and "ordinaries." In 1643, the General Court of Massachusetts granted Goody Armitage permission to "keepe the ordinary, but not to drawe wine,"[16] and throughout this century and the next the Boston town records show repeated instances of the granting of such licenses to women. In 1669, for example, "Widdow Snow and Widdow Upshall were 'approved of to sell beere and wine for the yeare ensuinge and keep houses of publique entertainment'," and there are records of the granting of similar permissions to other women on condition that they "have a careful and sufficient man to manage the house." Such licenses were granted most frequently to widows, but occasionally to wives. Thus the wife of Thomas Hawkins was given permission to sell liquors "by retayle" only because of "the selectmen consideringe the necessitie and weake condition of her Husband."

Shopkeeping was another of the early gainful employments for women in this country. The "New Haven Colonial Records" contain a most interesting account of a woman shopkeeper who flourished for a time during the first half of the seventeenth century, and then became involved in serious difficulties because of her method of systematic overcharging. In 1643 an indignant customer appealed to the court, charging that he had "heard of the dearnes of her commodities, the excessive gaynes she tooke, was discouradged from proceedinge and accordingly bid his man tel her he would have none of her cloth." He asked the court to deal with her "as an oppressor of the commonweale' and offered ten specific charges; among them, "that she sold primmers at 9 penee a piece which cost but 4 pence here in New England" and that "she sold a peece of cloth to the two Mecars at 23s. 4d. per yard in wompom, the cloth cost her about 12s. per yard and sold when wompom was in great request."[17] It is of interest that Higginson refers to this employment for women in

---

[16]"Massachusetts Colonial Records," ii, 46.
[17]"New Haven Colonial Records," i, 174-176, 147.

asking patronage for "sister Wharton's two daughters to help forward their shop-keeping"; and, he adds significantly that they "are like to continue as ancient maids I know not how long, Sarah being 25 or 26 years old!"

Other kinds of business attracted women in this same period. The raising of garden seeds and similar products seems to have been a common occupation.[18] Women were sometimes shrewd traders and, often, particularly in the seaboard towns, venturesome enough to be speculators. An interesting example of the way in which women along the coast sometimes risked their savings is to be found in an old memorandum of one Margaret Barton which belongs to the year 1705 and is preserved in the Boston Public Library's collection of manuscripts. This woman, who claimed to have served a full apprenticeship in the trade of "chair frame making" and to have worked at it for a time, seems to have made quite a fortune for those days in "ventures at sea." She was, however, a rather disreputable person, for the "Boston Selectmen's Records" show that she was "warned out of town," and her testimony may not be altogether reliable.

Among the other gainful employments for women in this period which were not industrial might be mentioned keeping a "dame's school" which, though a very unremunerative occupation, was often resorted to.[19] There were, too, many notable nurses and midwives; in Bristol a woman was ringer of the bell and kept a meeting-house, and in New Haven a woman was appointed to "sweepe and dresse the meeting house every weeke and have 1s. a weeke for her pains." The common way, however, for a woman to earn her board and a few pounds a year was by going out to service. But it should be noted that the domestic servant in the seventeenth and eighteenth centuries was employed for a considerable part of her time in processes of manufacture and that, without going far wrong, one might classify this as an industrial occupation. A servant, for example, who was a good spinner or a good tailoress, was valued accordingly, and advertisements in eighteenth-century newspapers frequently mention this as a qualification.

---

[18] See, for example, advertisments in the *Boston Evening Post,* January 25, 1745; *Boston Gazette,* April 19, 1748; *New England Weekly Journal,* March 10, 1741.

[19] There is a record of a woman keeping such a school in New Haven before 1656. See Blake, "Chronicles of New Haven Green," p. 184; and see also Sewall, "History of Wobum," p. 52, for a further note on such work.

There remain, however, a number of instances, in which women were employed in and were even at the head of what might, strictly speaking, be called industrial establishments. A woman, for example, occasionally ran a mill, carried on a distillery, or even worked in a sawmill. The "Plymouth Colony Records" note in 1644 that "Mistress Jenny, upon the presentment against her, promiseth to amend the grinding at the mill, and to keep morters cleane, and baggs of come from spoyleing and looseing." At Mason's settlement at Piscataqua, "eight Danes and twenty two women" were employed in sawing lumber and making potash.[20] In 1693 a woman appears with two men on the pages of the "Boston Town Records" "desiring leave to build a slaughter house." But all of these seem to have been unusual employments.

There were, however, a great many women printers in the eighteenth century, and these women were both compositors and worked at the press. Several colonial newspapers were published by women and they printed books and pamphlets as well. Women were also employed in the early paper mills, where they were paid something like the equivalent of seventy-five cents a week and board.

Although there is no doubt of the fact that women were gainfully employed away from home at this time, such employment was quite unimportant compared with work which they did in their own homes.

In considering minor industrial occupations within the home we find that a few women were bakers[21] and some were engaged in similar work, such as making and selling of preserves or wine.[22] But the great majority of women in this group were employed in the manufacture of textiles, which in its broadest sense includes knitting, lacemaking, the making of cards for combing cotton and wool, as well as sewing, spinning and weaving.

Some women must have found knitting a profitable by-employment. Knit stockings sold for two shillings a pair, and occasionally for much more. One old account book records that "Ann" sold a "pare of stockens for 16s." Sewing and tailoring were standard occupations and were variously remunerated, — one woman made "shirts for the

---

[20] Weeden, "Social and Economic History of New England" 1, 108, and see p 310 for note of a woman who bolted flour for her neighbors.

[21] See, for example, Felt, "Annals of Salem," ii, 152; and see also the mention of Widow Gray in *Boston News Letter*, January 21, 1711.

[22] *The New England Weekly Journal*, July 5, 1731, advertises a shop kept by a woman for the delusive sale of preserves and similar products.

Indians" at eight-pence each, and "men's breeches" for a shilling and sixpence a pair, and in addition to this work of tailoring she taught school, did spinning and weaving for good pay, managed her house, was twice married and had fourteen children.[23]

Spinning and weaving, the processes upon which the making of cloth depended, absorbed a great deal of the time of the women and girls of the period. This work was not uniformly organized according to any one industrial system. In the seventeenth century, the work was household industry; the raw materials were furnished by the household and the finished product was for household use; but so far as any part of it was marketed or exchanged at the village store, the system became closely akin to handicraft. The commodity that was exchanged or sold belonged to the woman as a true craftswoman, the material had been hers and the product, until she disposed of it, was her own capital. When the article was sold directly to the consumer, as frequently happened, even the final characteristic of handicraft, the fact of its being "custom work," was present.[24]

With the expansion of the industry, especially in the latter half of the eighteenth century, a considerable part of the work was done more in the manner of what is known as the commission system. As yarn came to be in great demand, many women were regularly employed spinning at home for purchasers who were really commission merchants. These men sometimes sold the yarn but often they put it out again to be woven and then sold the cloth.

The most important occupations for women, therefore, before the establishment of the factory system, were spinning and weaving. It is impossible to make any estimate of the number of women who did such work, or of their earnings, of the proportion of homespun which went to market, or of what part of it, even when exchanged by the husband, was manufactured by the wife and daughters. But it is quite safe to say that spinning for the household was a universal occupation for women, and that the number of those who used this, and later, weaving also, as a ⨍gainful employment" was very large.

Every effort was made to encourage children as well as women to engage in this work. As early as 1640, a court order in Massachusetts

[23]See Temple and Sheldon, "History of Northfield," p. 163.

[24]This discussion of industrial systems follows in the main Bücher's analysis in his "Industrial Evolution" (Wickett's translation), Chap. IV; and the introductory chapter in Unwin, "Industrial Organization in the Sixteenth and Seventeenth Centuries," in which Bücher's interpretation is related to the industrial organization of today.

directed an inquiry into the possibilities of manufacturing cotton cloth, "what men and woemen are skilful in the braking, spinning and weaving .... what course may be taken for teaching the boyes and girles in all towns the spinning of the yarne." A similar order in 1656 called upon every town to see that the "woemen, boyes and girles .... spin according to their skill and ability." In the same year Hull recorded in his *Diary of Public Occurrences* that "twenty persons, or about such a number, did agree to raise a stock to procure a house and materials to improve the children and youth of the town of Boston (which want employment) in the several manufactures."

There is, in short, no lack of evidence to show that it was regarded as a public duty in the colony of Massachusetts to provide for the training of children, not only in learning, but in the words of one of the old court orders in "labor and other imployments which may bee profitable to the commonwealth."

This experiment in Boston, of which John Hull made record in 1656, was the prototype of many attempts in the following century to make children useful in developing the cloth manufacture. In 1720, the same town appointed a committee to consider the establishment of spinning schools for the instruction of the children of the town in spinning, and one of the Committee's recommendations was a suggestion that twenty spinning wheels be provided "for such children as should be sent from the alms house"; while a generous philanthropist of the time erected at his own expense the "Spinning School House," which ten years later he bequeathed to the town "for the education of the children of the poor." There was much enthusiasm over the opening of this school, and the women of Boston, rich and poor, assembled on the Common for a public exhibition of their skill while an "immense concourse assembled to encourage them."

In the latter half of the eighteenth century, more persistent efforts were made to further the cloth-making industry, and much interest was manifested in the possibility of making children useful to this end. Two Boston newspapers announced in 1750 that it was proposed "to open several spinning schools in this Town where children may be taught gratis," In the following year the "Society for Encouraging Industry and Employing the Poor" was organized with the double purpose of promoting the manufacture of woolen and other cloth, and of employing " our own women and children who axe now in a great measure idle."

The Province Laws of the session of 1753-54 provided for a tax on carriages for the support of a linen manufactory which, it was hoped, would provide employment for the poor. The preamble of the law recites that the "number of poor is greatly increased .... and many persons, especially women, and children, are destitute of employment and in danger of becoming a public charge."

Although this scheme did not realize all the hopes of its promoters the policy was not abandoned. In 1770, Mr. William Molineux of Boston petitioned the legislature to assist him in his plan for "manufacturing the children's labour into wearing apparel" and "employing young females from eight years old and upward in earning their own support;" and the public opinion of his day commended him because, in the words of a contemporary, "The female children of this town .... are not only useful to the community but the poorer sort are able in some measure to assist their parents in getting a livelihood."

It was claimed that, as a result of the work of the spinning schools, at least three hundred women and children had been thoroughly instructed in the art of spinning and that they had earned a large sum as wages. Domestic industries became increasingly important during this period, and children as well as women were employed in the various processes of manufacture carried on in the household. The report of Governor Moore of New York in 1767 to the Lords of Trade, said with regard to his province, "every home swarms with children who are set to spin and card."

Spinning, however, for some time before this had been an employment which was fairly steady and remunerative. The "Salem Records," for example, show that in 1685, one John Wareing was loaned money "to pay spinners." In the eighteenth century, as the cloth manufacture developed, there was "an increased and reasonably steady demand for yarn, so that the earnings of women spinners were by no means inconsiderable for those days. In some localities women were paid eight cents a day and their "keep" for spinning. In the Wyoming Valley, six shillings a week seems to have been the standard wage of a good spinner.

The best idea, however, of what home work in the different processes of cloth manufacture meant to the individual, can probably be gained by a study of some extracts from two old memorandum books, one belonging to the seventeenth and the other to the eighteenth century. The first of these is from an old account book of a Boston shopkeeper which has been preserved in the manuscript collections of the Boston Public Library and which records to the credit of Mrs. Mary Avery during the years 1685-89, the following items:

	£	s.	d.
By 2 yard $\frac{1}{2}$ of buntin att	?	?	?
By yard $\frac{1}{2}$ of ditto att 14d.	0	3	3
By 3 yards $\frac{1}{2}$ of half thick Kersey att 3s.3d.	0	10	6
A coverlid	1	0	0
By 16 yards of druggett att — and a broom 3d.	1	17	7
By 20 yds. black searge at 4s. 6d.	4	10	0
By 20 yds. searge at 3s. 6d.	3	3	4
By 3 yds. of buntin at 3d.	0	3	3
By 18$\frac{1}{2}$ yards searge at 3/8	3	7	10
By a hatt 5-6	0	5	6
By 53 yds. of cotton and linnin at 2-9	7	5	9
By $\frac{1}{2}$ doz. of ? a carpett 30	2	14	0
By 7 hatts att 5-sd	1	16	9
By 4 yds. searge att ?	2	4	0
By 2 ditto at ?	1	10	0
By 4 yds. black searge	0	18	0
By searge	8	19	4$\frac{1}{2}$
By 34 yds. searge at 3s. 6d.	6	7	6
By 24 yards searge at ?	6	0	0

It should be said with regard to this account of Mrs. Avery that two or three of the entries are in her husband's name, which may mean either that they worked together or that he merely acted for her.

The illegibility of some of the entries makes it impossible to state accurately the sum total of Mrs. Avery's credit account during these years, but fifty pounds would seem to be a very safe estimate. There is, moreover, every reason to believe that this is a fairly typical account and that such work was commonly done by women throughout this period. Other account books for the same period show similar credits and the book from which Mrs. Avery's account is quoted records the names of several other women and the payments made to them for the same kind of work, although no record compares with hers in interest.

The eighteenth century account which is selected as of special interest, is one taken from the credit side of a merchant's book for

Table 3: ACCOUNT OF THEODORA ORCUTT

1781.	£	s.	d.
September (1780 ?). By spinning 11 Runs at 7/4—3 runs 7d.	0	9	1
February 11. By spinning 4 Runs for handkerchiefs	0	2	4
March 2. By spinning 8 Runs linen yarn at 7d.	0	4	8
" By spinning 5 Runs tow yarn	0	2	8
" 6. By spinning 1 Run fine tow yarn at 7d.	0	0	7
"13. By spinning 2 Runs woolen yarn	0	1	4
April 8. By spinning 13 Runs tow yarn at 8d.	0	6	11
" By spinning 14 Runs linen yarn	0	9	4
" 29. By spinning 9½ Runs fine tow yarn at 8d.	0	6	4
CARRIED FORWARD	2	3	3

1781 and shows the earnings for the year of a "spinner," Theodora Orcutt[25], who was probably, judging from her purchases, a wife and mother.

This account of Theodora Orcutt is especially interesting because it shows how many different kinds of yarn had a marketable value at this time, and how much women must have earned by trading the product of their labor at country stores, as well as "by selling it directly to the professional weavers and the small "manufactories."

Another interesting example of the way in which women exchanged the cloth which they made to purchase other articles is the list of goods which one Susannah Shepard of Wrentham tendered in part payment for a chaise. The contract and the credit were as follows:[26]

"Agreed with Mrs. Susannah Shepard, of Wrentham, to make her a chaise for £55, she finding the harness, the wheels, leather for top and lining, remainder to be had in goods, at wholesale cash price, of her manufacture.

"(Signed) STEPHEN OLNEY."
PROVIDENCE, November 13, 1795.

---

[25]Temple, "History of Whately," pp. 71, 72. "A 'run' of yarn consisted of 20 knots. A 'knot' was composed of 40 threads, and a thread was 74 inches in length or once round the reel. A 'skein' of yarn consisted of 7 knots. An ordinary day's work was 4 skeins when the spinner carded her own wool; when the wool was carded by a merchant she could easily spin 6 in a day."
[26]See Bagnall, "Textile Industries of the United States," i, 173-174.

Table 4: ACCOUNT OF THEODORA ORCUTT - *Continued*

1781			£	s.	d.
		BROUGHT FORWARD	2	3	3
May	13	By spinning 2 Runs fine thread			
		for stockings at 8*d*.	0	1	4
"		By spinning 4 Runs tow yarn			
		at 8*d*.	0	1	4
"		By spinning 3 Runs coarse tow			
		yarn at 4/ (O.T.)	0	1	7
"		By spinning 3 Runs coarse linen			
		yard at 6d.	0	1	6
June	19	By spinning 8 Runs fine yarn for			
		Lawn.	0	8	0
"		By spinning 22 Runs coarse linen			
		yarn at 6*d*.	0	11	0
"	24	By spinning 2 Runs linen yarn			
		at 8*d*.	0	1	4
July	5	By spinning 10 Runs tow yarn			
		at 4/ (O.T.)	0	10	4
"	9	By spinning 3$\frac{1}{2}$ Runs tow yarn			
		at 4/ (O.T.)	0	1	10
"	11	By spinning 10 Runs tow yarn			
		at 6*d*. (O.T.)	0	5	0
"	25	By spinning 3 Runs fine linen			
		yarn at 8*d*.	0	2	0
"		By spinning 2 Runs coarse linen			
		yarn at *6d*.	0	1	0
"		By spinning 2 Runs fine tow			
		yarn at 8*d*.	0	1	4
"	31	By spinning 1 Run fine tow			
		yarn at 8*d*.	0	0	8
August	24	By spinning 19 Runs coarse linen			
		chain.	0	9	6
September	11	By spinning 9 Runs coarse tow			
		yarn.	0	1	0
"		By spinning 2 Runs sent to Miss Graves &			
		By spinning 4 Runs tow by Do 8 Runs tow.	0	6	5
		TOTAL	4	8	5

18

Received of Mrs. Shepard on account of chaise.

	£	s.	d.
5½ yards of thick-set at 4s. 8d.	1	5	8
2½ yards of velveret, at 4s. 8d.	0	10	8
2¾ yards of satin bever, at 4s. 8d.	0	12	10
1 yard & 2 nails of carpeting, at 3s.	0	3	4½
13 yards carpeting	1	18	7½
2 handkerchiefs	0	7	0
	4	18	2

There was, too, at this time no small amount of spinning and weaving done by women as custom work. In one New England community, near Northfield, Massachusetts, a weaver by the name of Olive Moffatt, who was a descendant of the early Scotch immigrants, was famous for such work. She was employed by most of the well-to-do families in town, and for many years her loom was considered indispensable for wedding outfits. Her linsey-woolsey cloth was considered inimitable for evenness of texture; and no one else in town could weave such patterns of linen damask. She also understood perfectly how to color fine lamb's wool yarns a beautiful shade of red with madder. The use of logwood on indigo was common enough, but a "good red" like Olive Moffatt's was difficult to obtain. Her earnings must have been very considerable for that period for she charged six pence and seven pence a skein for fine linen thread and three pence a skein or eight pence a "run" for fine woolen thread. In general the work of women spinners became more profitable after the early "manufactories" were started, but an account of these primitive establishments and of their women spinners is reserved for the succeeding chapter.

In England, weaving was a man's occupation, but "spinning and the preliminary processes of cleaning, carding and roving were conducted in the early times by the women and children"[27]. In this country, although professional weavers seem to have been most frequently men, yet it is clear that weaving was not an uncommon occupation for women even in the early days.[28] As the cloth manufacture developed, it became a very important one, and, as a later

---

[27] Chapman, "The Lancashire Cotton Industry," p. 12

[28] An extract from an old account book, for example, shows a credit to "Sarah Badkuk (Babcock) for weven and coaming wistid," Weeden, i, 301; see also ibid,, ii, 855. Mrs. Holt's receipt for £1 5s., 11d., for spinning is a relic in Bailey,

chapter will show, it continued to give employment to a great many women well into the nineteenth century.

It is perhaps scarcely necessary to say by way of summary, that the gainful employment of women in different processes of manufacture in their own homes,[29] was common enough in the seventeenth and eighteenth centuries. In so far as the early spinners and weavers furnished their own material and disposed of their own product as custom work, they were true craftswomen, belonging to a system that has not survived to any extent in modern industry. When the product was disposed of at a country store, one of the essential elements of handicraft, "custom work," was lacking. But under whatever system they worked, these "women in industry" were an important factor in the industrial life of the period.

As the gainful employment of women during this period grew so largely out of their household duties, such training as they received for their work was, in a sense, part of their general education. Although girls as well as boys were apprenticed when they were very young, the girl's indenture, unlike that of the boy, failed to specify that she was to be taught a trade. Early laws provided for the binding out of the children of the poor, and in some towns where the custom of bidding off the poor prevailed, children were put to live "with some suitable person" until they were fourteen, at which age they were to be bound until they became free by law, but it was especially specified that "if boys [they be] put to some useful trade."[30] The poor law of Connecticut provided that poor children whose parents allowed them to "live idly or misspend their time in loitering" were to be bound out, a "man child until he shall come to the age of twenty-one years; and a woman child to the age of eighteen years, or time of marriage."

The girl's indenture seems to have been for the most part a mere binding out to service. She was trained doubtless to perform the do-

---

"History of Andover," p. 578. In the Moravian settlement in Pennsylvania, the light weaving was entirely "woman's work" (Bagnall, i, 27), and Virginia cloth was described as "Having been made of cotton and woven with great taste by the women in the country parts." Bishop, "History of American Manufactures," i, 343.

[29] Two other household manufactures of which mention might be made here, are the making of lace and the manufacture of the hand cards used for combing cotton and wool; that is, the preparing the fiber for spinning. Both of these industries, however, will be referred to again in a later chapter.

[30] Capen, "Historical Development of the Poor Law of Connecticut," p. 55.

mestic tasks of the housewife, and sometimes it was agreed that she was to be taught "the trade, art, or mystery of spinning woollen and linen" or knitting and sewing as well. Her indenture might require, too, that she was to be "learned to read," which was again unlike that of the boy, who was also to be taught writing and occasionally even "cypering." The Province Laws of Massachusetts which provided that poor girls as well as boys were to be bound out contain the provision that "males [be taught] to read and write, females to read as they shall respectively be capable." It is of further interest with regard to the training of girls and boys that the General Court of Massachusetts desired that boys as well as girls be taught how to spin and that both girls and boys who were set to keep cattle in the various towns,[31] should "bee set to some other impliment withall, as spinning up on the rock, kniting, weveing tape."

It seems clear, however, that although girls were called apprentices during the colonial period, this did not mean that they were consciously given any industrial training.[32] But it should, perhaps, be repeated that the ordinary experience of the girl in the colonial household tended to make her skillful in spinning and probably in weaving as well, so that she received preparation for the two most important occupations of that time without any specialized training or the serving of a formal apprenticeship.

In concluding this discussion of the employment of women during the colonial period, some reference must be made to the attitude of the public opinion of that day toward their work. The early court orders providing for the employment of women and children were not prompted solely by a desire to promote the manufacture of cloth. There was, in the spirit of them, the Puritan belief in the virtue of industry and the sin of idleness. Industry by compulsion, if not by faith, was the gospel of the seventeenth century and not only court orders but Puritan ministers warned the women of that day of the

---

[31] See "Massachusetts Colonial Records," i, 294; ii, 9.

[32] Attention may be called in passing to the fact that after two hundred and fifty years the opportunity of an apprenticed girl has increased very slightly. An industrial census today shows a very considerable number of girl apprentices, but the great proportion of them are in dressmaking or millinery shops where they are general service girls, learning only what will make them temporarily useful in the shop and not what is necessary to make them dolled workers in the trade. See, for example, the Bulletin "Sex and Industry," issued by the Massachusetts Bureau of Labor in 1903, which showed (p. 210) that only eighty-seven girls were serving any apprenticeship except in dressmakers' and milliners' shops. The number of apprenticed boys was 5,320.

dangers of idle living.[33]Summary measures were sometimes taken to punish those who were idle. Thus the "Salem Town Records" show (December 5, 1643) "It is ordered that Margarett Page shall [be sent] to Boston Goale as a lazy, idle, loytering person where she may be sett to work for her liveinge." In 1645 and 1646 different persons were paid "for Margarett Page to keep her at worke." Among the charges against Mary Boutwell in the "Essex Records," 1640, is one "for her exorbitancy not working but liveinge idly."

Perhaps the best expression of the prevailing attitude toward the employment of women at that time is to be found in one of the Province Laws of Massachusetts Bay for the session of 1692-93. The law ordered that every single person under twenty-one must live "under some orderly family government," but added the proviso that "this act shall not be construed to extend to hinder any single woman of good repute from the exercise of any lawful trade or employment for a livelihood, whereunto she shall have the allowance and approbation of the selectmen . . . any law, usage or custom to the contrary notwithstanding."

It is not, therefore, surprising to find that, in 1695, an act was passed which required single women who were self-supporting to pay a poll tax as well as men.[34]That this attitude was preserved during the eighteenth century, the establishment of the spinning schools bears witness. There was, however, the further point that providing employment for poor women and children lessened the poor rates, and the first factories were welcomed because they offered a means of support to the women and children who might otherwise be "useless, if not burdensome, to society."

The colonial attitude toward women's work was in brief one of rigid insistence on their employment. Court orders, laws, and public subscriptions were resorted to in order that poor women might be saved from the sin of idleness and taught to be self-supporting.

---

[33]See Winthrop's reference to the sermon of a Boston minister in 1636 in "History of New England," i, 186.

[34]"'Province Laws," 1, 213: "All edngle women that live at their own hand, at two shillings each, except such as through age, or extream poverty . . . are unable to contribute towards the publick charge." Men, however, of sixteen years or upwards were rated "at four shillings per poll."

Chapter III - The
Period of Transition

The effort to establish manufacturing industries in this country made little progress until after the year 1808 when the restrictive effects of the Embargo and Non-Intercourse Acts began to be felt, and, as a result of the exclusion of imported goods, our own manufactures began to assume considerable proportions. Some necessary preliminary steps, without which this industrial expansion would have been difficult, had already been taken; and during the period which covered roughly the years from1760 to 1808 there had been an unmistakable advance in industrial organization. This period is, therefore, one of distinct interest in our economic history as marking the transition from the old domestic system of production to the modern factory system.

During this time, the so-called "industrial revolution" was taking place in England. Machines for carding and spinning had been invented and the old hand processes in the making of cloth had been superseded. More wonderful, however, than any of the inventions, was the steam engine of Watts, which, together with the new labor-saving machinery, rapidly transformed the textile industries. Great factory towns grew up in the industrial districts, and women and children went to the factories to tend the machines instead of carrying on the processes in their own homes.

Although we attempted to introduce the new machine system in this country, our progress was slow and laborious. England's ambition was to become the "workshop of the world" and her way to accomplish this seemed clear if a monopoly of these inventions could be secured. The exportation of any of the machinery used in manufacturing and the emigration of work people who had learned to operate the machines were alike prohibited. We were, therefore, cut off from profiting by the work of English inventors and we were greatly handicapped in making similar experiments for ourselves because of the lack of capital and the scarcity of skilled workmen here. After 1775, persistent attempts were made to build machines like those in use in England, but it was not until 1789 when Samuel Slater's first cotton mill was established in Rhode Island, that all of the machinery necessary for spinning was successfully installed and operated in this country.

But for nearly a quarter of a century before this mill of Slater's was established, attempts were being made to organize and extend the cloth-making industry by the old methods. Societies "for Encouraging Manufactures" were formed in Boston, New York, Philadelphia, and Baltimore; and so-called "manufactories" were established although not very numerous, were useful in stimulating public interest in our industrial development. In them, however, neither the new machinery nor power was used and they are, on that account, to be carefully distinguished from the factories of the later period.

Most of these "manufactories" were merely rooms where several looms were gathered and where a place of business could be maintained. The spinning was done by women in their own homes, and they delivered the yarn at the establishments and were paid there for their work. Sometimes the yarn which was returned was woven in the home and the finished cloth was then returned as the yarn had been. Some establishments seem to have marketed the yarn as a finished product without having it woven and they were, therefore, merely commercial agencies.

While the great bulk of the cloth making was still carried on, as it had been, without any connection with the "manufactories," yet they must altogether have employed a considerable number of women. Thus it was said that in 1764 a Philadelphia establishment for the manufacture of linen employed more than one hundred persons in spinning and weaving, and certainly a large proportion, if not all, of the pinners were employed at home. The New York "Society for the Promotion of Arts, Agriculture and Economy" whose linen "manufactory" was commended because it had relieved "numbers of distressed women now in the poor house," employed, in 1767-68, "above three hundred poor and necessitous persons" spinning and

weaving. In Philadelphia, in 1775, the first joint stock manufacturing company was established in this country. This "United Company
of Philadelphia for Promoting American Manufactures" employed
some four hundred women, most of whom seem to have worked in
their own homes. In an interesting advertisement[35] this company
offered to "employ every good spinner that can apply, however remote from the factory, and, as many women in the country may
supply themselves with the materials there and may have leisure to
spin in considerable quantities, they are hereby informed that ready
money will be given at the factory, up Market Street, for any parcel,
either great or small, of hemp, flax, or woolen yarn. The managers
return their thanks to all those industrious women who are now
employed in spinning for the factory." In 1777 a Rhode Island paper noted that "one gentleman at Barnstable has set up a woolen
manufactory and receives from the spinners 500 skeins of yarn one
day with another."[36] The cotton "manufactory" at Bethlehem, Connecticut, advertised for good linen yarn "from three to seven runs
to the pound, for which, merchant's price will be paid from 9 pence
to one shilling per run" [37]

The Pennsylvania "Society for the Encouragement of Manufactures and the useful Arts" in 1787 also kept two to three hundred
women at work spinning linen yarn, and the New York "Society for
Encouraging American Manufactures" was employing one hundred
and thirty spinners in 1789.

In some of the "manufactories" part of the women and girls
worked on the premises instead of in their own homes. One of
the best examples of such an establishment is the sail duck manufactory, established in Boston in 1788. In that year the *Boston
Centinel* noted that the "manufactory of sail cloth and glass" would
soon be completed and "give employment to a great number of persons especially females who now eat the bread of idleness." In 1789,
a New York paper,[38] the *Gazette of the United States*, in describing
the same factory, referred to the fact that "sixteen young women
and as many girls under the direction of a steady matron are here
employed"; and later in the year, when Washington visited the estab-

---

[35] *Pennsylvania Packet and Gazette* quoted in Bagnall's "Textile Industries of
the United States," i, 70, 71; and see pages 52, 53-54, and 63-70, 78, in regard
to the other companies mentioned.
[36] Recopied in the *Boston Newsletter* and *City Record*, December 31, 1825.
[37] Bagnall, i, 197.
[38] Ibid,, 113-114.

lishment, he recorded in his diary that he saw there "girls spinning with both hands" and with smaller girls to turn the wheels for them. In contrast with the arrangements of this factory, he noted on the same trip that, at Haverhill, he found a similar establishment, where "one small person" turned a wheel which employed eight spinners; "whereas at the Boston manufactory of this article each spinner" he said, "had a small girl to turn the wheel."

This Boston factory was a large and unique establishment, and it is not surprising that it attracted Washington's attention. A two-story building, one hundred and eighty feet long, had been erected on Frog Lane by the company, and it was said that in 1792 there were four hundred persons employed. Many of the spinners must have worked in their own homes, but there was an unusual feeling of solidarity among the work people wherever they were employed. Mutual aid societies were formed both among the weavers and the spinners. "The spinners admitted none into their company except by vote"; and it was said that "their measures to promote industry and self-government were very successful." President Washington at the time of his visit said of them: "They are daughters of decayed families, and are girls of character — none others are admitted."[39]

Another interesting example of an early "manufactory" with a large number of employees, was an establishment also situated in Boston, which made the "card" used for combing wool and cotton. The making of these cards had become a well-organized industry toward the close of the eighteenth century, but even after the establishment of "manufactories" the most tedious part of the work continued to be done by women at home. New machinery had been introduced for cutting the leather and making, even cutting and bending, the wire for the teeth, which were inserted separately by hand. The materials were then distributed, and the women and children in the neighborhood worked at "setting teeth." In some places whole families were dependent on this work as their only means of support. The Boston card factory, however, was the largest one in existence and it was considered of great value to the community, because it employed "not less than twelve hundred persons, chiefly women and children."[40] When the cards were returned to the factory

---

[39] Quoted in Bishop, "History of American Manufactures", i, 419, 420.

[40] "Topographical and Historical Description of Boston," *Massachussetts Historical Society Collections*, First Series, ii, 279. Professor Levasseur in a reference to this establishment ("The American Workman," Adams's translation,

the women were paid at a fixed rate for every dozen they made. A few women were employed in the factory, too, examining the cards that were returned and correcting the imperfect work.

Records of careful descriptions of these early "manufactories" are extremely difficult to find, but it is evident that they were conducted according to a variety of methods. Some of them were equipped only with looms, while others carried on all of the processes of cloth making, and, in these, women seem to have been employed in various capacities. In general, however, a small number of women worked on the premises of the employer and a very much larger number were employed to work in their own homes. After the introduction of the machine system and the substitution of the modern factory for the primitive manufactory, the situation was reversed. Women continued in the same occupations, but the great majority of them worked away from home. It should be noticed, however, that the factory system was introduced much more slowly into some industries than others. The application of labor-saving machinery to the manufacture of shoes, for example, was made nearly three quarters of a century after the revolution in the textile industries.

It should be noted here that throughout the nineteenth century and even at the present time, large numbers of women have continued to work very much as they did in the days of the "manufactories." The tenement workers in the so-called "sweated trades" today are, so far as the method of their employment is concerned, the direct descendants of the women who were employed in weaving, or in making cards for the "manufactory" of the eighteenth century. Although the women of the earlier period did their work at home, their materials were often furnished and they were employed by a manufacturer to whom they returned the product when finished and by whom they were paid for what they had done. It should be said top that while the primitive manufactories which have been described had little in common with the factory system of the succeeding century, yet the factory and the "manufactory" were alike dependent on women's labor.

In the earliest mills in which successful experiments were made with the new machines, women were among the operatives and the establishments were in part encouraged for this reason. In 1789, a

p. 337) seems to magnify the importance of the industry and to assume that because these women were employed *by* the factory they were employed *in* the factory.

petition in behalf of the first cotton factory of Massachusetts, that of Beverly, stated that it would "afford employment to a great number of women and children, many of whom will be otherwise useless, if not burdensome to society." In this earliest prototype of the modern cotton mill there were forty employees — both men and women. In a letter written in 1790 by one of the proprietors,[41] complaint was made that both the Worcester and the Rhode Island "undertakers" had bribed the Beverly women that had been taught to use the machines to leave at a time when they were most needed, — an interesting letter, because it indicates that Beverly was not the only place where women were employed as operatives.

It has already been pointed out that in Rhode Island, Samuel Slater, the "father of American manufactures," established the first mill in which a complete set of the new machinery was used. An interesting story is told of his method of obtaining the labor which he needed. A man by the name of Arnold was living with his wife and ten or twelve children, a few miles away in the woods, in a den formed by two rocks and some rough slabs of wood. When the woman was asked by Mr. Slater if she would come and work with her children in his new mill she consented upon the express condition that she should be provided with as good a house as the one in which she then lived. The first time lists for the mill, for the winter 1790-91, which have fortunately been preserved, contained the names, therefore, of Ann, Torpen, Charles, and Eunice Arnold.[42] Smith Wilkinson's account of this mill, which was published many years later, describes all of Slater's operatives as being between seven and twelve years of age. "I was then," he says, "in my tenth year and went to work for him tending the breaker." [43]

Another interesting factory of the period was Dickson's, at Hell Gates, near New York. When Henry Wansey, an English manufacturer, visited it in 1794, he found a good equipment in the way of machinery, and noted in his "Journal of an Excursion to the United

---

[41] "George Cabot to Benjamin Goodhue," in Rantoul, "The First Cotton Mill," *Collections of Essex Institute*, xxxiii, 37, and see also p. 40.

[42] White, "Memoir of Samuel Slater" (1836), p. 99. In the early factory with which Moses Brown experimented before Slater's arrival, the billies and jennies were driven by men, but "cotton for this experiment was carded by hand and roped on a wooden wheel by a female." Batchelder, "Introduction and Early Progress of the Cotton Manufacture in the United States" (1868), p. 19.

[43] See Bagnall, "Samuel Slater and the Early Development of Manufactures," pp. 44, 45.

States," "they are training up women and children to the business, of whom I saw twenty or thirty at work" The same factory advertised in 1793 for "apprentices either boys or girls" who "will be found in everything during their apprenticeship and taught the different branches of the cotton business."

With regard to all of these early establishments, it should be clearly understood that they were only spinning mills and that their product was not cloth, but yarn. This yarn was put out in webs and woven by hand-loom weavers for the factory, or sold in country stores for purposes of household manufacture. The processes carried on in the first factories were those of carding and spinning, and the women and girls, therefore, who went into the factories to operate the new machines, were doing what had always been women's work. They had taken over no new employment, but the manner of carrying on the old had been changed.

Weaving did not become a factory occupation in this country until after 1814, when the power loom was first used here. [44] But the flying shuttle, which was used in Providence, Rhode Island, as early as 1788, and which greatly facilitated hand weaving, had come into common use long before this time. [45]The improvements in spinning which greatly increased the supply of yarn, created a new demand for weaving and as a result of the fact that this had become an occupation requiring less physical strength than formerly, women were more and more frequently employed as weavers. In 1814, the year in which the power loom was introduced, Trench Coxe, called attention to this fact in his "Digest of Manufactures." "Women," he said, "relieved in a considerable degree from their former employments as carders, spinners, and feeders by hand, occasionally turn to the occupation of the weaver with improved machinery and instruments, while the male weavers employ themselves in superintendence, instruction, superior or other operations and promote their health by occasional attentions to gardening, agriculture and the clearing and improvements of their farms."

An incident which occurred in the town of Leicester, Massachusetts,

---

[44]See Appleton, "The Introduction of the Power Loom and the Origin of Lowell," (1868). The power loom had been invented in 1785 by the Rev. Dr. Edmund Cartwright, but it was a long time before it was perfected and its superiority to the hand loom proved. See Taylor, "The Modern Factory System," pp. 431, 433.

[45]Bishop, i, 333, 401, 410; for the use of the flying shuttle in England, see Cunningham, "History of English Industry and Commerce" (1903), ii, 502, 503.

in the same year, is of interest as an illustration of the extent to which weaving was then considered "women's work." One of the early clothiers of the town enlarged his business in 1814 and began to manufacture woolen cloth. The weaving was done by men in his shop, on hand looms, but "the employment of men in what had been before regarded as within the peculiar province of females" created an unusual degree of comment and these men weavers were said to be regarded in much the same light as were the first men milliners and dressmakers of a later day.

The history of the employment of women in the cotton mills of this country will be traced in some detail in a later chapter and a more extended account will be given of the relative numbers of men and women employed in weaving and in other departments. In conclusion, however, it should be emphasized that the earliest factories did not open any new occupations to women. So long as they were only "spinning-mills" there was merely a transferring of women's work from the home to the factory, and by the time that the establishment of the power loom had made weaving also a profitable factory operation, women had become so largely employed as weavers that they were only following this occupation, too, as it left the home. It may, in brief, be said that the result of the introduction of the factory system in the textile industries was that the work which women had been doing in the home could be done more efficiently outside of the home, but women were carrying on the same processes in the making of yarn or cloth. The place and conditions of labor had been changed, but women's work continued to be an important factor in the industry.

Chapter IV - The Establishment of the Factory System

The relation of women and children to the early factory system can be understood only in connection with the whole labor situation as it existed at the close of the eighteenth and the beginning of the nineteenth century. The labor problem of that period was fundamentally different from ours of today. The ease with which any man could become a freeholder and the superior chances of success in agriculture made it difficult to find men who were willing to work in manufacturing establishments and it was questionable whether sufficient labor could be found to run the new mills when they were constructed. Moreover, as a question of national economy, fear was expressed regarding the possible injury to our agricultural interests if much labor were diverted from the land. Manufactures, if they were to be established, must not, it was emphatically said, be built up at the expense of agriculture.

It has already been pointed out that, in many respects, the situation in England was quite different from our own. There the manufacture of cloth had become an industry of large proportions before the industrial revolution; and the establishment of the factory system created a disaffected class of unemployed workmen who were jealous of the new machinery which could be easily managed by women and children and which was taking the work away from them. In this country, however, a comparatively small number of persons were employed, and because of the absorption of our male laborers in agriculture, in so far as there was such an industry, it was for the most part in the hands of women and girls.

The establishment of the factory system, therefore, substantially meant, with us, the creation of new work, and made imperative a large increase in our wage-earning population. Moreover, this new work was identical with the work which women had long been doing in their own homes, and it was inevitable that the difficulties caused by the scarcity and high cost of male labor should be met by the employment of women. So long as land remained cheap and agriculture profitable, it was taken for granted that men could not be induced to work in the new mills and factories; and just as confidently it was expected that women could be counted on to continue, in the mills, the work they had formerly done at home.

The economic ideals of our early statesmen must also be taken into account as a factor of importance, Hamilton and his followers had visions of the complete development of the virgin resources of the new republic; and they hoped to formulate a policy for obtaining the maximum utility, not only from our territory, but from our population. It was logical, therefore, that Hamilton, in his famous "Report on Manufactures," should argue that one great advantage of the establishment of manufactures was "the employment of persons who would otherwise be idle. ... In general," he said, "women and children are rendered more useful by manufacturing establishments than they otherwise would be." He also pointed out that "the husbandman himself [would experience] a new source of profit and support from the increased industry of his wife and daughters, invited and stimulated by the demands of the neighboring manufactories."

In 1794, when Trench Coxe found it necessary to reply to the argument that labor was so dear as to make it impossible for us to succeed as a manufacturing nation and that the pursuit of agriculture should occupy all our citizens, he at once called attention to the fact that the importance of women's labor must not be overlooked, since manufactures furnished the most profitable field for its employment. And in the early part of the last century, a new factory was called a "blessing to the community," [46] among other reasons, because it would furnish employment for the women of the neighborhood. Later it was said that women were "kept out of vice simply by being employed and instead of being destitute provided

---

[46] "History of Dorchester" by a Committee of the Dorchester Antiquarian and Historical Society (1859), p. 632.

with an abundance for a comfortable subsistence." The availability of women's labor to meet the demand for hands to police the new machines was one of the arguments with which the early protectionists most frequently met their opponents. The objection that American labor was more profitably employed in agriculture than in manufactures and that to "abstract" this labor from the soil would be unwise and unprofitable, was answered by pointing to the women and children. In the pages of *Niles's Register* this is done again and again. The work of manufactures does not demand able-bodied men, it is claimed, but "is now better done by little girls from six to twelve years old." To the "Friends of Industry" as the early protectionists loved to call themselves, it was, therefore, a useful argument to be able to say that of all the employees in our manufacturing establishments not one fourth were able-bodied men fit for farming;[47] and the question was raised, Would agriculture be benefited if "on the stopping of the cotton and woolen manufactures, these women returned to idleness!"[48]

During the period following the close of the War of 1812, when the tariff was, for a time, the most important subject of public discussion, the fact that women formed so large a proportion of the employees in the "infant industries" proved a valuable protectionist argument, Niles and Matthew Carey frequently made use of it, and memorials to Congress during the period called attention to the additions to the national wealth and prosperity made possible by the utilization in factories of women's labor which had hitherto been less advantageously employed.[49] In 1815, a group of manufacturers, in a petition to Congress urging the prohibition of the importation of coarse cottons, pointed out that their establishments had afforded "the means of employment to thousands of poor women and chil-

---

[47]M. Carey, "Address of the Philadelphia Society," "Essays in Political Economy," p. 69. The "Report on Protection to the Manufactures of Cotton Fabrics" said, "not one-ninth or perhaps one-tenth are able-bodied men," "American State Papers: Finance," iii, 34. See also *Niles's Register*, ix, 365.

[48]*Niles's Register*, xi, 367. In x, 99, manufactures are lauded because of their "subserviency to the public defense; their employment of women and children, machinery, cattle, fire, fuel, steam, water, and even wind — instead of our ploughmen and male laborers."

[49]See, for example, a petition from Connecticut citizens, 1820, "American State Papers: Finance," iii, 453; "Address of the American Society," 1816, p.11; "Philadelphia Memorial," *Niles's Register*, xlii, 177; "Address of the New York Convention," 1831, p. 138; "Petition from Citizens of the United States Engaged in Manufactories on Brandywine" (pamphlet, 1815), pp. 4,5.

dren for whom the ordinary business of agriculture [supplied] no opportunities for earning a livelihood," and that any loss to manufacturing interests would mean that hundreds of poor women would be "thrown back on the community for support." Thus the charge that manufactures would produce pauperism had already been met and it was only necessary to repeat that the number of those unable to earn their own subsistence was decreased when new or more remunerative occupations for women were provided.[50]

During the tariff controversy of the early thirties, free traders and protectionists alike agreed in commending the manufacturing industries which had furnished employment for women. It was no new thing for the "Friends of Industry" to argue that the decline of our manufacturing interests would mean that the women employees would become "the tenants of charitable institutions or be consigned to prisons and penitentiaries by the vices contracted during idleness." But to have their opponents obliged to yield this point, was, in its way, a considerable victory.

Precisely this happened, however, in 1831, when in the "Memorial for the Free-Trade Convention" of that year, Gallatin frankly admitted that although labor generally was less productive in manufactures than if applied to other pursuits, there was one exception which seemed "to alleviate the evil." Women's work in the cotton and woolen industries was, he said, "much more productive than if applied to the ordinary occupations of women." And, he added, that with the fund out of which they had been previously supported thus set free, large accumulations might be annually added to the wealth and capital of the country. Gallatin even proceeded to make a precise computation as to the additional quantity of productive labor put in motion, and concluded that the surplus product obtained by the employment of women in a single cotton mill of two hundred employees was $14,000 annually.[51]

---

[50] "Report of the Committee on Commerce and Manufactures, 1821," "American State Papers: Finance," iii, 601.

[51] Gallatin made his estimate on the following basis: "Their wages vary from $2 to $3 a week; and to estimate the difference between this and what might be earned in their usual occupations at $1.50 a week, or $78 a year, is certainly a large allowance.[...]In a flourishing cotton factory at Lowell, Massachusetts, where annual sales amount to $210,000, there are 20 men and 180 women employed. The surplus product obtained by the labor of [the women] beyond what it would otherwise have been, amounts therefore, to $14,000, or $6\frac{1}{2}$ per cent, upon the annual amount of sales. The ratio, as deduced in the same manner from the Committee on Manufactures, of the amount of the annual sales and

That the convention, in its official memorial, should be obliged to make an exception which included so large a proportion of the total number of employees, was a distinct concession to the protectionists.

The committee on cotton of the "Convention of the Friends of Industry" which was held in New York in 1831, reported similarly that "thirty-nine thousand females" were employed in the various cotton factories of the United States, their aggregate wages amounting to "upwards of four million dollars annually." In the words of the committee: "This immense sum paid for the wages of females may be considered so much clear gain to the country. Before the establishment of these and other domestic manufactures, this labor was almost without employment. Daughters are now emphatically a blessing to the farmer. Many instances have occurred within the personal knowledge of individuals of this committee in which the earnings of daughters have been scrupulously hoarded to enable them to pay off mortgages on the parental farm."[52]

It was in short, easy to point out that there was a clear economic gain to the community in the establishment of factories in which women's labor, which was very unproductive in agriculture, could be advantageously employed. Thus a writer in the Boston Centinel attempted to summarize the situation. "In Europe as in America," he said, "machinery not only facilitates labor in a tenfold ratio, but enables women and children who are unable to cultivate the earth to make us independent of foreign supplies." Matthew Carey argued similarly: "The services of females of the specified ages (10-16-25) employed in agriculture, for which above one half of them are too young or too delicate, are very unproductive. At manufactures they are far more valuable and command higher wages."

In brief, it was claimed that "thousands of persons were turned from the consuming to the producing class"; that a maximum return was more nearly obtained from the country's labor force; that the national prosperity was increased by making women "a source

---

the number and wages of women employees in the Taft, Shepherd, Wolcott, and Pierce's woolen manufactories is $6\frac{1}{4}$ per cent, on the annual sales." (Gallatin in Taussig, "State Papers and Speeches on the Tariff," p. 130).

[52] "Address and Proceedings of the Convention of the Friends of Domestic Industry" 1831, p. 110. One of the resolutions passed at a Philadelphia tariff meeting declared that any injury to "the manufacture of hats, caps and bonnets destroys a large amount of labor generally considered a clear gain to the country, vis., that of females which in these articles alone produces an annual value of nearly three million dollars." *Niles's Register*, xliii, 277.

of wealth, rather than an incumbrance"; and that their work represented so much clear gain to society, an argument to which, as we have seen, even so able a free-trader as Gallatin could not reply.

Another point of interest in connection with the employment of women in the early mills and factories is that their work in these establishments was approved on social as well as on economic grounds. It has already been pointed out that in the colonial period great apprehension existed lest women and children, particularly those who were poor and in danger of becoming a public charge, should fall into the sin of idleness. This old Puritan fetich of the virtue of industry survived long into the nineteenth century and in some quarters the introduction of cotton machinery was regarded with disfavor "from the fear that the female part of the population by the disuse of the distaff should become idle."

Public attention was, therefore, frequently called to the fact that women found increased rather than diminished opportunities for employment as a result of the introduction of machinery and the establishment of factories. The new system, it was thought, not only gave women a chance of earning their livelihood, but educated them in habits of honest industry. The rise of manufactures was said to have "elevated the females belonging to the families of the cultivators of the soil in their vicinity from a state of penury and idleness to competence and industry." It was pointed out that young women who, before the introduction of the factory system, were "with their parents in a state of poverty and idleness, bare-footed and living in wretched hovels," had "since that period been comfortably fed and clothed, their habits and manners and dwellings greatly improved"; and they had in general become "useful members of society."

In the same spirit of unreasoning exaggeration the women in villages remote from manufacturing centers were described as "doomed to idleness and its inseparable attendants, vice and guilt." [53] A picture of a village where "free, independent and happy workmen with their wives and children were employed," [54] was a sign of prosperity that seemed to arouse no misgivings in the first quarter of the last century.

Matthew Carey, one of the well-known philanthropists of his day,

---

[53] "Petition from Citizens of Pennsylvania (1820)," in "American State Papers: Finance," iii, 456.

[54] Address of the Philadelphia Society for the Promotion of Domestic Industry, 1819, p. 27.

declared in a public address, in 1824, before the Philadelphia "Society for Promoting Agriculture" that one half of the "young females" in the cotton mills, "would be absolutely or wholly idle but for this branch of business," and although his account of the beneficial effects of their work there was absurdly extravagant, it is an interesting illustration of the point of view of the times. "They contract," he said, "habits of order, regularity and industry, which lay a broad and deep foundation of public and private future usefulness. They become eligible partners for life for young men, to whom they will be able to afford substantial aid in the support of families. Thus," his crowning argument was, "the inducement to early marriages ... is greatly increased and immensely important effects produced on the welfare of society."

The employment of children in the early factories was regarded from much the same point of view as the employment of women. Philanthropists, who still cherished colonial traditions of the value of an industrious childhood, supported statesmen and economists in warmly praising the establishment of manufactures because of the new opportunities of employment for children. They pointed out the additional value that could be got from the six hundred thousand girls in the country, between the ages of ten and sixteen, most of whom were too young or too delicate for agriculture," and in contrast called attention to the "vice and immorality" to which children were "exposed by a career of idleness."

The approval of child labor was, in short, met with on all sides. Early inventors worked to discover possible means of using the labor of children as well as women. Commendation was solicited for Baxter's machines on the ground that they could be turned, one sort by children from five to ten years and the other by girls from ten to twenty years. [55]

Governor Davis of Massachusetts called attention, in a message in 1835, to the fact that not only machines in the textile manufactures but "thousands of others equally important, were managed and worked easily by females and children." Mr. E. B. Bigelow of Boston, in 1842, patented a series of devices "for making the carpet loom automatic, so that the costly labor of man might be dispensed

---

[55]See *Niles's Register*, vi, 16, where it is claimed as a great advantage that the carding, roving and spinning machines are separate and distinct machines; "the first (carding), worked by a girl or woman and fed by a child; the second (roving), worked by a child; the third worked by a child or girl."

with, and the whole process of weaving be conducted by women and boys."

Tariff arguments, too, made use of the fact that children as well as women were employed in large numbers in the new mills. One protectionist carefully worked out in the pages of *Niles's Register* the exact gain that came to a typical village from the fact that its children could find work in neighboring textile factories. He came to the conclusion that " if we suppose that before the establishment of these factories, there were two hundred children between seven and sixteen years of age, that contributed nothing toward their maintenance and that they are now employed, it makes an immediate difference of $13,500 a year to the value produced in the town!" [56]

Now and then an interesting document is found which throws light on conditions which prevailed at this time. The memorandum from the "Poignaud and Plant Papers" showing the wages paid to Dennis Rier for himself and his family of children and to Abigail Smith and " her daughter Sally, 8 years of age and son, Samuel, 13 years of age," which is quoted in a later chapter dealing with wages, is of interest from this point of view. Of similar interest is a wages book for the year 1821, still in the possession of the agent of the Waltham cotton mills, which shows that one Gideon Haynes in that year, came regularly to collect the wages of his children; for Cynthia Haynes, who worked in the cloth room, two dollars and a quarter a week; for the three children who were employed in the card room, Ann, one dollar and a half a week. Sabre, two dollars, and Sophia, two dollars and eight cents. Samuel Longley also came to collect the three dollars and a half, which represented the joint weekly earnings of his daughters Sarah and Rebecca.

In general, however, it should be said that a relatively larger number of women and fewer children were employed in the mills of eastern Massachusetts and in New Hampshire than in Rhode Island and Connecticut, where the so-called "family system" prevailed. This point, however, will be dealt with in some detail in a later chapter dealing with the early mill towns.

A brief summary of the industrial situation during the first part of the last century so far as it concerned the employment of women may be useful, even at the risk of repetition. The introduction of

---

[56] *Niles's Register*, xi, 86. Children under seven are carefully excluded from the computation on the ground that, at this age, they are "incapable of any employment other than the little services they can render in domestic affairs!"

machinery had created new and great industrial possibilities, but we were confronted with the problem of establishing manufactures in a country where labor was scarce and dear and where there was a strong national prejudice against "diverting labor from the land." This problem was solved by the employment of women and children to police the new machines, a natural solution since the "machines were doing work which women had been doing in their own homes. Moreover, to have the women of the country fully employed meant the more complete utilization of the country's labor force, which was a clear economic gain to the nation and in line with the policy of achieving the maximum utility not only from our boundless and unexplored territory, but from our population. It should be noted, too, that in addition to the fact that an economic justification was found for the employment of women in the new mills and factories, there was no social prejudice against it. Following in the wake of Puritan tradition which loathed idleness as a vice and cherished ideals of industry and thrift, anything which offered new opportunities of employment for either women or children was eagerly welcomed.

Chapter V - The Early Field of Employment

ALTHOUGH the first factories in which labor-saving machinery was used in this country were established in the closing decade of the eighteenth century, these early establishments were crude and experimental, and employed very few hands, and it has been pointed out that it was not until the year 1808 that any real impetus was given to the "infant industries" of this country.

The years from 1808 to 1840 have been well described as the period of the domestication of the factory system. [57] Machinery was gradually applied to a large number of different industries. The Patent Office registered from year to year a constantly increasing series of new inventions; the number of our manufacturing establishments grew with equal rapidity; and the value of our manufactured products, which was estimated in 1834 to be equal to three hundred and twenty-five million dollars a year, bore witness to our industrial progress.

But we are concerned here only with one phase of the economic history of this period, — the effect of the development of the factory system upon the position of women in industry. Succeeding chapters will trace in detail the history of the most important changes in several different industries in so far as they have affected women's work, and, as a preparation for these special studies, a general survey will be attempted of the field of employment for women at this time, together with some account of the occupations in which they were

---

[57] See the very interesting chapter with this title in Bogart, "Economic History of the United States," pp. 142-154.

engaged and some discussion of the extent to which factory work had superseded employment in the home.

No list of the industries in which women were employed during the period following the industrial revolution that can lay the smallest claim to completeness has been heretofore accessible, and it has been easy to be misled into believing that we are unable to obtain any such information for a period earlier than 1860. A prize monograph of the American Economic Association, published in 1891, confessed "defeat and discouragement" with regard to "well-nigh every step of the attempt to reach any conclusions regarding women workers in the early years of the century"; and announced that it was "to the United States Census of 1860 that we must look for the first really definite statement as to the occupations of women and children." [58]

One statement, however, regarding the early employment of women which is frequently met with, is misquoted from Harriet Martineau's "Society in America," to the effect that, when she visited America in 1836, but seven occupations were open to women. This alleged enumeration contains teaching, needle-work, keeping boarders, work in the cotton mills, typesetting, bookbinding, and domestic service.[59] Miss Martineau's statement, however, was that for the poor woman, "before the opening of the factories, there were but three resources — teaching needle-work and keeping boarding-houses or hotels. Now," she said, "there are the mills; and women are employed in printing offices as compositors as well as folders and stitchers."[60]

There can, clearly, be no doubt of the fact that this was merely a casual *obiter dictum* on the part of Miss Martineau, and that she had no thought of making a careful enumeration of women's occupations. She did not, for example, include domestic service in the list, although she so often refers to it in other parts of the book, and she also omitted shoe binding, which she mentions in a chapter on manufacturing labor, and which she must have known to be an occupation much more important than bookbinding or typesetting.

But this casual statement of the meager opportunities of employment for working women in 1836 has come in recent years to be

---

[58]Helen Campbell, "Women Wage Earners," pp. 95, 96. For a similar statement, see Mabel Hurd Willett, "Women in the Clothing Trades," p. 24.

[59]See Wright, "Industrial Evolution of the United States," p. 202; and Levasseur, "The American Workman," p. 337.

[60]Harriet Martineau, "Society in America" (1837), fourth edition, ii, 257.

treated as a final word on the subject of the early employment of women and has lent convenient color to vague and comforting generalizations regarding the multiplication of industrial openings for women that has come with our years of progress.

Fortunately it is not so impossible to secure information regarding occupations for women in this early period as it has been represented to be, and, in particular, some of the official reports on manufacturing industries are useful for this purpose. From a study of three such reports belonging to the period from 1820 to 1840 it appears that, instead of seven, there were more than one hundred industrial occupations open to women at this time. One of these reports is the United States industrial census [61] of 1822; another is a series of "Documents Relative to the Manufactures of the United States," collected in 1832, by the Secretary of the Treasury; [62] the third is the industrial census of Massachusetts for 1836-37.[63]

Both the "Digest" of 1822, and the "Documents" of 1832 were disappointing as attempts at a census of manufactures,[64] but from the three reports together, however unsatisfactory each may be alone, it is possible to obtain some interesting information relating to the employment of women during these years. The total number of women employed in all of our industrial establishments, or even in any one

---

[61] "Digest of the Manufacturing Establishments in the United States," issued as an additional volume of the "Fourth Census" 1823, conveniently available in "American State Papers: Finance," iv, 28-224.

[62] "House Executive Documents," Twenty-second Congress, First Session, i and ii.

[63] "Statistical Tables Exhibiting the Condition and Products of Certain Branches of Industry in Massachusetts for the Year Ending April 1, 1837."

[64] Of these the 1832 collection is unquestionably the most important. As a census of manufacturing industries it was a failure, and no attempt was made to tabulate the data or prepare a summary of the results. Save in the New England States, little information is given, except for a few leading industries like cotton, wool, glass, and iron, and even for these the returns are fragmentary; but for the New England States some valuable and detailed information is given. In 1822, the attempt to prepare a "digest" of the manufacturing industries had been similarly disappointing. Niles called it a "miserable exhibit" (*Niles's Register,* May 3, 1823), and said that "to bring forth a summary for general purposes of reference and remark we esteem as an impossibility and were not, therefore, surprised that none is given." For our purpose, however, these reports are extremely valuable, because of the fact that the schedules called for the number of "men, women and children" instead of the baffling "number of persons" employed. Frequently the designation in the schedules was disregarded and only the fact that the "number of employees" returned; but in a large proportion of cases it was faithfully observed.

one industry, cannot be ascertained; neither can a complete list of occupations be compiled; but the data furnished by these documents affords abundant evidence of the fact that the employment of women in such industries as had been established at that time, was common enough.

For example, the "Digest" of 1822 shows that in that year women were employed in the manufacture of anchors, beer, brass nails, books, barrels, boats, button molds, buttons, brushes, bagging (hemp), bakery products, beds, boots and shoes, candles and soap, coaches, cheese, combs, cigars, cotton cloth, cordage and twine, chairs, clocks, cards, cooper's ware, clothing, carts, earthenware, furniture, flour, floor cloth, gloves, goldleaf, gunpowder, gun stocks, fur and wool hats, hardware, leather, lace, lumber, machinery, maple sugar, morocco leather, medicines, millstones, oil (flaxseed), paper, rope, salt, saddles, saddletrees, stoves, straw hats, shovels, silver and gold ware, saltpeter, tinware, tobacco and snuff, types, woolen goods, yarn, whips, whisky and gin. While a list of this sort is tedious, it does, perhaps, enable one to realize more vividly in how large a variety of industries women worked in the first quarter of the nineteenth century.

In the "Documents" of 1832, the New Hampshire returns show that they were employed in the manufacture of brushes, bobbins, books, batting, cigars and snuff, gum, garden seeds, glass bottles, fur and wool hats, leather and morocco leather, musical instruments, paper, starch, straw hats, roots and herbs, tin-plating, wire, wheelheads, whips; as well as in printing, tailoring, and cloth dressing, and of course in cotton and woolen mills and in the manufacture of boots and shoes.

The Connecticut investigation found women also employed in brass foundries, in silversmith work, in the manufacture of buttons and combs, cabinetware, coaches and wagons, caps, clocks, cotton webbing and cotton wicks, iron nails, jewelry, line twine, metal clasps, razor strops, stoneware, suspenders, and pocketbooks.

Putting together such returns for Massachusetts as are included in the "Documents" and the state industrial census of 1837, the list of industries may be extended to include the manufacture of boxes, bedcords and clothes lines, blacking, children's carriages, cards, chocolate, cordage and twine, candles and soap, cork cutters, cigars and tobacco, chairs, chair stuff, crackers, carpets, curtains, cheese and butter, copperas, furs, furniture, flax, flint glass, fishing nets, gimlets, hair cloth and hair beds, hosiery, hooks and eyes, india rubber, lead, lead pencils, lace, letter boxes, locks, looking glasses, paper hangings, pails, rakes, stocks, tacks, types, thread and sewing silk, umbrellas, window blinds; and women were also engaged in millinery, tailoring, and mantua-making, making of instruments wool-pulling, gold-beating, silk and wool dyeing, lithographing, bed-binding and upholstering; and they were also employed as silversmiths, and in publishing houses.

Returns from other States were not detailed enough to add any other industries to this list, which would have been greatly extended if the documents relating to New York had even approached in completeness those of Massachusetts.

The exact number of industries given in all of these lists cannot be accurately estimated, for some of the expressions used are clearly redundant and the same industry may be counted more than once. On the other hand, it is clear that with such very incomplete returns from important manufacturing states like New York and Pennsylvania, any estimate will be under the correct number. The lists, too, might have been considerably extended, if, instead of keeping within the limits of these official reports, contemporary newspapers had been resorted to for supplementary information. It may, therefore, be repeated there were more than one hundred different industries which had women employees at this time, and that the field of employment for women in industry was much wider than has been generally supposed.

The reports from which this enumeration of industries was compiled included returns from industries in various stages of development, and it is of interest that women were employed not only in a large number of industries, but in industries carried on according to a variety of methods.

Some of them were still hand trades in which much of the work was done in the homes or in small shops and was probably "given out" by manufacturers in the larger towns; others were carried on in small factories, which had little or no machinery, and employed very few hands. This is evident from the fact that in answer to the schedule inquiry regarding the "value of tools, machinery, etc.," as apart from real estate, buildings, and fixtures, sums under fifty dollars were frequently reported and in other cases their value was merely described as "inconsiderable." There were, of course, some large establishments, but save in the cotton and woolen industries the number of these was relatively small.

As late as the decade 1830-40 several large women's industries were carried on very much as clothmaking had been before the introduction of the factory system. The most important of these were the various branches of the clothing industry, especially the manufacture of men's shirts and trousers, the work done in connection with boot and shoe making, and the making of straw hats and bonnets — the last an industry which flourished in Massachusetts. Special chapters will deal later with the manufacture of clothing, and of boots and shoes, so that it has seemed worth while to select straw hat making as an illustration of the extent and importance of home work at this period.

The manufacture of straw braid for hats and bonnets was begun as early as 1798, in Dedham, Massachusetts, where a twelve-year-old girl by the name of Betsey Metcalf discovered a method of making braid for bonnets "from oat straw, smoothed with her scissors and split with her thumbnail." A bonnet of seven braids "with bobbin inserted like open work, ... in imitation of the English straw bonnets, then fashionable and of high price," was much admired and many duplicates were demanded, since a bonnet like Betsey's could be sold at half the price of a similar imported one. Young women came from neighboring towns to be "instructed in the art" of straw braiding and the foundation of a flourishing industry was laid, not only in Massachusetts but in other New England States, and at the close of the first quarter of the nineteenth century making straw braid and bonnets and palm-leaf hats, had become an occupation numerically very important for women.

In 1821, a Connecticut woman received from the London Society of Arts, a silver medal and twenty guineas "on condition that she would put the society in possession of some of the seed and the process of bleaching with a description of the whole treatment of culm." In 1827, the "Report of the Harrisburg Convention in the Interests of Domestic Industry" contained the statement that "25,000 persons (nearly all females) make straw hats and braid in Massachusetts." The statement was probably an exaggerated one, but there can be no question of the fact that the industry had grown prosperous. In 1830, the annual value of the product was said to be more than a million and a half dollars.

Some New Hampshire women claimed the secret of making leghorn bonnets, and one of their samples sold in Boston at auction for fifty dollars. The fine bonnets were generally expensive. Those which were made from rye in Boxford, Massachusetts, sold regularly in the large cities at from ten to fourteen dollars each, although the cost was but two or three; and fine straw and grass bonnets in imitation of leghorn often sold for thirty or forty dollars each.

The industry was given some attention in other parts of the country. In 1824 a school was established at Baltimore "for the instruction of poor girls in the various branches of straw-plaiting from simple braid to finished bonnets"; but it was in New England, and particularly in Massachusetts, that the industry centered. The "Documents" of 1832 contain many reports with regard to straw hat making in Massachusetts towns, Foxborough reported that "as to straw and palm leaf hats, they say that a large proportion of the braid is collected from the neighboring towns, and probably 8,000 females are employed in the business." Dealers in Franklin were said to employ "1,333 females in various places"; Wrentham reported 4,000 women engaged in this work, Medfield 500, Milford 500, Upton 400, Ware 500. [65]

Other towns made no attempt to estimate the number of persons employed and there are many such returns as the following: "Made by females eight years of age and upward for eighteen cents a hat"; or, "Braided in families at seventeen cents each"; or, perhaps, "Made by women and children for goods at retail price." This latter form of payment seems to have been common enough when the manufacturer or contractor also kept a retail store. [66]

---

[65] Many of the towns in which a considerable amount of work was done, did not attempt to estimate the number employed because of the irregularity with which many of the women worked. Thus the town of Enfield reported: "There are brought annually to three traders in this town by females in this or the adjoining towns, 50,000 palm leaf hats, which manufacture, like that of covered buttons, has sprung up within about six years; in which time it has driven the foreign article from our market and supplied us with a substitute of greater beauty and value for less than one-third the price formerly paid. The hats are made in private families, the coarser kind by quite small children. It is impossible to estimate, with perfect accuracy, the extent of this manufacture. . . . The number of females employed in this and the adjacent towns amount to about two hundred."

[66] Some towns reported not the actual number of women who did this work but the number who would have worked if the employment had been regular and constant, and sometimes more detailed reports are given. North Bridgewater, for example, added the following explanatory note regarding the industry: "Considerable straw is braided in this town, say to the amount of fifteen thousand dollars, which is done by women and young girls; and it is very difficult to

Straw hat making was, however, by no means exclusively home work, although the number of women employed in factories was small compared with the number who worked at home. The largest establishment of the time was probably that of the Messrs. Montague in Boston, who had from 150 to 200 looms and kept about 300 women constantly employed in the weaving of silk warp with filling of imported Tuscan straw,[67] In 1837 the value of the palm leaf hats and straw bonnets made in Massachusetts was estimated at nearly two thousand dollars.[68] In 1846, in an account of the industry in *Fisher's National Magazine and Industrial Record*, it was said that "the best workwomen" could not earn more than fifty cents a day and that the average was only twenty-five cents; and it was added, "the braid is generally made by children varying in age from six to twelve years"

The estimate then made was that Massachusetts alone employed 13,311 hands in the manufacture of straw bonnets, braid, and palm leaf hats, and that the total value of the product was $1,659,496.[69] It was not long, however, before it became customary to import straw braids so that a considerable amount of the work done by women and children was no longer necessary, and the industry gradually came to be a much less important one for women, numerically.

Another interesting local industry which. was carried on "home work" at this time was the manufacture of buttons. The molds were made by machinery "carried by water power and tended by females," the lasting was imported from England and the silk from France. The women who did the covering received all of their materials from the manufacturers to whom they returned the finished product; and they were paid by the gross for the work. The industry began in 1827 and centered about Easthampton, Massachusetts, where as many as a thousand families were employed. [70] In 1833-34, the manufacture of buttons by machinery was attempted and in the summer of 1834 the first covering machine was in operation. Local historians report

---

obtain any very accurate account of it, or of the number of persons employed in it. ... It is done in almost every family occasionally, and by part only of the day, week, month or year, when not occupied in household and family cares."

[67]Bishop, ii, 393. These were probably hand looms in which the straw was woven after the Tuscan fashion. In the issue of May 17, 1834, *Niles's Register*, p. 191, describes an interesting factory near Boston employing "between 160 and 200 persons, chiefly females, in weaving straw by hand looms"; but this may be the same factory as the one described above.

[68]"Tables of Industry, 1837," p. 181.

[69]*Fisher's National Magazine and Industrial Record*, ii, 1152, 1153.

[70]Lyman, "History of Easthampton," p. 56.

that Miss Elvira Clapp of Southampton was the person who covered the first buttons by machinery.[71]

While it is not possible to make any exact statement of the number of women who worked either in their own homes, or in factories, before 1850, it is clear that women's labor was an important factor in a large number of industries. It is of further interest that the demand for women "hands" was frequently greater than the supply. In 1827 a prominent manufacturer said, in writing to a friend: "I have no doubt that it would be more profitable to employ young women in our factories generally, except for overseers, if they could be obtained."[72] And the scarcity of women operatives which is implied here is also referred to in one of the "Documents" of 1832, and is interesting evidence of the great demand for women employees. Among the replies from manufacturers published in the "Documents" is a letter from Smith Wilkinson, written, as he said, out of his twenty-five years of experience as a manufacturer: "Our greatest difficulty at present," he declared, "is a want of females — women and children — and from the great number of factories now building, [I] have my fears that we shall not be able to operate all our machinery another year."[73]

---

[71]Other button factories were also in existence at this time, according to the "Documents" of 1832. Three establishments in Waterbury, Connecticut, which made gilt buttons, employed 140 men at $1.00 a day and 100 women at $2.25 a week in 1831. Sometimes buttons and combs were made in the same factory. Four such establishments in Connecticut employed 207 men and 104 women. Comb making as a separate industry, however, employed about a thousand women in Connecticut and Massachusetts. In Leominster, in the latter state, there were 17 comb factories which had together 150 men at work for 75 cents a day and 75 women employees at 40 cents; the same industry in Newburyport employed 85 men at 80 cents, 20 boys at 30 cents, and 85 women at 35 cents; in Haverhill 25 men at 70 cents, 3 boys at 21 cents, and 23 women at 25 cents; at Lancaster, 55 men at 75 cents and 17 women at "two shillings and sixpence."

[72]White, "Memoir of Slater," p. 129.

[73]This complaint of the scarcity of women operatives is an interesting one since the familiar situation today is that of great competition within the relatively restricted field of employment open to women. But there were, of course, overcrowded trades then as now, and there were many difficulties in the way of women who wished to be self-supporting. One of the comments of Miss Martineau at the time of her visit in 1836, is a statement of the other side of the situation: "One consequence, mournful and injurious, of the 'chivalrous' taste and temper of a country with regard to its women is that it is difficult, where it is not impossible, for women to earn their bread. Where it is a boast that women do not labor, the encouragement and rewards of labor are not provided. It is so in America. In some parts there are now so many women dependent on

Another interesting statement made in the same decade regarding the employment of women is that of the economist, Henry Carey, who said in 1835, in his *Essay on Wages*, "The improvements of the present times tend very much to reducing the demand for children and men and increasing that for young women, a change that cannot be otherwise than advantageous." Carey also called attention in another connection to the fact that in the cotton manufacture a very much larger proportion of the employees were women in this country than was the case in England. "At first sight," he said, "it might be supposed that this should cause wages to be lower here, the labor of men being generally more productive than that of women. . . . Such is not, however, the case, women being employed *here* because everything is done to render labour productive, while *there* a large portion of the power of the male operatives is wasted."

In the year 1842, another economist, Amasa Walker, presided over a convention of the "manufacturers, dealers and operatives" in the shoe and leather trade of the State of Massachusetts. An address was issued by the convention protesting against possible changes in the tariff which, it was claimed, would affect a large number of prosperous industries. "There is one class," the address declared, "upon which the weight of this calamity will fall with peculiar severity. That class is the women of our country who get their living as many hundreds and thousands now do with great comfort and respectability, by the work of their own hands. This large and interesting class, heretofore not overpaid for their services, must not only experience a great falling off in price, but in many instances an absolute annihilation of demand for their labor."[74] While this statement may not seem to be of special interest, it is significant that so important a convention at that time should have demanded protection not merely for the workingman, but for the workingwoman as well.

Comparisons between the field of employment today and that of

---

their exertions that the evil will give way before the force of circumstances. In the meantime the lot of the poor woman is sad."

[74]"Proceedings of the Convention of the Manufacturers, Dealers and Operatives in the Shoe and Leather Trade in the State of Massachusetts" (Boston, March 2, 1842, p. 70). The convention address added with regard to the women employed: "They cannot subsist if compelled to work in competition with the laboring females of Europe, who receive from four to six cents a day for their services . . . what an amount of privation and suffering must be involved in the turning out of employ or in employment at half price, of this immense number of industrious women."

the first half of the last century must be made with caution. The data for the earlier period which have been the subject of this discussion are obviously too fragmentary for this purpose. The first national industrial census that is in the least complete is that of 1850 and such information as has been collected for the earlier years relates chiefly to Massachusetts. Moreover, since so many of the women were employed in their own homes, the total number of women employees would inevitably include a large number who worked only a portion of the time.

It should be noted, too, that a large proportion of the industries enumerated in the lists which were given employed only a very few women and were, therefore, relatively insignificant. But the same comment may be made upon the long list of industries in which women are employed today. In 1900 women were found in 295 out of the 303 employments enumerated in the census.[75] Women were, for example, reported to be carpenters, masons, blacksmiths, "quarrymen," plasterers, well borers, coal and gold and silver miners, and the like, but it is clear that such work for women is the rare exception and that such occupations have no significance when the real field of employment for women is considered. There is, however, little doubt that the field of employment for women has been widened in the last half century, and there is great need that this should be so. The female population over ten years of age has increased from 4,265,812 in 1830 to 28,246,384 in 1900, nearly seven-fold. No positive statement can be made as to whether the number of women who are competing for industrial employment, out of every one hundred of this population has increased or not. But even had there been, no change, which is, of course, highly improbable, the need of new occupations would still exist, unless the old had become seven times as important; and this, as succeeding chapters will show, is not what has happened; on the contrary, some of them have become very much less important.

The census of manufactures which was taken in 1850, which, as has been said, is our first reasonably complete industrial census, showed 225,922 women and 731,137 men employed in manufacturing industries in establishments whose annual product was valued at five hundred dollars. In 1850, then, 24 per cent of the total number of employees reported were women. The last census of manufactures does not furnish statistics which are exactly comparable

---

[75]For a list of these occupations, see Appendix E.

with these earlier data. The total number of persons, however, reported employed in manufactures in 1905 was 6,157,751. Of these, 4,801,096 were men over sixteen, 1,194,083 were women over sixteen, and 167,066 were children, boys and girls under sixteen. That is, in 1905, 78 per cent of the total number of employees were men, 19 per cent were women, and 3 per cent were children. These percentages seem to indicate that relatively fewer women in proportion to the number of men (19 per cent in 1900 in comparison with 24 per cent in 1850) are now employed, but these census data, although superior to the statistics for the period before 1850, are not sufficiently accurate to warrant an exact comparison and any conclusions based on them are, therefore, likely to be unsafe.[76]

Some of the difficulties in the way of comparing these statistics are discussed in Appendix B, but the fact that there has been no

---

[76]The following table showing the relative numbers of men and women employees reported by each succeeding census since 1850 is given in the 1905 "Census of Manufactures" and is here reprinted. The percentage which women formed of the total number of employees at each decade has been computed and is added to the table. The data for 1850, which are omitted from the 1905 census, are also added here:

COMPARATIVE SUMMARY OF ALL INDUSTRIES (FACTORY, MECHANICAL, AND NEIGHBORHOOD). FROM 1905 CENSUS OF MANUFACTURES, I, XXXVI.

	1905	1900	1890	1880
Men	4,801,096	4,110,527	3,327,042	2,019,035
Women	1,194,083	1,029,296	803,686	531,639
Child'n*	167,066	168,583	120,885	181,921
Total	6,162,245	5,308,406	4,251,618	2,732,595
% of women employed†	19	19	19	

	1870	1860	1850
Men	1,615,598	1,040,349	731,137
Women	323,770	270,897	225,922
Child'n*	114,628		
Total	2,053,996	1,311,246	957,059
% of women employed†	16	21	24

* Not reported separately for 1850 and 1860.

† In 1870 and after, the percentage of women means percentage of women over sixteen (or fifteen). See Appendix B.

substantial change in the proportion of women employed in the last few decades is significant and should be noted here.

It is, however, to be emphasized that the proportion of both men and women employed in manufacturing industries is. larger than formerly. In 1850 eighty-seven men and twenty-eight women out of every one thousand persons of each sex in the population over ten years of age were employed in manufacturing industries; in 1900 one hundred and forty-two men and thirty-nine women were so employed.[77] That is, within fifty years the number of men in "manufacturing and mechanical pursuits" increased relatively much faster than the number of women. There is, then, a very evident fallacy at the bottom of the popular superstition that the increase in the number of women employed in factories has meant "driving out the men." Against an increase of eleven in every one thousand women must be set an increase of fifty-five in every one thousand men.

But the question of greatest interest is not whether there has been a general displacement of women by men, or of men by women, in industrial occupations, but what specific changes have occurred in specific trades and why these changes have taken place. Such questions, however, cannot be answered in a general discussion of the whole field of industrial employment, and it has seemed best, therefore, in the succeeding chapters to treat separately the history of each of the important industries in this country which employ large numbers of women. In the most recent census of manufactures, which was taken in 1905, the "hand trades" (which, of course, included millinery and dressmaking) were omitted, but more than a million women were reported to be employed in establishments conducted under what is known as the factory system. The following table shows the total number of women employed and the number in each of the industries employing the largest number of women. Along with the number of women employed, the number of men and of children are given in order that the importance of women in the industry may be more correctly understood.

---

[77] According to the "Census of Occupations" these figures would have been, for 1900, 194 out of every thousand men, and 46 out of every thousand women. The figures for 1900, which are given above in the text, were obtained from the 1900 statistics given in the preceding table, with the number of children apportioned as indicated in Appendix B. In any case the numbers are only approximate, since there are no statistics for 1850 which are properly comparable with those for 1900.

Table 5: TOTAL NUMBER OF PERSONS IN MANUFACTURING INDUSTRIES IN 1905, AND THE NUMBER IN THE FIVE INDUSTRIES EMPLOYING THE LARGEST NUMBER OF WOMEN.

	MEN.		WOMEN.		CHILDREN.	
1. The textile industries						
Total	273,822		298,910		68,456	
Cotton and Manufactures		147,283		128,163		40,428
Hosiery and Knit Goods		25,167		68,867		9,681
Silk and Silk Goods		27,037		45,198		7,366
Woolen Goods		44,452		24,552		3,743
Wortsted Goods		29,883		32,130		7,238
2. The Clothing Industry						
Total	101,373		147,710		3,812	
Men's Clothing		58,759		75,468		2,963
Women's Clothing		42,614		72,242		849
3. Tobacco and Cigars	72,970			57,174	5,274	
4. Boots and Shoes	95,257			49,535	5,132	
5. Printing and Publishing						
Total	142,110		37,503		5,001	
"Book and Job"		65,293		19,975		2,478
"Newspapers and Periodicals"		76,817		17,528		2,523
Total Number of Persons Employed in Five Industrial Groups	685,532		590,832		87,675	
Total number of Persons Employed in all industries	4,801,096		1,194,083		167,066	

53

According to this table, five industries or groups of industries, textiles, cigarmaking, "boots and shoes," the clothing trades, and printing and publishing,[78] employed half of the one million women; and, in the succeeding chapters, an attempt will be made to follow in detail the history of each of these industries in relation to the problem of women's work.

Fortunately these five industries are not only those which employ the largest numbers of women, but they have been, at the same time, quite different in their technique and method of development ; and they present, therefore, in their several histories, various phases of the adjustment made necessary by the introduction of machinery and the establishment of the factory system. Studies will, therefore, successively be made of the cotton manufacture as the most important representative of the textile industries which belonged historically to women, but in which women are now being displaced by men; of the manufacture of boots and shoes, historically a trade for men, but one in which women's labor has for a hundred years been an important factor; of cigar making, which is not a historic industry at all, but which began early in the nineteenth century in a small way as a by-employment for farmer's wives, and then became a trade for immigrant men and later for immigrant women. Somewhat briefer accounts will be given of the sewing trades, which have always been numerically the most important women's industry; and of printing, the latter of special interest because it is a skilled trade in which women have long been employed, but in which they have been so largely outnumbered by the men that they have with difficulty held their own.

---

[78]The next largest number of women found in any one industry is very much smaller than the smallest number given in the table above, viz., 14,844, the number employed in the manufacturing of "bread and bakery products." It should be noted that along with the 14,844 women, 64,580 men are employed, an interesting example of the way in which women's work has been taken over by men. The explanation of the displacement of women is the fact that the work is extremely heavy and that much of it is night work.

Chapter VI - The Cotton Industry

An account has been given in an earlier chapter of the establishment, in the closing decade of the eighteenth century, of the first cotton mills in which the new spinning machinery was used in this country. An attempt has also been made to give a sufficient account of the early labor situation to explain the great demand for women operatives and, in some measure, perhaps, the public approval of their work. It remains, therefore, for this chapter to deal with the effect on the employment of women of the development of the cotton manufacture in the nineteenth century.

The rapid growth of the industry between 1800 and 1815 is indicated by the increased consumption of raw cotton; in 1800, only five hundred bales were used in our American mills, one thousand bales were used in 1805, ten thousand in 1810 and ninety thousand in 1815.[79] The number of spindles in use was only 4,500 in 1805, but there were 8,000 in 1807, 31, 000 in 1809, 87,000 in 1810, and 130,000 in 1815.[80]

This expansion meant the employment of increased numbers of women and children in the new and enlarged mills. In 1810, returns from eighty-seven mills were received by Secretary Gallatin before he published his "Report on Manufactures" and, on the basis of the data furnished, he estimated that in 1811 the cotton mills of this

---

[79] See "Report of the Committee on Protection of Manufactures," "American State Papers: Finance", III, 82.

[80] Taussig, "Tariff History of the United States," p. 28, note.

Table 6: NUMBER OF PERSONS EMPLOYED IN COTTON MILLS IN
1816

MALES FROM SEVENTEEN UP	10,000
WOMEN AND FEMALE CHILDREN	66,000
BOYS UNDER SEVENTEEN	24,000
TOTAL	100,000

country would employ 500 men and 3,500 women and children.[81]
According to this official estimate, which, although made on the basis of very imperfect data, is undoubtedly a valuable one, women and
children formed eighty-seven per cent of the total number of persons
employed in the cotton mills in the second decade of the last century.
That this was not considered an unusually high percentage for that
period is indicated by other similar estimates which were made a few
years later. In 1814 Trench Coxe, in the "Digest of Manufactures,"
prepared for the Secretary of the Treasury, said, in discussing possibilities for the industry, that about 58,000 persons would produce
50,000,000 pounds of yarn, and "of these not more than one eighth
part ought to be adult males; the remaining seven eighths might
be women and children." He estimated also that 100,000 women,
"less than one sixth of our adult females," might with perfect ease
weave all of this yarn with the fly shuttle. But a more satisfactory
statement of the employment of women is found in a report of a con-
gressional committee[82] in 1816 showing, in the form of the following
table, the number of persons employed in the cotton mills in that
year:

No other estimate for the whole country was made until 1831, but
some records showing the number of operatives in various isolated
mills are preserved, and these indicate for the most part a very high
percentage of women operatives.

At the Waltham factory in 1819 there were 14 men and 286
women and children. In the same mill in 1821 there were 353 employees, 299 women and 54 men; all of the overseers were men as
well as the painters, machinists, teamsters, card coverers, general
laborers and the like. A factory at Pishkill on North River had from

---

[81]Gallatin's estimate was based on a theory that 800 spindles employed 40
persons, 5 men and 35 women and children ("American State Papers: Finance"
ii, 427).
[82]"American State Papers: Finance" iii, 82.

Table 7: PERCENTAGE OF WOMEN EMPLOYEES IN MILLS

Date	Place	Per Cent which Women formed of Total number of Operatives
1818	LANCASTER	88
1819	WALTHAM	95
1821	WALTHAM	85
1822 (PROBABLY)	FISHKILL	83
1825	LANCASTER	83
1827	NEW MARKET	90
1827	LOWELL	90
1833	LANCASTER	85

seventy to eighty employees, five sixths of whom were women and girls. The Poignaud and Plant factory at Lancaster had, in 1825, 39 women, 7 men, and an overseer, and in 1833, 35 women, 5 men, and an overseer. In the factories at New Market, New Hampshire, 250 girls, 5 boys, and 20 overseers and assistants formed the working force in 1827. In the same year. Kirk Boott prepared a statement showing that six Lowell mills employed 1,200 persons, "nine tenths of those females, and twenty from twelve to fourteen years of age."

A summary of these statements showing the percentage which women formed of the total number of employees in the different mills is given in the following table :

It is also of interest to know that the proportion of women employed in our cotton mills was not only very large, but that it was considerably larger in this country than in England. Henry C. Carey estimated on the basis of statistics for 1831 that there the number of women was about 9 per cent greater than the number of men employed, while in this country it was about 110 per cent greater. "The great disproportion," he said, "between the two countries in the employment of male and female labor cannot fail to strike the reader." A manufacturer of the same period said with regard to this point: "The perfection to which machinery is brought enables the proprietor to avail himself more extensively of female labor than is the case in Europe. The labor of the females is much more productive [here] and they consequently receive higher wages."

Much more interesting, however, than the number of women employed in the new mills is the work which they did and the question of the division of occupations, in so far as there was any at this time, between women and men.

Then, as now, the two chief occupations in the mills were spinning and weaving. Spinning, as has been pointed out, had always been women's work in the home, and the early spinning frames in the factories were exclusively tended by women. It was undoubtedly due, in part, to the scarcity of male labor and to the fact that women were willing to work in the mills that the spinning machinery in this country was adapted to their use. Thus frame spinning was the rule and mule spinning the exception here, although the mule was extensively used in England.

Mule spinning has always been awkward work for women because their movements in following the mule are so much impeded by their skirts, and the scarcity of male labor in this country was probably one reason why mule spinning came so slowly into use. There is reason to believe that the mule was introduced in Rhode Island as early as 1817, but it was not adopted in Lowell nor in Massachusetts generally until much later, and as late as 1840 was little used. Henry C. Carey, writing in the thirties, said the mule was not used in any of the Lowell factories, "and the consequence is that female labor here takes the place of male labor in England." And the comment of James Montgomery was that "in neither [Waltham nor Lowell] nor in any of the mills that followed their system was mule spinning introduced until after 1830." There is reason to believe that attempts were made to employ women as tenders when the mules were first being adopted in this country, but it was found to be more suitable work for men. An old Waltham operative who tells of seeing mule spinning for the first time in the early forties, remembers a woman spinner and girl piecers working in the mule room at Lawrence when he was employed there. Later the same woman with her girls came to Waltham where mules were introduced later, but she was obliged to leave. "The men made unpleasant remarks and it was too hard for her, being the only woman"!

It has already been explained that, while weaving was not so exclusively women's work before the introduction of machinery, yet after the fly shuttle had come into use and the "spinning mills" had greatly increased the demand for weavers, large numbers of women were employed in weaving, not only for their households but for factories and local dealers; and the sign "weaving given out" was common over shops at this time. A manuscript volume which was used to record the quantity of yarn given out, cloth returned, and the payments made to the persons who wove in their own homes for the Poignaud and Plant factory in Lancaster, is still preserved; and on the pages of this old "Weaver's Book" appear the names of Ivory Wildes, Nabby Fife, Patty Wilder, Polly Barker, Prudence Buttrick, Consider Studley, Dolly Maynard, together with those of some forty other women who wove for the factory from 1812 to 1816. The number of men weavers was larger than the number of women but in many cases the men undoubtedly acted as agents for their wives who did the weaving, but who left to their husbands the work of calling for the yarn and returning the cloth.

Later in 1818, an English traveler in another part of New England noted the large number of "female weavers" and was astonished at their independence in dealing with their employers. "Some of them," he said, "who have no other means of support except service (which is unpopular in America) lodge with farmers, and give half the produce of their labor for their board and lodging."[83]

In the year 1814 the power loom was first successfully used in the Waltham factory and the modern cotton mill which converted the raw cotton through all the processes of manufacture to cotton cloth was at last constructed. Power loom weaving became at once the most profitable occupation for women in the mills. The old wages book for the year 1821, which is preserved in the Waltham mills, shows that all of the 138 weavers were women, although the six overseers were men. The first power loom weaving at Lowell was done by Deborah Skinner,[84] who, according to the old Waltham book had been the best weaver there before she was brought to Lowell by the Merrimack Corporation to teach their girl weavers the use of the new loom. In Fall River, where three of the looms were started in 1817, all of the weavers were women or girls, and one of the latter was Hannah Borden, the daughter of a large stockholder in Pall Elver's first cotton mill, and the best weaver of her day.

A further word may be said here about Hannah Borden who is one of the most interesting of the remarkable women who worked in our early cotton mills. She learned to weave on the hand loom when she was eight years old, and at fourteen, when she went into the mill to work, she was an excellent weaver. After the power loom was introduced she ran two looms, and wove thirty yards of

---

[83]Fearon, "Sketches of America," 1818, p. 101.
[84]"Contributions to Old Residents' Historical Association" (Lowell), vi, 71.

cloth a day. She worked from five in the morning to seven in the evening in a weaving room which was rough and unplastered, very cold and with only one small stove for heat. Part of the time she did "custom weaving," running only one loom, with extra care, so that a finer cloth was produced ; but for this, of course, she received extra pay.[85]

The tending of power looms continued to be done almost exclusively by women for a period of nearly fifty years. In Henry Carey's "Essay on Wages," written in 1835, power loom weaving is discussed as a women's occupation and from James Montgomery's account of the industry written a few years later, it seems clear that the custom of having girl weavers was universal here. Some of the oldest employees in the New England mills today say they can remember when weaving was so universally considered women's work that a "man weaver" was held up to public ridicule for holding "woman's job." As late as 1860, in the discussions of the New England Cotton Manufacturers' Association, a weaver is uniformly referred to as "she,"[86] An interesting old employee of the Waltham mills, a man who has worked continuously there since the forties, says he cannot remember having seen any "men weavers" until about the time of the Civil War. He believes that the first men to work in the weaving rooms in Waltham were immigrant English weavers. Mechanical improvements, however, have gradually led to the substitution of men for women until at the present time weaving threatens to become "men's work." The number of looms which a single operative can tend has constantly increased, and the tendency has been all along to a higher and higher rate of speed. When the power loom was first introduced, a weaver tended only a single loom and that loom ran from 80 to 100 picks a minute. It was not long before the invention of the rotary temple made it possible for an operative to tend two looms instead of one and those looms ran at a higher speed so that the result was about 260 picks a minute. In 1850 four looms with a total of about 600 picks a minute could be watched by a single weaver. In 1895 one operative could tend eight looms which ran a total of about 1,500 picks a minute. The invention of the automatic loom enormously increased the number of looms to an operative un-

---

[85] Other details of Hannah Borden's life are to be found in an address by Miss S. H. Wixon which was published in the *Fall River Evening News*, May 28, 1903

[86] "Reports of New England Cotton Manufacturers' Association," October 21, 1860, pp. 28, 29.

Table 8: COTTON MILL WEAVERS

	Number of Weavers in the United States.	Number of Weavers in the State of Massachusetts.
Men over sixteen	48,248	14,554
Women over sixteen	48,325	16,473
Children under sixteen	2,238	531

til today a single weaver may tend as many as twenty looms running more than 4,500 picks per minute.[87]

The effect of the introduction of these new looms has been to reduce still further the number of women employed. The statement in the census of 1900 that the "improved high-speed and automatic looms many of which are put under the charge of one weaver, can be operated most efficiently by men," [88] is borne out by the following table, showing the number of men and women employed as weavers in 1905. Data are given separately for Massachusetts, the state in which the industry has had the longest history because the situation there is of special interest.

This table[89] is of very great interest since it shows that the number of men and of women weavers is now substantially equal. In 1900 the "Census of Manufactures" said with regard to this point: "It is well known to those conversant with the industry that only a few years ago the weaving of cotton goods was regarded as peculiarly the work of women. The introduction of improved and fast looms has led more and more to the employment of men as weavers. The tendency is so marked that the next enumeration should show the men in a majority."

The number of men, however, has been increasing not only in the weaving rooms but in the spinning department as well. The number of mule spinners in this country has never become very large, but mule spinning has remained exclusively an occupation for men. On the other hand, the spinning frame is now tended by men as

---

[87] On this point see a little volume called "Labor-Saving Looms," 1905, published by the Draper Company, which manufactures these looms. See also the 1905 "Census of Manufactures," iii, p. 50.

[88] "Twelfth Census (1900): Manufactures," Pt. iii, 32.

[89] Data for this and following table are from the 1905 "Census of Manufactures," iii, 50.

Table 9: COTTON MILL WEAVERS

	FRAME SPINNERS.	MULE SPINNERS.	TOTAL.
MEN OVER SIXTEEN	10,709	4866	15,575
WOMEN OVER SIXTEEN	25,701	...	25,701
CHILDREN UNDER SIXTEEN	19,078	...	19,078

well as by women, and the result has been, as the following table indicates, that a very considerable number of men are now employed as spinners.

There are now, then, more than fifteen thousand men employed in the cotton mills at spinning, an occupation which belonged historically to women in the home and an occupation which in the early days of the machine system was equally their own in the factory. While it is not possible to follow in detail all of the changes in the technique of an industry so elaborate in its mechanical processes, the changes in another important occupation, that of "dressing" or sizing the yarn, may be noticed as a further illustration of the way in which improvements in machinery have tended to displace women in favor of men operatives.

"Dressing" was long one of the best paid occupations for women in the mills but in the year 1866 a new machine for sizing yarn known as the slasher, was imported. Before this time the work had been done by the dressing machines worked by women. The slasher was found to be very successful as a means of saving labor and was rapidly installed. When the New England Cotton Manufacturers Association met in 1869, the new machine was discussed and the question was raised by one member, "Do ladies or gentlemen tend the slashers?" The answer was, "My impression is that we can use girls, in part, but we have not tried them."[90] But the work proved to be physically exhausting and the substitution of men slasher-tenders for women who had worked at the dressing machines was inevitable. In an interesting book of reminiscences, Mrs. Robinson, one of the early mill girls of Lowell, reports as one of the changes which she found in going back to the old mill where she worked nearly half a century before, that the room in which the girls of her day had tended the dressing machines was filled with men, who were, of

---

[90] "Transactions New England Cotton Manufacturers' Association," 1869, p. 14.

course, operating slashers.

The tendency toward a decrease in the proportion of women employed in the mills is also indicated by the census statistics for the industry as a whole. It has already been pointed out that early statistics of employment are extremely incomplete. It is impossible to obtain any statement, even approximately accurate, of the absolute number of women employed until the close of the third decade of the nineteenth century. But a failure to obtain the total number of employees does not necessarily mean that it is impossible to find a basis for estimating the percentage which women formed of that total. For if a census gives the relative numbers of men and women operatives for the factories reporting, then even if a great many establishments fail to report and make the totals so incorrect as to be useless, still the percentage of women is likely to be very much the same in the establishments that do not report as in those that do. That is, the percentage which women form of the total number of employees, is not likely to change much, even with a great change in the totals themselves. It is important to note, too, that so far as errors may exist in the reports sent in, they are likely to be in the direction of an underestimate rather than in an overestimate of the number of women; for factories sending in careless returns after the manner of census-taking in the early years, often reported only the "number of employees" without indicating the number of each sex. Such returns would invariably be entered as "men employed" and the percentage of women operatives be made to appear smaller than it really was.

Some of the estimates of the number of men and women employed in the mills before 1831 have already been given. In 1831, when the convention of the "Friends of Industry" met in New York, a Committee on the Cotton Industry was appointed, which returned some interesting statistics, a part of which, those relating to the number of employees, are reproduced in the table on the following page. For the period between 1831 and 1850 no data relating to the number of men and women operatives in the whole country have been found; but from 1850 to the present time the federal census has furnished statistics which are fairly reliable; and for convenience, these data from the census, with the two most useful of the earlier estimates, have been incorporated in the table 10 on page 65. In order to show not only the change in the proportion of men and women employed, but the relative importance of the cotton industry at different periods as furnishing an occupation either for men or women, the number of employees out of every ten thousand persons in the population over ten years of age has also been computed.

To accompany these statistics for the country as a whole, a table has been prepared from data for Massachusetts, showing the number of employees for each decade since 1831, which has been throughout the whole period the most important cotton manufacturing state. A study of statistics for the state[91][92]where the industry has the longest history and where it is most concentrated is, in some respects, more illuminating for a historical study of this kind than statistics for the country at large[93].

A study of these tables points to some interesting conclusions: (1) That for three quarters of a century, the period for which data for a comparison are available, the proportion of men in the cotton mills has been steadily increasing while the proportion of women has been as steadily decreasing. In this, the most important women's industry, the women are being slowly displaced by men. Women formed, in round numbers, from two thirds to three fourths, and in some districts as high as nine tenths, of the total number of operatives in the first half of the century; but this proportion has been

---

[91]Data for 1831 from the "Report of the Committee on Cotton," "Address and Proceedings of the Convention of Friends of Industry at New York" (1831), p. 112. Other data are from the State Industrial Census from decade to decade until 1905; the 1905 industrial census is not yet available and statistics for that year are from the Federal, 1905, "Census of Manufactures," children eliminated as in the former table.

[92]With respect to the figures for 1895, an enumeration taken on the day when the greatest number of operatives were employed counted more men than women, i.e., men, 43,705; women, 43,247 — women forming only 40 per cent of the total. "Massachusetts State Census: Manufactures," 1895, p. 537.

[93]Figures for 1811 from Secretary Gallatin's "Report on Manufactures," "American State Papers: Finance," ii, 427.

Figures for 1816 from "Report of the Committee on Commerce and Manufactures," *idem*, iii, 82.

Figures for 1831 from "Report of the Gonmuttee on Cotton," "Address and Proceedings of the Convention of the Friends of Industry at New York" (1831), p. 112.

Figures for 1850 from Statistics from "U. S. Seventh Census (1850): Manufactures."

Figures for 1860 from Statistics from "U. S. Eighth Census (1860): Manufactures."

Figures for 1870-1905, statistics from the "U.S. Census of Manufactures" for different decades, with the number of children eliminated. For the method used in obtaining these statistics, see Appendix B.

Table 10: STATISTICS OF EMPLOYMENT FOR THE AMERICAN COTTON INDUSTRY IN THE LAST CENTURY

DATE.	NUMBER OF EMPLOYEES		NUMBER OF COTTON MILL EMPLOYEES OUT OF EVERY 10,000 IN POPULATION OVER TEN YEARS OF AGE		PERCENTAGE WOMEN FORMED OF ALL EMPLOYEES
	Men.	Women.	Men.	Women.	
1811	500	3,500	..	..	..
1816	34,000*	66,000*	..	..	..
1831	18,538	38,937	53	111	68
1850	33,150	59,136	39	74	64
1860	46,859	75,169	41	69	62
1870	54,031	81,337	38	58	60
1880	75,081	99,579	40	55	57
1890	100,319	118,557	41	51	54
1900	154,642	148,219	52	52	49
1905	166,284	149,590	..	..	47

*Estimates only

Table 11: STATISTICS OF EMPLOYMENT IN THE COTTON INDUSTRY - MASSACHUSETTS

Date	Number of Employees		Percentage of
	Men.	Women.	Women.
1831	2,665	10,678	80
1837	4,997	14,757	75
1845	6,303	14,507	70
1855*	...	...	...
1865	9,102	15,024	62
1875	24,814	35,362	59
1885	27,033	33,099	55
1895	41,184	41,925	50
1905	46,186	41,847	48

*The census taken in 1855 does not furnish these data.

declining until, in the twentieth century, the men outnumber the women.

This relatively greater increase in the proportion of men has, moreover, been officially recognized for some years; and the census has more than once stated emphatically that there is a decreasing proportion of women employed in the cotton mills. Thus in 1900 the "Twelfth Census," after discussing various statistics relating to the cotton industry, pointed out that one important fact resulting from their examination was "that the tendency is more and more to the employment of men."[94]

The more recent 1905 "Census of Manufactures" makes the interesting comment that "the ratio of the number of men employed [in the cotton industry] to the total number of wage earners has been constantly increasing since 1870. The increase in this ratio, amounting to 15 per cent, was made largely at the expense of the women wage earners, whose ratio has decreased 10.8 per cent during the thirty-five years." The census also calls attention to the fact that "without any concert of action— perhaps unconsciously to the general body of manufacturers — there is a slow but steady displacement of women by men. In the New England States in twenty-five years the proportion of women employed has dropped from 49.7 per cent to 45 per cent; that of men has risen from 36.2 per cent to 49 per cent."[95] Had a longer period been selected for a comparison, these differences would have been even more marked.

The second conclusion of interest is that the cotton manufacture now employs a relatively smaller proportion of the total number of women in the country than formerly. It is clear that the men have not only gained numerically from the expansion of the industry, but they have gained at the expense of the women. But since this has been such a rapidly expanding industry, it would not necessarily follow that work in the cotton mills had become a relatively less important occupation for women merely because women formed a smaller proportion of the total number of persons employed. 10would seem, however, to indicate that this has been the case. While in 1831 about one hundred out of every ten thousand women over ten years of age, and in 1850 about seventy out of the same number worked in the cotton mills, when the last census was taken but fifty women

---

[94]"Twelfth Census (1900): Manufactures," Pt. iii, 32.
[95]1905 "Census of Manufactures," Pt. iii, 30, and Pt. i, lxxxii.

Table 12: PERCENTAGE INCREASES FOR EACH DECADE FROM 1850 TO 1900 IN THE NUMBER OF COTTON-MILL EMPLOYEES AND IN THE POPULATION OVER TEN YEARS

Decade.	Women.		Men.	
	Cotton Mill Operatives. Per Cent Increase.	Population over 10 Years. Per Cent Increase.	Cotton Mill Operatives. Per Cent Increase.	Population over 10 Years. Per Cent Increase.
1850-1860	27	37	41	37
1860-1870	8	27	15	24
1870-1880	22	29	39	31
1880-1890	19	28	34	30
1890-1900	25	22	54	22

were so employed.[96] It will appear in the chapter dealing with conditions of life and work, that a marked change in the employment of women began to be noted toward the close of the decade 1840-50, and it is probable that the decline has been constant since that time. Percentage increases for each decade since 1850 in the number of cotton-mill operatives and in the population have also been computed and are given in the table[97] below.

It is clear from this table that the rate of increase in the number of women cotton operatives has been smaller than the rate of increase in the female population over ten years of age until the last decade, when the statistics seem to point to a slightly greater increase. Even during the last decade it should be noted that the rate of increase is fifty-four per cent for men operatives and but twenty-five per cent for women operatives, while the male and female population increased at the same rate.

It is true that these census data, when carefully examined,[98] are seen to be in many respects faulty and unsatisfactory for purposes of comparison over a long term of years. They do not, therefore, furnish any exact statistical expression of the decrease in the pro-

---

[96]Round numbers, instead of those indicated in the table, are purposely used because it is desired to emphasize the fact that absolute accuracy cannot be obtained from such data as exists.

[97]Percentages computed from statistics of employment in 10 and statistics of population from federal census.

[98]See Appendix B, which discusses the census statistics in greater detail.

portion of women employees; and, indeed, it must be recognized that no accurate percentage measure of this change can ever be obtained. But these data are, with all their imperfections, of very great interest and significance; and they have been used because they are sufficiently trustworthy to indicate a general tendency, and the tendency to which they point unmistakably is the growing preponderance of men in the mills.

In general it may be said that there are two important reasons explaining the displacement of the woman operative. The first, which has already been discussed, is the fact that in the progress of mechanical invention in the industry cotton machinery has tended constantly to become heavier and to be operated at an increased speed, demanding, therefore, greater strength and more nervous energy on the part of the employee. To quote the census again: "The number of places in which women can profitably be employed in a cotton mill in preference to men, or on an equality with them, steadily decreases as the speed of the machinery increases, and as the requirement that one hand shall tend a greater number of machines is extended." The second explanation, which will be dealt with in the succeeding chapter, is the change in the available labor supply, the increase in the number, of men wanting work as a result of immigration, and the decrease in the relative number of women desiring work in the mills, due to the widening of the field of employment for educated women. This is, obviously, the more important of the two reasons for if male labor had remained as scarce as it was in the first twenty-five years during which our mills were operated, the machinery would, of necessity, have been adapted to the employment of women. But the men who are in the cotton mills today are almost exclusively of the immigrant class — either foreign born or of foreign parentage — a class that scarcely existed in the first quarter of the nineteenth century, when women first followed their work from the home to the mill.

Chapter VII - Early Mill Operatives: Conditions of Life and Work

Turning from the more technical questions connected with the employment of women in the mills to the social aspects of their work, some interesting changes are to be noted. There is a traditional belief that the early cotton industry was carried on under idyllic conditions in this country, particularly in New England. Lowell, the famous "City of Spindles" of the period from 1825 to 1850, when Lucy Larcom and her friends worked in the mills and published the *Lowell Offering*, is frequently compared with the Lowell of the twentieth century, where only eight per cent of the inhabitants are of native parentage, and where the mills are filled with Irish, French-Canadians, Armenians, Portuguese, and Poles; and as a result it is charged that the factory population of New England has deteriorated. In attempting, however, to trace the history of the changes that have been brought about, it is necessary to consider conditions of life and work apart from the character and nationality of the operatives. With regard to the former, we find so many unmistakable improvements, such as shorter hours, and more sanitary conditions in mills and towns alike, that if the same class of operatives had remained, we should record a large measure of progress.

But the most striking feature in the evolution of the New England factory town is the change in the character of the operatives — the fact that the women in the mills today are not the deteriorated descendants of the girls who formed Improvement Circles and attended Emerson's Lyceum lectures. The granddaughters of the first mill girls are now to be found in the women's colleges, while the women who have taken their places in the mills are immigrants or the children of immigrants — in the terms of the well-known census classification "foreign-born or of foreign parentage."

Lucy Larcom once said that "there was, indeed, nothing peculiar about the Lowell mill girls, except that they were New England girls of the older and hardier stock." This one point of difference, however, is so fundamental that it made the mill town of that time a different world from the immigrant factory city of today. And it is further symptomatic of the line of delimitation that is now drawn between occupations for middle-class and occupations for working-class women. Before 1850 this line was scarcely discernible in New England, and work in the mills involved no social degradation. There was, indeed, no "field of employment" for educated women, and opportunities for training practically did not exist. A few months' term as a schoolmistress was a very unremunerative occupation, and as will be pointed out, this was frequently combined with mill work as a sort of by-employment.

Then, too, the old respectable domestic occupations had been taken away from the household. Spinning and weaving were no longer a source of income except as factory work. Tailoring was still left, and a few minor employments, but to be self-supporting in the home was difficult.[99] It was these daughters of New England farmers — girls with energy, perseverance, and ambition to do not only for themselves but for others, who for a period of nearly half a century (roughly from 1810 to 1860) formed the great body of cotton-mill employees in certain parts of New England.

These girls were the sisters of the young men who were "going West" to the great states of the prairie country, and they had something of the pioneer spirit themselves — a willingness to venture into a new industrial world, and confidence in their ability to make it a world in which they could live with dignity and self-respect. They had attended the common schools, and some of them were saving their hardwon earnings to enter the well-known women's academies

---

[99] The *Lowell Offering* v, 279, contains an interesting account of the occupations of well-to-do fanners' daughters in the thirties.

70

or seminaries of the day. Lucy Larcom wrote that "for twenty years or more Lowell might have been looked upon as a rather select industrial school for young people. The girls there," she said, "were just such girls as are knocking at the doors of young women's colleges today. They had come to work with their hands, but that could not hinder the working of their minds also." Some of them were able to attend such schools as Bradford Academy half the year, by working in the mills the other half and "Mt. Holyoke Seminary broke upon the thoughts of many of them as a vision of hope."

In short, the underlying cause which made the first great "City of Spindles" so exceptional was the presence in the mills of young women of character and ability, to whom at that time few other employments were open. When an opportunity suddenly came to them to satisfy their desire for pecuniary independence and their longing for educational advantages by engaging in factory work, there was no reason for hesitation, save a vague prejudice against factory labor which had grown up out of stories of English mill towns. This did, for a time, perhaps, act as a deterrent, and many girls preferred to go on working at some more "genteel" employment at seventy-five cents a week and board but the influence of the bolder spirits was soon felt and steady work at high wages became an attraction too great to resist. There was, after all, no reason why they should not do together work which their mothers had been doing in their own homes. They went eagerly, therefore, long distances to Lowell,[100] to Waltham, to Manchester, and other early mill cities. Statistics for "1840 showed that of 6,320 women in the Lowell mills, only one eighth were from Massachusetts, while the great majority were from Maine, New Hampshire, and Vermont. This association with girls from different places, in a period when traveling was almost unknown, was considered one of the delightful features of factory life in Lowell.

Since their operatives were for the most part young women from good families living temporarily away from their homes, the corporations, if they wished to keep this highly desirable body of employees, were obliged to provide suitable living accommodations for them in

---

[100]Special attention is given to Lowell in this discussion because it was the most conspicuous of the early mill towns, and throughout the history of the cotton industry, and still at the present time, an important and typical one. Other towns in the "Lowell district," which included Maine and New Hampshire, were modeled after it. In Rhode Island and the district about Providence, the "family system" prevailed, and conditions were much less satisfactory. See Appendix B.

the new factory towns. To meet this need the corporation boarding house was devised. Rows of brick tenements to be used as boarding houses were built near the mills of the corporation, and women of known respectability and even of genuine refinement were put in charge of them. The Merrimack corporation at Lowell in 1849 owned 178 houses, 35 boarding houses for women operatives, 10 for men, and a large number of company tenements.

Perhaps the most typical head of a "company boarding-house" was a widow who was left with family to provide for, and whose own daughter could work in the mills. Lucy Larcom's mother provided for her eight children by moving to Lowell and taking mill-girl boarders in a corporation tenement and Harriet Hanson's[101] aunt and mother are other examples of these notable "house-mothers," or "boarding-women" as they were often called. Such women were, of course, likely to be very much interested in everything connected with the welfare of the girls under their care. But the corporations themselves were not lax in the matter, and had rules drawn up regarding the conduct of the girls in their boarding houses. Thus they not only regulated the dwelling places and food of their operatives, but dictated the time of going to bed and the rules of social intercourse.[102] For the most part, the operatives in the early days seemed to have made few objections to the system but occasionally a considerable measure of opposition is found. In one of the early factory tracts, issued by the Female Labor Reform Association of Lowell,[103] complaint is made of the wearisome extent of corporation control. At the close of the day's work, the operative was said to be watched to see that her footsteps did not "drag beyond the corporation limits" and whether she wished it or not she was subjected to the manifold inconveniences of a large crowded boarding house, where, too, it was said that the price paid for her accommodation was so utterly insignificant that it would not insure to her the common comforts of life.

This was the high tide of corporation paternalism in New Eng-

---

[101]Harriet Hanson, later Mrs. Robinson, afterwards became distinguished in the woman suffrage movement, and is the author of the book of Lowell reminiscences, "Loom and Spindle," which is frequently referred to in this chapter.

[102]Appendix D contains copies of the rules used in Lowell and in the Poignaud and Plant boarding houses at Lancaster.

[103]This "association" is interesting as an example of an early labor organization among women. It presented a written address at the first Industrial Congress of the United States (New York, 1845).

land, when the girls not only slept in company houses, but went to company churches and frequently spent their earnings at company stores.[104] When a girl entered a Lowell mill, she was required to sign what was known as a "regulation paper," binding herself to attend regularly some place of public worship. On the Merrimack corporation, during the period known as "Bark Boott's reign," every person employed was obliged to pay a regular monthly fee for the support of St. Anne's, an Episcopalian church established by Mr. Boott without regard to the different religious beliefs of his operatives, who, of course, greatly resented this "company church." The agent of the corporation let the pews to persons who were employed in the mills or who occupied company houses; he also made the contract with the rector and paid his salary and the other expenses of the church, and in return reserved from the wages of each operative a fixed sum for "purposes of public worship, no matter whether they attended this church or not."[105]

There had grown up, in short, a thoroughgoing system of corporation control, and it was in harmony with that system that boarding-house keepers, as well as overseers, were to be directly responsible to the agent for the moral as well as the physical welfare of those in their care. It was a rule that no immoral person should be employed in any capacity in the mills, and there is every reason to believe that it was rigidly enforced. Indeed, abundant evidence exists to show that "from the beginning, Lowell had a high reputation for good order, morality, piety, and all that was dear to the old-fashioned New Englander's heart."

It followed as a matter of course that these capable, ambitious girls did not stay long in the mills. James Montgomery described them as farmers' daughters who came into the factory for "perhaps a year or two, and frequently for but a few months," and then went home. "There were," he said, "great numbers of inexperienced hands in every factory." Many of them were working to get money for some cherished purpose; to send a brother to college or to prepare him for

---

[104]Company stores were not a feature of the Lowell system, but they were common enough in the early factory days throughput New England. See Chapter XII

[105]See Justice Hoar's opinion in the case of the Attorney General *ex. rel.* the Rector, etc., of St. Anne's Church vs. the Merrimack Corporation, 14 Gray (Mass.) 586. See also Robinson, pp. 78 and 21, Larcom in *Atlantic Monthly,* xlviii, 599, and the rules of the Lowell Manufacturing Company in Appendix D of this volume.

the ministry; to pay off a mortgage on the paternal farm, or to earn money for their own education that they might become superior school-mistresses or even missionaries.

Girls of this latter class were, moreover, often eager to avail themselves of the "opportunities" which a city like Lowell offered, and from which they were quite shut off in lonely farmhouses and country villages. In Lowell there was the Lyceum, which brought John Quincy Adams and Edward Everett and Ralph Waldo Emerson there to lecture, and which was said to be "more patronized by the mill people than any mere entertainment" of that day; indeed, the women operatives formed two thirds of the Lyceum audiences. There were "lending-libraries," too, and as a further means of culture a "debating club"; and the churches with their female benevolent societies, female charitable societies, female education societies, female missionary societies, indeed, "female" circles of every kind, furnished an outlet for activities of many sorts.[106]

More definitely their own were the French or German classes which some of the girls maintained in their factory boarding house, and the famous "Improvement Circle" of whose work the columns of the Lowell Offering bear lasting testimony.[107]Symptomatic, too, of the intellectual interests of the operatives is the fact that rules were needed to prevent reading in the mills. Bringing books with them when they came to work was strictly forbidden, and among an old list of discharges the following, evidently typical, case appears:

"March 14, 1839. Ann —, No. 2 spinning room; discharged for reading in the mill; gave her a line stating the facts."

With real Puritan zeal the girls tried to evade the rule by refusing to believe that the Bible could be among the forbidden books,

---

[106]See, for example, the list in Benjamin Floyd's "Supplement to the Lowell Directory of 1836, Containing Names of the Females Employed and Places of Employment in the Various Manufacturing Establishments in this City, etc." (Lowell, 1836).

[107]The *Lowell Offering: A Repository of Original Articles Written Exclusively by Females Actively Employed in the Mills*, 1841-1845, 5 vols., and the *New England Offering: A Magazine of Industry Written by Females Who are or Who Have Been Factory Operatives*, Harriet Fariey, editor, 1845-50, 3 vols., were preceded by an earlier periodical, *The Operatives' Magazine*, 1840-41, edited by Lydia S. Hall and Abby A. Goddard. The magazine was published by "an Association of Females," but contributions were solicited from "operatives of both sexes." See Lucy Larcom, "Mill Girls' Magazines," *Atlantic Monthly* , xlviii, and Robinson, "Loom and Spindle," Chapters VI, VII. A famous collection of extracts from *The Lowell Offering*, "Mind Among the Spindles," was published in London and contained an introductory tribute by Harriet Martineau.

and so persistently were the Scriptures taken into the mill that an overseer who "cared more for law than for gospel" reaped a harvest of confiscated bibles. To large numbers of earnest and ambitious New England girls in the second quarter of the last century, the cotton mill spelled opportunity and opened for them paths of knowledge and independence of which in the past they had only vaguely dreamed.

Work in the mills competed as an alternative employment with teaching, and it was very common to find the schoolmistress in the mill during part of the year at least.[108] On the Merrimack corporation alone there were at one period more than one hundred and fifty women operatives who had been at some time engaged in teaching school.[109] Some of them still taught in the summer and returned to factory work for the winter months. Miss Larcom tells us that an agent who came from the west for school teachers was told by her own pastor that five hundred could easily be furnished from among the Lowell mill girls.[110] And the ranks of the primary and grammar school teachers in Lowell were frequently replenished from among

---

[108] In Lucy Larcom's "An Idyl of Work," one of the characters thus described herself and her associates:

"In plain words,

I am a schoolma'am in the summer time

As now I am a Lady of the Loom.

. . . inside those factory walls

The daughters of our honest yeomanry,

Children of tradesmen, teachers, clergymen,

Their own condition make in mingling."

[109] Statement of superintendent of the Merrimack Mills, quoted in "Fifth Annual Report of Massachusetts State Board of Education," p. 98. The Superintendent added: "The average wages of these ex-teachers I find to be $17\frac{3}{4}$ per cent above the general average of our mills, and about 40 per cent above the wages of the twenty-six who cannot write their names." A similar statement in "Massachusetts House Document No. 98," p. 14, estimates the number of teachers at 180.

[110] "New England Girlhood," p. 256. It is scarcely necessary to add that many did go, and that this and similar "openings" operated to withdraw girls of this class into superior occupations.

the mill operatives.

Teaching was far from being a satisfactory employment for women in the first half of the century. The expediency of employing more women teachers was urged upon the various towns in Massachusetts in 1837, but a decade later, when Horace Mann issued his final report, he was obliged to call attention to the fact that schoolmistresses were still so inadequately paid that women in many occupations in mills and factories earned six or seven times as much as women teachers. Higher salaries and more permanent employment would be necessary, he said, before school committees could "escape the mortification which they now sometimes suffer, of being overbid by a capitalist who wants them for his factory and who can afford to pay them more for superintending a loom or a spinning frame."

The mills offered not only regular employment and higher wages, but educational advantages which many of the operatives prized even more highly. Moreover, the girl who had worked in Lowell was looked upon with respect as a person of importance when she returned to her rural neighborhood. Her fashionable dress and manners and her general air of independence were greatly envied by those who had not been to the metropolis and enjoyed its advantages.[111]

The women operatives were pretty uniformly of the same age at this period, few of them being younger than sixteen or older than twenty-five, and the great majority in the early twenties. Although the practice of employing very young children in cotton mills was common enough at this time, yet in Lowell, Waltham, and similar places where the company boarding-house system was maintained, the employment of children was unprofitable, since the cost of board was more than a child could earn. In Rhode Island and the adjoining parts of Massachusetts and Connecticut, the "English" or "family system" of hiring operatives was the rule, and it meant, of course, a much larger number of children among the employees than were to be found where the system of hiring individual operatives prevailed.[112] Kirk Boott's estimate for Lowell, it may be remembered, was that in 1827, in six mills employing twelve hundred persons, nine tenths of the operatives were females, and only twenty were from twelve to fourteen years of age. Certainly there must have been some children under twelve, for. Mrs. Robinson was only ten years old when she

---

[111]See, for example, the *Lowell Offering*, passim, and Scoresby, "American Factories and their Female Operatives," 1845, Chapter III, Sec. 2.

[112]See Appendix A.

Table 13: CONJUGAL CONDITION OF WOMEN IN COTTON MILLS, 1900

Married	19,688
Widowed	5,381
Divorced	485
	25,554
Single or Unknown	95,049
Total	120,603

began work in the Lowell mills, and Lucy Larcom was just eleven.

Extreme youth, however, was no more rare than age. Out of a thousand women employed by the Lawrence corporation, there were only thirty who were either married or widowed. In striking contrast is the Lowell of today, where thirty per cent of all the women in the cotton mills are married, widowed, or divorced, and where fewer than half fall within the age group of sixteen to twenty-four, which contained practically all of the women of the early period.[113] Census statistics do not show, for cities like Lowell, how large a proportion of the married women operatives are foreign-born or of foreign parentage; but such statistics are given for the United States, and are of interest in this connection. The following tables[114] show the conjugal condition of women in the cotton mills of the United States :

From these data, which show that, of the 19,688 married women, 13,017 were either foreign-born or of foreign parentage, it is clear that the presence of married women in the mills and a great numerical. increase in the higher-age groups are unquestionably a result of the employment of immigrant women.

Since so large a proportion of the inhabitants of Lowell in its

---

[113]See statistics from the "Twelfth Census (1900): Occupations" p. 600, which contains the following data regarding the age and conjugal condition of the women cotton-mill operatives of Lowell in 1900:

Age 10-15: 206; Age 16-24: 2,049; Age 25-44: 2,144; Age 45-64: 482; Age 65 up: 36 (Total 4,931). Married: 1,112; Widowed: 364; Divorced: 14; Single 3,441 (Total 4,917).

Age groups in the same industry for the United States as a whole show a much larger percentage of women operatives under twenty-five. This is of course due to the wide extent of child labor in some sections.

[114]"Twelfth Census (1900): Occupations," p. ccxxii. and p. ccxxiv respectively.

Table 14: PARENTAGE OF MARRIED WOMEN IN COTTON MILLS

Native white, native parents	6,610
Native white, foreign parents	2,337
Foreign white	10,680
Negroes	61
Total	19,688

Table 15: POPULATION OF LOWELL

	In 1830		In 1840	
	Men.	Women.	Men.	Women.
Under 10 years	495	504	1,865	1,865
10-20 years	405	1,182	1,369	3,464
20-30 years	958	1,792	2,143	5,568
30-40 years	358	353	1,128	1,605
40-50 years	111	164	520	650
50-60 years	37	57	224	318
More than 60 years	21	29	92	170
Total	2,385	4,081	7,341	13,640

first decades were mill hands, early census data which show the distribution of the whole population in age groups supply to some extent the lack of data showing the ages of those employed. For 1830 and 1840 we have the following age distribution of its inhabitants[115]:

In the decade 1830-40, therefore, women formed nearly two thirds of the population of Lowell, and from eighty to eighty-five per cent of all the women were under thirty years of age. Undoubtedly the fact that so large a proportion of the inhabitants were young and vigorous recruits from New England farms explained the low death rate of Lowell. By contemporary supporters of the system, however, the satisfactory condition of her bills of mortality was pointed to with pride as an evidence of the healthfulness of factory work and the superior conditions under which the operatives lived. As a matter of fact, it does not seem as if the conditions either in the mills or in the boarding houses could have been healthful, but the girls stayed so short a time, and brought such good constitutions with them from the farms, that they seemingly escaped ill health as a result; or, if

---

[115]Data from Table XXXV, in "Brief Remarks on the Hygiene of Massachusetts, but More Particularly of the Cities of Boston and Lowell," 1849, p. 681

78

they became ill, they at once went back to their homes, and Lowell's bill of health was left clean.[116] Many of them, too, worked only eight or ten months of the year and spent the rest of the time in their country homes.

Conditions of work in the cotton mills of the first J half of the nineteenth century were, in fact, far from being as superior as the early body of operatives. The mills of this period were badly constructed, from the point of view of sanitation, or safety, or comfort. They were for the most part narrow and extremely high buildings, sometimes with seven stories; they were low-studded, heated by stoves, badly ventilated, and badly lighted; weavers depended on the old "petticoat lamps," as they were called, which were fastened to the loom and filled with whale oil, to be ready when the light failed. Moreover, slight attention was given to apparatus for removing the fine dust which is so unhealthful in cotton mills, or to any artificial means of ventilation.[117] Dr. Josiah Curtis, in his very able study of hygienic conditions in Lowell in 1849, said quite emphatically that bad ventilation in the mills was "the most prolific source of deteriorated health" among the mill hands of Lowell and the neighboring factory towns. "In winter," he said, "for four months, when the windows are closed and generally double, each room has fifty solar lamps burning morning and evening, which assist not only in impairing the confined air, but also in raising the temperature frequently to 90° F. before closing work at night."

The hours were notoriously long, often from five in the morning till seven at night. In Lowell, except during very brief periods in the year, the girls went in for two hours' work before breakfast and returned to the mills again in the evening after supper. The meager half hour allowed for breakfast at seven o'clock and for dinner at noon was much complained of by the operatives and by physicians in their behalf. While fourteen hours was sometimes the period of work, twelve and three quarters was probably the average length

---

[116] An extract from the *Offering*, which was inclined to be most optimistic, is of interest: "The daughter leaves the farm, it is said, a plump, rosy-cheeked, strong, and laughing girl, and in one year comes back to them — better clad, 'tis true, and with refined manners, and money for the discharge of their little debts and for the supply of their little wants — but alas, how changed! . . . This is a dark picture, but there are even darker realities, and these in no inconsiderable numbers." — *New England Offering*, April, 1848, p. 4.

[117] Edward Atkinson writes very forcibly as to most of these points in the "Tenth Census" (1880), ii, 953.

of the working day before May 1, 1847. "Overtime," too, was not unknown, and the lamps were sometimes kept burning until nine or ten o'clock; but it was claimed as a justification that "overtime was always voluntary."[118]

In Fall River the hours must have been even longer. For example, Hannah Borden's day, which, however, belongs to an earlier period, seems to have been as follow ; she rose at four, took her breakfast with her to the mills, and at five had her two looms under way. From seven-thirty to eight-thirty she had an hour for breakfast, at noon half an hour, and the looms did not stop again until half past seven at night. It was eight o'clock before the Fall River girls of this period reached their homes, and they were said to be so tired that it was not unusual for one to fall asleep at the supper table.

In some Lowell mills the working day varied with the season of the year from twelve hours in the winter to fourteen in the summer. It is an evidence of the temporary character of their employment that some of the girls who were on piece-work rates preferred the longer hours since their object was to gain a certain fixed sum of money and then leave the mills, and the higher earnings that were the result of the longer hours meant an earlier release. One skilled and intelligent girl, in answering charges made in a political speech about the abuses of the mills, said: "We never work more than twelve and a half hours a day; the majority would not be willing to work less, if their earnings were less, as they only intend working a few years, and they wish to make all they can while here." It is significant, too, that an editorial in the *New England Offering* said with regard to this point: "Every overseer and girl in the New England mills knows perfectly well, or may know, that the majority, if not the whole body of the weavers and spinners, prefer to work as long as they can. . . . They enter the factories to make money."[119] Conditions in the corporation boarding houses varied much with the character of the woman in charge, but in any case the bedrooms were crowded and

---

[118]Miles, "Lowell as It Was and as It Is" 1847, p. 108. He adds: "The young woman, who is able, is generally willing to engage in it, as she draws the pay, to the extent of the extra work, of two girls, while she incurs the expense of the board of but one."

[119]See also the *New England Offering,* pp. 48, 79: "One overseer said that the girls would rather work more hours than less. When Mr. G. gave them three quarters of an hour for breakfast, they shut the gates to keep the girls out; and ... in twenty minutes from the time they came out, one hundred were there on the bridge waiting — and not very patiently either — for the gates to open."

uncomfortable, and little, if any, better ventilated than the mills. The comment of Dr. Curtis was that the condition of the sleeping apartments would not be endured so passively if the occupants had not first become habituated to such unwholesome air while at work. Another physician. Dr. Gilman Kimball of the Lowell Hospital, made an official complaint, not only of the lack of ventilation, but of the "manifest disregard of cleanliness" and of the overcrowding in some of the corporation boarding houses.[120] Often six or eight girls occupied a single bedchamber, and the descriptions in the *Operatives' Magazine*,[121] of rooms so "absolutely choked with beds, trunks, bandboxes, clothes, umbrellas, and people, that one finds it difficult to stir, even to breathe freely," were probably not exaggerated. This was particularly trying when the girls were not congenial, and stories in the *Offering* indicate that this was frequently enough the case. But it was easier to bear patiently with unsatisfactory conditions, when one was to have only a very temporary connection with them, than to take either the time or trouble to remedy them. Complaints of the "long hours, the close workrooms, the crowded chambers," were not wanting, but it was following the line of least resistance to treat these as the inevitable discomforts of an occupation which was to be followed for a very short time at most. Thus, Miss Larcom, writing many years later, says emphatically: "Certainly we mill girls did not regard our own lot as an easy one, but we had accepted its fatigues and discomforts as unavoidable, and could forget them in struggling forward to what was before us."[122] They even took pride in the fact that they were above complaining about the physical discomforts of their work. The editor of the *Offering* says of the contributors: "They have done honor to their heads and hearts. They have shown that their first and absorbing thought was not for an advance of wages, or a reduction of labor hours. They have given the impression that they were contented

---

[120]"Report of the Lowell Hospital from 1840-1849," made to the Trustees, June 12, 1849, by Gilman Kimball, M.D., 1849, p. 14. For further statement as to unwholesome conditions in sleeping rooms of corporation boarding houses, see "Bill of Mortality of City of Lowell for 1854," p. 22.

[121]Vol. ii, p. 100; and see Curtis, p. 33, and Scoresby, p. 57.

[122]Larcom, in *Atlantic Monthly* xlviii, 610. She says further: "The mistaken impression went abroad that a paradise of work had at last been found. Romantic young women came from a distance with rose-colored pictures in their minds of labor turned to pastime, which were doomed to be sadly blurred by disappointment."

even with their humble lot. . . . They have striven for improvement of head and heart before that of situation. They have attended more to self-reformation than to the reformation of society."

When it was charged that the editorial policy of the magazine was to present only the bright side of factory life and therefore to convey an essentially false impression, the answer of the editor was: "Happy indeed are we, if our eyes can turn involuntarily to the sunny side of the objects which arrest our gaze."[123]

All of this is, of course, an illustration of the familiar fact that a labor movement is born only when a definite wage-earning class is created which is concerned with the permanent improvement in the condition of that class and is willing to make sacrifices in its behalf. To quote Miss Larcom again : "This feeling, that they were at work in the mills for a little while, only to accomplish some special purpose, gave them contentment without any sacrifice of independence. Reductions of wages would often bring rumors of intended 'strikes,'[124] but the quiet, steady-going ones formed a large majority who gave no aid or sympathy to violent measures, and the murmur of disaffection soon died away. What reason had these young girls for

---

[123] See the closing editorial, *New England Offering,* i, 376: "We have been accused by those who seem to wish us no ill ... of unfaithfulness to ourselves as exponents of the general character and state of feeling among the female population of this city. They say the *Offering* . . . does not expose all the evils and miseries and mortifications attendant upon a factory life. It speaks, they say, on only one side of the question; and they compare us to poor caged birds, singing of the flowers which surround our prison bars, and apparently unconscious that those bars exist."

[124] Occasionally there was more than a rumor of a strike, and ("turn-outs" or "flare-ups," as they were called, occured. See, e.g., Condy Raguet's old *Journal of Political Economy,* i, 73, for note of a "turn-out" in 1829, and Robinson, "Loom and Spindle," for a Lowell "turn-out" in the thirties against a reduction of wages. The *Boston Evening Transcript* of March 25, 1836, contains the following interesting paragraph: "The factory girls of Amesbury have had a flare-up, and turned out. . . . The girls were told they must tend two looms in the future, by which they would weave double the number of yards that they now weave on one loom, and this without any advance of wages. . . . They proceeded to the Baptist vestry, chose officers, and passed resolutions, pledging themselves under a forfeiture of five dollars, that they would not go back without all. The agent, finding them determined to persevere, sent a written notice that they might come back!" Mention has already been made of an early strike against the first reduction of wages in Lowell; and in 1836-7, in Dover, N. H., a proposed reduction of wages caused a "turn-out" in which all of the women seem to have participated. This strike lasted but three or four days, during which the girls "placarded the fence of the mill-yard and door of the office with rhymes composed for the occasion" (McNeill, p. 89; see also pp. 103, 104).

nursing a sense of injustice, with all New England beckoning them back to their native hills, to the homes that were missing them, and would overflow with rejoicing when the absent sister or daughter should see for herself that it was no longer worth while for her to stay away."

Moreover, these girls were compensated in some measure by the sense of being pioneers, and successful pioneers. They had a clear vision of the future, and saw that pecuniary independence with the opening of a large and remunerative field of employment for women held for them the promise of a new world. They had a conscious pride, too, in upholding the dignity of labor, in demonstrating that in a republic "work with the hands is no disgrace," and, above all, perhaps, in "clearing away a few weeds from the overgrown track of independent labor for other women. They practically said by numbering themselves among factory girls that in our country no real odium could be attached to any honest toil that any self-respecting woman might undertake."

The poet Whittier, who saw many evils connected with the early cotton industry, found compensation for the hardships suffered in the mills in the fact that there, more than in any other mechanical employment, woman's labor was placed essentially upon an equality with man's. Writing from Lowell, he said: "Here, at least, one of the many social disabilities under which woman, as a distinct individual unconnected with the other sex, had labored in all times, is removed; the work of her hands is adequately rewarded; and she goes to her daily task with the consciousness that she is not spending her strength for naught."[125]

On the whole, then, it seems fair to say that conditions in early Lowell,

> That wonderful city of spindles and looms,

> And thousands of factory folk,

as it appeared to many girls at that time, were far from being so idyllic as those who are prone to idealize the past would have us believe. Long hours, unsanitary mills, crowded boarding houses, compulsorily supported corporation churches, all of these things are

---

[125]See the description of Lowell, "The City of a Day," in Whittier, "Prose Works," i, 351-384.

forgotten, and the young factory town seems to us, as it seemed to Dickens and other early visitors, sufficiently justified because of the remarkable intelligence and refinement of its operatives. But their presence there was not symptomatic of ideal conditions in the mills, but rather of the lack of alternative occupations for women of education or superior abilities at that time. Harriet Martineau, with her keen powers of observation, saw the situation truly when she wrote: "Twice the wages and half the toil would not have made the girls I saw happy and healthy, without that cultivation of mind which afforded them perpetual support, entertainment, and motive for activity. Their minds were so open to fresh ideas as to be drawn off from thoughts of themselves and their own concerns."

It should, perhaps, be asked at this point: How far were the girls of the Improvement Circle typical of the whole body of Lowell operatives? And how far was Lowell a typical example of the mill towns of the period? The first question is raised by the editor of the Lowell Offering herself. Have these factory "blues," as they loved to call themselves; represented the factory operatives as a class? she asks; and replies: "In truth it is such a promiscuous class that it would be impossible for any one magazine or paper, ... to represent them. It is generally conceded that they represent the more intelligent portion of them."

But certainly Emeline and Lucy Larcom, Margaret Foley and Harriet Farley would have been exceptional in any group of women; Miss Larcom, writing later of her early associates, says in her quiet, truthful way that hundreds of the thousands of girls that were employed there did not care at all for either books or study, but worked at Lowell just as they would have worked earlier "at the family sewing or at any household toil at home."

It has already been pointed out that conditions in the mill towns in southern New England, particularly in Rhode Island, were essentially different from those which prevailed in towns of the Lowell type. The "family system" made the corporation boarding houses unnecessary, and the operatives were clearly drawn from a lower social stratum.[126] That Lowell itself was an ordinary mill town, except

---

[126]Many points of contrast between Lowell and these mill towns of the south might be found. For example, Seth Luther's rather inflammatory "Address to the Workingmen of New England" 1836, contains an account of the corporal punishment of one of the women operatives in a Rhode Island mill by an overseer in a spinning room — an incident which resulted in the prosecution and conviction of the man in the Court of Common Pleas. Such an incident could

for its size, and was much like a large number of other towns in the district which followed more or less the same system, is probably true. Waltham was the "Parent of Lowell" and cherished as high a reputation for morality.[127] The "Rumford Institute" of Waltham, a system of popular lectures, founded in the interest of the factory operatives and much patronized by them, was the first lyceum in the country. And not only Waltham, but Lancaster, Chicopee, Manchester in New Hampshire, and Newmarket, Exeter, Portsmouth and Dover in the same state, and many other mill towns, seem to have cared for their operatives in carefully supervised corporation boarding houses like those of Lowell. The rules of the Lancaster boarding house, which have been preserved, are not unlike those prescribed by Kirk Boott for Lowell.[128] The *Lowell Offering* opened its pages to operatives from other factory villages, and contributions were printed that came from various towns, not only in Massachusetts, but in New Hampshire, Maine and even Rhode Island;[129] but in the south of New England the mill towns were far inferior to those of the Lowell and Waltham type.

But since the exceptional fame of early Lowell and the towns like it was due to their having a unique body of operatives and not to any superiority of their mills or boarding houses, so the withdrawal of the girls who represented the best of the older New England farm life meant the close of a remarkable period in the history of the American cotton manufacture.

By the year 1850 the old order was quite obviously passing away. The days when printed regulations were necessary to prevent the bringing of books into the mills, when young girls pasted their spinning frames with verses to train their memories to work with their

---

not possibly have happened in Lowell.

[127] See, for example, the section in Miles, pp. 21-24, on "Waltham, the Parent of Lowell."

[128] See Appendix D for a reprint of these rules.

[129] It is an interesting instance of "community of interest" that the Lowell Circulating Library, which was so lavishly patronized by the mill girls, seems to have been transplanted almost in its entirety, with its two thousand volumes, from Dover, one of the well-known New Hampshire mill towns. (See the note on the title-page of the old catalogue which is still preserved in the Boston Public Library.) Attention might also be called to the fact that bathing rooms had been established by corporations in Manchester, New Hampshire, before they were instituted in Lowell. There are, in fact, many little points which seem to show that the other towns of the same type were not unlike Lowell except that they were smaller.

hands, when mathematical problems were pinned up in the "dressing room" — these were the days which Lowell was soon to know no more. The new body of operatives were not like these daughters of the Puritans, who debated earnestly with their consciences as to whether it was "right to be at work upon material so entirely the product of slave labor as cotton," and cheerfully paid out of their own hard earnings not only their pew rents, but liberal subscriptions to missions and charities of many sorts.

The women who came over in the earliest wave of Irish immigration did not compete directly with the girls in the better-paid factory occupations. Domestic service was the first great field of employment for immigrant women, though some of them found places at very low-grade work in the mills. Lucy Larcom tells of an Irish woman who was employed as a waste picker on the corporation where she worked as a child, and who was regarded as a great curiosity by the other operatives.

But the moving of the New England girls of the old stock out of the mills into higher-grade occupations, and the filling of the vacant posts by Irish women, had become common enough in the latter half of the forties. As early as 1845, several of Lucy Larcom's friends had emigrated to the West as teachers or missionaries, and the New England Offering was obliged to call for support not only from "those who are," but from "those who have been factory operatives"'; references to the mill girls who had permanently given up factory work for teaching became frequent; and letters were published in the Offering from former mill girls who had found positions in Missouri, Arkansas, and Illinois.

The crisis of 1848-49, with its accompanying reduction of wages, gave a quickening impulse to the changing order. Changes which were already in progress came more rapidly in the wake of to Industrial depression. High wages had been the chief attraction of the mills, and without this the most intelligent of the women operatives, who now saw other opportunities for work opening to them, found nothing to keep them in Lowell.[130] As early as 1851 an English traveler noted that the great demand for operatives had "gradu-

---

[130]An article in the *Offering*, December, 1848, on "The Rights and Duties of Mill Girls" makes the following reference to their departure: "New England cotton mills are, and for the last six months have been, running at a positive loss, and therefore lowering speed and lessening wages . . . the girls are leaving the mills by the thousand here and elsewhere."

ally introduced black sheep into the workshops, and disreputable neighbors in the crowded streets."[131] Irish Women who would have entered domestic service during the first decade after Irish immigration began, gradually drifted into the mills during the forties, and in the early fifties, when James Robertson visited Lowell he found that half of the operatives were Irish and that the former high tone of the place had been lowered. "In consequence," he said, "the reputation of the employment has suffered in the estimation of those whose daughters, under more favorable circumstances, would have become workers in the place."

Miss Farley, in the pages of the *New England Offering*, lamented this exodus of her New England sisters and foreshadowed the permanence of the change in the body of operatives. She saw the "great West open for our girls away there, with all this clamor for teachers, missionaries, and wives," and she felt that with only "the Irish and low-class New England girls" remaining, a great and deplorable change of conditions in Lowell would result.[132]

Later in the year the evidences of the substitution of low-grade Irish help had become more marked, and the *Offering* complained that so many of the best operatives had either gone west or settled permanently into some other kind of work, that "now the good old times will not return even if the good old wages are again held out as an inducement."[133] Other signs of change appeared. An overseer noted that there was an increasing number of illiterate operatives who "made their mark" because they could not sign their own names. Shopkeepers and boarding-house managers declared that they found themselves dealing with a new mill population.

The reduction of wages was not, of course, wholly responsible for this " downward tendency," as it was called in Lowell. It was inevitable that the opening of occupations for educated women

---

[131] Johnston, "Notes on North America," 1851, p. 423.

[132] Wages, she thought, would come down as a result of the comparative unprofitableness of the new employees, and "they will submit, since they have little energy, few aspirations to be ministered unto by their gains, and having poor homes, or little of the home sentiment, they will stay, and wages may be reduced again and again."

[133] Article by Miss Farley on "The Present Crisis," in the *New England Offering*, Miss Farley adds in her editorial that other causes than the reduction of wages have brought about the "downward tendency" — among these, less watchfulness over the morals of the operatives by superintendents and boarding-house keepers and less care as to the morals of the male sub-ordinates in the mills. She felt that there was, in general, much immorality in the city.

should mean their withdrawal from mechanical employments of a lower grade. The reduction of wages hastened, but did not cause the movement. The fact that there were increasing opportunities for women as teachers was also in part responsible for the change. From 1838 to 1847 the increase in the number of women teaching in Massachusetts was 1,647, while during the same time the number of men in the profession increased but 67. In 1850 the number of women teachers in the State was more than twice the number of men teachers. Moreover, there had been three normal schools established, which made it easier for a woman to fit herself for teaching. By the close of the first half of the nineteenth century the cotton mill had ceased to be the preparatory school for the women teachers of Massachusetts, and during the ten years preceding the Civil War, the proportion of educated women among the operatives constantly decreased.

In the following decade, 1860-70, the effect of the war was to hasten the withdrawal of educated women from the mills. In many directions there was an increased demand for the work of women of this class. They were wanted as nurses and for teaching posts left vacant by men who had gone to the front, and for clerical positions of many kinds. Moreover, the prosperity of the farming population, particularly in New England, diminished the necessity for the employment of the daughters. Immediately after the war, the lure of the West, of the vast riches of its unexploited mines and prairies, was felt; and energetic and ambitious women pushed out to earn the high wages that were being offered to teachers.

This outward movement of New England women into new professions and into new sections of the country was further stimulated by the prolonged depression in the cotton industry which was caused by the war. The Merrimack, the oldest and largest of great Lowell corporations, dismissed its operatives and discontinued its purchases of cotton. Many other companies followed the same policy and allowed their mills to stand idle while they waited for peace. Experiments were made in some cases with other branches of manufacture. In Lowell, the Suffolk and Tremont corporations attempted, unsuccessfully, to manufacture cassimeres, the Lawrence turned to the hosiery industry, the Hamilton threw out part of its cotton machinery and prepared for the manufacture of woolen goods. Thousands of cotton operatives were dismissed, and the position of those who remained was less desirable since there was not a sufficient increase in wages to correspond with the sharp up ward movement of prices. As a result, when the war ceased, the most capable and intelligent of the old body of operatives had entered other occupations, and, with the reopening of the mills, such difficulty was found in obtaining competent women employees that lower-grade immigrant labor was resorted to.[134]

At a meeting of the New England Cotton Manufacturers' Association, in 1869, complaint was made of the scarcity of skilled labor, although "ordinary help" seemed to be abundant.[135] Many manufacturers testified to a decrease in the efficiency of labor after the war. It was estimated by Commissioner David A. Wells,[136] in the summer of 1866, that the produce of the cotton mills of New England was variously reduced from five to twenty-five per cent, because of the impossibility of finding women operatives; "an unusual scarcity of female operatives . . . particularly in the manufacturing districts of New England . . . has not been remedied by a large advance in wages." Wages of course had risen during the war, but cost of living had increased so disproportionately that real wages were much less, and the attraction of the mills was correspondingly decreased.

Not only the native-born, but the immigrant Irish operatives were seeking higher-grade employments, and a new wave of immigration was beginning to fill their places with less skilled and less efficient hands from the French-Canadian provinces. In 1872, when Mr. Harris-Gastrell made his report[137] to the English Government, he found the labor chiefly Irish, but the French-Canadian operatives conspicuous enough to be mentioned. The report of the Mas-

---

[134]The following comments of a local historian, written soon after the war, are of interest: "... nine of the great corporations of Lowell, under a mistaken belief that they could not run their mills to a profit during the war, unanimously, in cold blood, dismissed ten thousand operatives penniless into the streets. . . . When these companies resumed operations, their former skilled operatives were dispersed, and could no more be recalled than the ten lost tribes of Israel. Their places were poorly filled by the less skilled operatives whom the companies now had to employ." — Cowley, "History of Lowell," revised edition, 1868, pp. 60, 61. For another criticism of the mills for shutting down, see J. C. Ayer, "Some of the Usages and Abuses in the Management of Our Manufacturing Corporations," 1863, p. 22.

[135] *Transactions* of the Association (1869), p. 5. See also the testimony in the "Weeks Report," "Tenth Census," (1880) xx, 346, 361.

[136]Report of the special commissioner of revenue, "Senate Documents, Second Session, Thirty-ninth Congress," i, 21 ff.

[137]In "Reports on the Condition of the Industrial Classes in Foreign Countries and the Purchase Power of Money," etc., 3 parts, 1870-72.

sachusetts Bureau of Labor in 1870 speaks of the Irish element in the mills as "falling off" and of a new class, "the French-Canadians who are coming into New England and New York by thousands of families and making permanent settlement among us." Some over-seers, it appeared, preferred "foreigners," who, instead of coming from country homes, lived in the town as the Irish did, and could be relied on to work in the mills the year round "without bothering about vacations."

In 1873 attention was called to the fact that there was clearly being created "what the founders of Lowell never looked for — a permanent body of factory employees, composed in part of American stock, but more largely of Irish and French-Canadian elements."

Complaint was made of more and more crowded boarding houses; twelve persons were reported by a woman operative to be sleeping in one room in the boarding house where she lived, and the room was uncomfortable in other respects. But with the decrease in the number of operatives who came from the country to reside temporarily in Lowell and a corresponding increase in the number of those who resided permanently, in many cases with their families, the need for corporation boarding houses largely disappeared.

Many of them have now been entirely given up and turned into storehouses. The immigrant woman[138] has no interest in operatives' magazines, improvement circles, or lending libraries. She has no theories about making labor or laborers alike self-respecting and respected. And it must not be forgotten that the operatives have changed not only in nationality but in age. The fact that there are

---

[138]The following percentages computed from statistics in the "Twelfth Census (1900): Occupations," Table 43, show the percentage of foreign born and those "foreign born or of foreign parentage" among cotton mill operatives:

	Massa-chu-setts.	Lowell.	Fall River.	Law-rence.	New Bed-ford.
Percentage of foreign-born operatives:					
Men.	72	73	71	70	78
Women.	68	68	74	62	70
Percentage of operatives "foreign born or of foreign parentage":					
Men.	95	91	96	93	96
Women.	95	92	97	94	96

more of the old and of the very young in the mills, more married women and more children, is in itself symptomatic of the existence of an inferior factory population. Moreover, as has been pointed out in the preceding chapter, the men are now outnumbering the women.

With the formation of a fairly permanent body of factory operatives, other changes have come. Attempts have been made gradually to bring about improvements in working conditions which did not seem worth the struggle to the early operatives who were there only for a brief term of service.[139] Thus the organized movement for a shorter, working day, which the superior transient factory population refused to undertake, has long been in progress and has achieved some notable results. Trade-unionism has been slowly taking root as a growing class consciousness has recognized the need of fostering a permanent organization to protect class interests as such.

The community, too, has awakened to a greater sense of its responsibility for unhealthful industrial and social conditions, as it has come face to face with the fact that large numbers of people will always live and work in them. The law has compelled mill owners to improve ventilation in the mills, to fence machinery, to shorten the hours of labor for women and children; and the law and scientific progress have improved the sanitary conditions not only of the mills but of the towns.

In conclusion, it should perhaps be emphasized that while it is unquestionably true that the Lowell of the twentieth century impresses the visitor more unfavorably than did the Lowell of fifty or seventy years ago, yet the changes are due primarily to one fact: the substitution of immigrant operatives for the educated New England women who first filled the mills. The educated woman has passed from mechanical occupations into various professional employments, and the number of these which have been opened to her in the last

---

[139]In contrast, for example, with the little "flare-ups" and "turn-outs" of an earlier day which have already been described, was the part played by women in the strike of the Fall River weavers in 1875. In 1874 the men weavers had met without the women and voted to accept a marked reduction of wages; but the women at a meeting of their own, at which no men except reporters were admitted, decided to strike, beginning with three mills only, so that some could go on working and support those striking. This was a very bold step, for they were acting in opposition to the decision of the men weavers and they did not know whether they would receive any support from the men. Their action, however, was indorsed by. the men's committee and the great strike of 1875 began.

half century is the measure of the new opportunity that the world has offered her.

Chapter VIII - The Manufacture of Boots and Shoes

Unlike the manufacture of cloth, the making of I boots and shoes was not historically a woman's industry. Shoemaking or cobbling had always been considered "men's work" almost as universally as spinning was looked upon as work for women. Yet in this country throughout the nineteenth century, women found one of their most important occupations in the manufacture of boots and shoes, and according to the 1905 "Census of Manufactures," it ranks second after the textile industries in the number of its women employees. Women, however, were never "shoemakers" in any proper sense of that term, and their relation to the industry only begins with the introduction of a system of division of labor which was in use for more than half a century before machinery and the factory system revolutionized the industry.

The application of laborsaving machinery to the manufacture of boots and shoes belongs to a comparatively recent chapter in our industrial history. There is no other of our important manufacturing industries in which machinery has so recently displaced hand methods and in which the displacement has been so swiftly successful and complete. Although for more than fifty years after the establishment of the first cotton mill in Massachusetts, shoes continued to be made after primitive hand methods, at the present time even the smallest details of the process of manufacture are done by machinery.

The history of the manufacture of boots and shoes in this country divides itself into three different periods: (1) The colonial period, in which the work was done entirely by men — village shoemakers, or cobblers, or cordwainers; (2) a period which extended, roughly, from the latter part of the eighteenth century through the first half of the nineteenth, and in which, under a system of division of labor, women became an important factor in the industry; (3) the modern period, which has witnessed the introduction of machinery and the establishment of the factory system, and in which women's labor has become increasingly important.[140]

Of the first period little need be said. Boots and shoes were made by the village shoemaker, who kept a shop or went from house to house repairing and making shoes for the family once a year. Sometimes he procured a little leather and made it into shoes which were bartered at a neighboring store, and it gradually became customary for storekeepers to carry a few ready-made shoes for sale.[141]

In the latter half of the eighteenth century more of this ready-made work was done and a considerable wholesale trade developed. During the Revolutionary War the domestic industry was able to furnish shoes for the Continental army; and it was not long before Southern planters began to depend on Massachusetts to supply the brogans which were worn by the negroes. By 1795, 300,000 pairs of ladies' shoes were produced in Lynn, and it was estimated that 200 master workmen and 600 journeymen were employed there.[142] From 1800 to 1810 the population of Lynn was reported to have increased 50 per cent, an increase attributed to the growing opportunity for employment in the boot and shoe industry.

This large and prosperous trade, however, could not have been worked out on the village cobbler system alone. Along with the expansion of the industry, a system of division of labor was developed, which greatly increased the possible output. This system came into

---

[140]In Mr. H. P. Fairchild's article on shoemaking in Shaler, "United States of America," ii, 178, these periods are more exactly defined. The first period, the period of the cordwainer, is said to extend from 1629 to 1752; the second period, "from a trade to a manufacturing industry," from 1750 to 1850; the third period, "the steam-power factory," from 1850 to 1892. See also the "Thirteenth Annual Report of the Commissioner of Labor" on "Hand and Machine Labor," i, 13, for a somewhat different account of the periods through which the industry has passed.

[141]See Kingman, "History of North Bridgewater," 1866, pp. 402, 403.

[142]"One Hundred Years of American Commerce," ii, 567. The article on the "Boot and Shoe Trade" is by William B. Rice.

existence very gradually, and the latter half of the eighteenth century was a time of transition from the period of the individual shoemaker making the whole boot or shoe to the period of the "team," when the work was subdivided and one man carried on only a single process.

During the first period and, for the most part, during the experimental time of transition, the industry was exclusively in the hands of men. Journeymen and master workmen alike were men, and no women were employed at any part of the work. Shoe shops large enough to accommodate the three or four members of a team soon became common in the more enterprising shoe towns. Prosperous shoemakers became manufacturers in a small way by hiring a few neighbors to work with them in the shop. It was natural, under the circumstances, to make some division of labor, and it became customary to have the cutting of the leather done by one man, the work of fitting and sewing the uppers done by another, and to have still another exclusively employed in fastening the uppers to the soles. This system, in which each workman carried on a single process, was found to be vastly superior to the more primitive method of having the whole shoe made by a single workman.

Shoemakers were not slow in discovering that under the new system the labor of the women and children in the family could be utilized by giving them the uppers to be stitched and bound in the home and then returned to the shop to have the soles put on by the men. "Stitching and binding" thus came to be exclusively women's work during the first half of the nineteenth century. Work in the shops was confined to cutting, bottoming, finishing, and packing to send to market; and all through eastern Massachusetts, women in or near the "shoe towns" became in a measure self-supporting by getting shoes to bind. As early as 1810 it was reported that the women binders of Lynn alone had earned $50,000 in the course of that year.[143] From the beginning, Lynn made a specialty of the manufacture of ladies' shoes,[144] and this perhaps accounts in part for the large proportion of women always employed there; for the work of these Lynn shoemakers was much lighter and less fatiguing than the heavy work of the old cobblers or of the makers of men's shoes.

---

[143]Hurd, "History of Essex County," i, 284.

[144]The work of making ladies' shoes is still kept more or less segregated. Just as Lynn has always been the center of the manufacture of ladies' shoes, Brockton makes a specialty of manufacturing men's shoes.

A change of some importance followed the invention of the wooden shoe peg in 1811. The new peg filled a great need. Premiums had been offered for the invention of machines which would enable shoe-makers to work standing and thus relieve the pressure upon the breast which came from holding the shoe and the fatigue caused by the stooping position which was necessary while sewing;[145] but improvements came slowly. After the introduction of the pegging machine, however, the work of "bottoming" became much easier, so that boys and even women could peg shoes, although they could not be advantageously employed on the heavy-sewed work.

With the impetus given by the success of the attempts at a division of labor, the industry grew rapidly, and many so-called "factories" were established in the large centers. These factories, however, were merely small buildings where the large dealers or manufacturers, as they were called, accumulated materials, had the different kinds of leather cut into "uppers and understock," and given out to be made up all through the surrounding country in shoemakers' shops or binders' homes. The finished shoes were then returned to the factory, and, after being packed in boxes, were distributed to the various markets throughout the country.

But it is clear that very little, if any, of the work was done in the so-called factory. Shoes were still made in the little "eight-by-ten" shops, where the shoemaker and his sons, or a few neighbors, made a team; and in the home, where the women and girls did the stitching and binding and, for fancy slippers, the trimming and ornamenting. In the shop, although cutters were not needed when the stock was received from the factory ready to be made up, work was still found for a team. One man did the lasting, the necessary stretching and fitting of the upper to the sole, another did the pegging, "the boys, and sometimes the girls, were taught this branch, and still another the eye setting, but all was done by hand."[146]

While much of the work was given out by "factories" which employed a large number of work people and marketed the product on a large scale, there were many petty employers in the trade at this time. The men who were known as "bag-bosses" were of this class,

---

[145] 1905 "Census of Manufactures," iii, 242.

[146] "One Hundred Years of American Commerce" ii, 567. Other accounts of the industry at this period are to be found in the "Twelfth Census (1900): Manufactures," iii, 754-755, and in the "Thirteenth Annual Report of the Commissioner of Labor," i, 113.

and their name originated from their custom of taking one or two dozen pairs of shoes in a bag to Boston to be traded off for whatever could be got in exchange.[147]

With the increased efficiency which followed as a result of the improved methods of production, the manufacture of boots and shoes became a large and prosperous industry in spite of the lack of labor-saving machinery. The work continued to be done almost exclusively by hand until after the close of the first half of the nineteenth century, and during this time shoemaking was still regarded as a skilled trade, a craft to which boys were regularly apprenticed for a term of seven years.

This fact of the boy's long apprenticeship illustrates the difference between the relation of men and women to the trade. Although the labor of women was an important factor in the development of the industry, they were almost exclusively employed in sewing or binding, and their position was very different from that of the men who had learned all the processes. The women carried on a single, narrowly defined part of the work, for which little or no skill was required and for which they were never apprenticed; the men knew the whole trade and had been rigidly held down to a long period of training.

Since the women did the work in their own homes, much of it was done only at times when they were not engaged in household duties. Any statements, therefore, of the total number of women employed in the industry must have included a large number who did not give full time to the work, but such early statistics of the number of women shoebinders and stitchers as are available are of interest, even if they are only estimates. In 1829 the city of Lynn contained sixty-two factories, which were said to employ 1,500 "mechanics" and about the same number of women. The latter, said a local historian, "are engaged in binding and trimming, and by their industry and economy contribute to the support and respectability of their families."

The factories of Lynn, however, gave out a great deal of work to the women of the neighboring towns and villages as well as to those within the city. In the fishing villages of the coast, where shoemaking was a winter occupation for fishermen, their wives and daughters found employment at shoebinding through a great part

---

[147] Johnson, "Sketches of Lynn," 1880, p. 14. The "bag-bosses" belonged to the period about 1830.

of the year. The village of Marblehead in 1831 reported 51 men, 134 women, and a considerable number of boys engaged in the boot and shoe industry. Lucy Larcom in an early poem, "Hannah at the Window Binding Shoes," describes one of these shoebinders forever watching for the return of. the lover who has been lost at sea:

> Poor lone Hannah Sitting at the window binding
> shoes;
>
> Faded, wrinkled, Sitting stitching in a mournful muse,
>
> • • • • •
>
> Spring and winter. Night and morning, Hannah's at the
> window, binding shoes.

Further information regarding the extent to which women were employed in the manufacture of shoes is found in the collection of data in the "Documents Relative to the Manufactures of the United States,"[148] which were gathered in 1832 by the Secretary of the Treasury. The industry at this time was largely confined to the towns of eastern Massachusetts, and some interesting statements of the number of men and women working at the trade and the wages they were receiving are given for these shoemaking centers. While it must be recognized that these statistics are for the most part very crude estimates, the enumeration of some of them may be useful as a means of giving a more concrete idea of the extent to which women were engaged in this work.

At Haverhill, one of the oldest shoe manufacturing towns in the State, 586 men, 130 boys, and 265 women were employed ; and it is of interest that most of the women earned twenty cents a day, while the men earned seventy cents; at Salem, there were 300 men at "five shillings and sixpence" a day, and 250 women at "two shillings" a day; at Maiden, 275 men at one dollar a day, 200 women at twenty-five cents, and 25 boys at fifty cents; at Randolph, 470 men at eighty cents, 300 women at forty cents, and 200 boys at the same wages as the women; at Newbury and Newburyport, 155 men were getting from seventy to eighty-four cents a day, and 120 women from fifteen

---

[148]"House Executive Documents," Twenty-second Congress, First Session, i and ii.

to twenty-five cents;[149] at Marblehead, where more than 130 women were reported employed, many of them earned only eight or nine cents a day, though the majority got as much as twelve cents a day.

More than 1,600 women and girls were reported employed in Lynn, and their wages ranged from twelve cents to fifty cents a day, although very few were employed either at the highest or at the lowest wage; about the same number of men were employed for wages ranging from thirty-five cents to $1.83, but few received less than seventy cents or more than a dollar a day. From Boston it was reported that the industry there was so intimately connected with that of the neighboring counties, Essex and Norfolk particularly, that it could not very well be separated. Many of the principal establishments in Boston also had shops in the country to which they furnished the stock and from which they received the manufactured product.

For the state as a whole the most reliable estimate of the number of persons employed in the industry is found in the industrial census of 1837. According to the "Tables of Industry" for that year, 15,000 women were engaged in the manufacture of boots and shoes, and in the same year there were 14,757 women employed in the cotton factories. While it might appear from this census that shoebinding had become numerically a more important occupation for women than work in the cotton mills, it was really much less important when considered from other points of view. Binding shoes, like other kinds of home work, was done irregularly. This was due in part to the fact that many women binders worked only in the intervals of household duties, and in part because work was not always furnished regularly by the factories and "bosses." It is of course true that employers make a much greater effort to provide work constantly for factory employees than for home workers, since the latter are not paid for any of the time which is unemployed.

A large proportion, therefore, of the 15,000 women reported to be engaged in the manufacture of boots and shoes worked only in

---

[149]Similar statements are reported for a large number of other towns; thus at Stoneham 200 men were employed at 75 cents, 120 women at 33 cents, and 50 boys at the latter wage; at South Reading 350 men at 75 cents, 100 women at 25 cents, and 50 boys at 30 cents; at Stoughton, 160 men at 83 cents and 100 women at 40 cents; at Abington, 300 men at 75 cents, 150 women at 25 cents, and 200 boys at 33 cents; at Weymouth, 300 men at $1, 100 women at 50 cents, and 50 boys at the same wage; at Reading, 238 men at 65 cents, 150 women at 25 cents, and 72 boys at the same wage.

the intervals of other duties, and their earnings were correspondingly small. The data for 1832 which have been given show that some of these women binders did not average more than eight or nine cents a day, and, while many more earned from thirty to forty cents, very few earned as much as fifty or sixty cents. Women cotton operatives, on the other hand, worked in factories and were regularly employed at what were considered very good wages for women. Moreover, in the cotton mills some women were employed at highly skilled work, so that a capable, ambitious girl could make very good wages indeed. In general, it would not be far wrong to say that what were regarded as "high" earnings for shoebinders corresponded roughly with the "low" earnings of women in the cotton mills.

The class of women who worked in the two industries seems to have been, on the whole, pretty carefully differentiated, although they were all alike Americans of "good New England stock." Young, ambitious, unmarried women who could leave home preferred the cotton mills, which offered to those who were industrious, skilled work, steady employment, and high wages. Married women and widows, on the other hand, preferred work which could be done in their own homes and could be neglected when household cares were pressing. Other women who could not "be spared" at home or those who still cherished a social prejudice against "factory hands" also preferred home work to mill work.

Social conditions in the towns and villages in which the making of boots and shoes had become an important industry, were on the whole very favorable during this period. The trade had centered in eastern Massachusetts, and much of what has been said regarding the factory operatives of this region is also true of the men and women who were shoemakers and binders. In these "shoe villages," most of the workmen owned their own homes and had quite a little adjoining land for vegetable gardens and fruit. There were said to be three times as many freeholders among the operatives in the boot and shoe industry as among the employees in the cotton, wool, or iron manufacture.[150] How far this statement is trustworthy it is not possible to say, but it is certainly true that the textile industries employed a larger proportion of women and offered much better opportunities to women than did the manufacture of boots

---

[150]"Proceedings of the Convention of the Manufacturers, Dealers, and Operatives in the Shoe and Leather Trade in the State of Massachusetts" (Boston, 1842), p. 30.

and shoes. The latter was much more a men's industry, demanding skilled men employees, and offering practically no skilled work for women. It was only natural, therefore, that the largest proportion of freeholders should be found in this industry, which employed the largest proportion of skilled men. That both the men and women, however, formed a superior class of work people, native born of good stock, intelligent and reliable, there can be no question.

Amasa Walker in an address before the Convention of Manufacturers in the Shoe and Leather Business in 1842, said emphatically, that no villages "stood higher than the shoe villages of New England in the moral, social, and intellectual condition of their inhabitants. The population engaged in the trade was," he thought, "distinguished for general intelligence. The business was a social business, the people were not crowded together in factory buildings; their conversation was not drowned by the noise of machinery; there were many and great opportunities for reading and instruction and mutual improvement."

The women binders unfortunately did not have the advantages that came from working in groups as the men did. Every shoemaker's shop at that period was said to be a center of instruction and a place where political questions were threshed out. A statement frequently repeated at the time that "every shoemaker in Lynn was fit to be a United States senator" illustrates contemporary opinion of the craft.

Both shoemakers and shoebinders suffered in common with most of the working people of that day from the truck system.[151] Some "bosses" paid their binders exclusively in orders on dry goods stores where they were mercilessly overcharged for what they bought, and a man who would advertise to "pay cash" had no difficulty in getting work people at any season. In general, however, higher rates were paid when orders were given.

In striking contrast to these New England women and the conditions under which they were employed were the poor shoebinders of the larger cities, who worked in wretched tenement homes and who were really the victims of an early sweating system. Matthew Carey, the early philanthropist and publicist, in an open letter of remonstrance regarding "the inadequate payment which females receive for their labor," said that the work for which women were notoriously underpaid both in New York and in Philadelphia included the

---

[151]See later for an account of this system in the cotton industry.

folding and stitching of books, the sewing of carpet rags, the work done for the army and navy, and the binding of shoes.[152] These were what one might call the "sweated trades" of the first half of the nineteenth century, and it is clear that, so far as working conditions were concerned, there was little in common between the shoebinders of the Massachusetts towns and villages and the shoebinders of the cities. The condition of the latter was pictured as one of extreme wretchedness, and the "garret bosses" under whom they worked were undoubtedly heavy taskmasters.[153]

But the work of women shoebinders everywhere, together with the work of the shoemakers, was destined to be completely revolutionized. In the year 1845 the first important labor-saving machine to be used in the manufacture of boots and shoes was introduced, and the third period in the history of the industry may be said to have begun. This period has been marked by a long series of remarkable mechanical inventions, the long-delayed establishment of the factory system, and the bringing to an end of the old primitive methods of work in the shoemakers' shops and the binders' homes.

The machine which was invented in 1845 was for leather rolling, and was therefore not directly connected with the making of shoes and did not in any way affect the work which women were doing. But within a few years the invention of the sewing machine brought about the most radical change in the industry which has affected their work. It was soon discovered that the sewing machine could be successfully used with dry thread for the work of binding and stitching which women had been doing by hand, and in 1852 the first machine for stitching shoe-uppers was used in Lynn. The machine was a "Singer patent" and a woman operator was employed to run it. When its superiority to the old method of closing and binding uppers by hand had been demonstrated, the machine soon came into very general use. The amount of work which a binder could do in a given period of time was, of course, vastly increased, and other changes necessarily followed. In Lynn, stitching shops were started in various parts of the city; and everywhere, as steam power was substituted for foot power in the running of the machines, it became inevitable that the work should be transferred from the home to the factory.

---

[152]M. Carey, "Essays on the Public Charities of Philadelphia," 1830.
[153]For an account of the system to which the "garret bosses" belonged, see Freedley, "Philadelphia and Its Manufactures," 1867, p. 178.

Table 16: NUMBER OF WOMEN EMPLOYED IN THE MANUFACTURE
OF SHOES IN THE STATE OF MASSACHUSETTS

	City of Lynn.			State of Massachusetts.	
	1845	1855		1845	1850
Men.	2,719	4,545	Men.	27,199	29,252
Women.	3,209	6,476	Women.	18,678	22,310
Total.	5,928	11,021	Total.	45,877	51,562

Just before the introduction of the machine an increase not only in the number but in the proportion of women employees in the industry had been noted. This is indicated in the table[154] given below, which shows the number of women employed in the manufacture of shoes in the State of Massachusetts and in the city of Lynn at the beginning and at the end of the decade.

No very great weight can be attached to conclusions drawn from this table, since the data are probably none of them very accurate. It is nevertheless interesting that the proportion of women employed in the industry increased from fifty-four to fifty-nine per cent for the city of Lynn and from forty to forty-three; per cent for the state as a whole. This slight increase in the proportion of women can perhaps be explained as the result of the introduction of the leather-rolling machine in 1845. With this machine it was said that "a man could do in a minute what would require half an hour's hard work with a lapstone and hammer." The increase in the proportion of women, therefore, probably did not mean that the kind or the quantity of work done by women had been changed, but merely that one of the processes carried on by men required fewer hands than formerly.[155] There had been no change up to this point in the division of labor between men and women.

In comparing the statistics given in the census of 1850 with those

[154]Data for 1845 from Massachusetts "Tables of Industry."
Data for 1855 from *Hunt's Merchants' Magazine*, xxx, 126.;
From census data for 1850.
[155] A writer in *Hunt's Merchants' Magazine*, xxxiii, 126, said, in commenting on this increase in the number of women employed: "Increased skill and intelligence have been brought to bear upon the manufacture, by which female now accomplishes results greatly surpassing those of male industry in the former period, and also that in the face of a very important rise in hides and other raw materials, and of a large advance in wages."

103

Table 17: NUMBER OF WOMEN EMPLOYED IN THE MANUFACTURE OF SHOES IN THE UNITED STATES AND IN THE STATE OF MASSACHUSETTS

	United States.			Massachusetts.	
	1850	1860		1850	1860
Men.	72,305	94,515	Men.	29,252	43,068
Women.	32,949	28,515	Women.	22,310	19,215
Total.	105,254	123,030	Total.	51,562	62,283

from the census of 1860, the results of the introduction of the sewing machine are seen in the decrease both in the number and in the proportion of women employed. Data are not available for Lynn, but they are given for the United States and for the State of Massachusetts.

The percentage which women formed of all employees decreased, for the country as a whole, from thirty-one per cent in 1850 to twenty-three per cent in 1860, and the census of 1860, in commenting upon this change, attributed it correctly enough to the use of the sewing machine.

The year 1860 was a significant one in the industry because of the great shoemakers' strike in Lynn during that year. It was charged that the whole trade was "in an unhealthy condition," probably in part because of the necessity of rapidly adjusting it to new conditions. The object of the strike was higher wages, and, while no attempt can be made here to follow the various labor difficulties in the industry, this one is of special interest because the shoebinders were also on strike. A contemporary account relates that in several instances, at one time during a snowstorm, "large bodies of females appeared in the ranks." On one occasion hundreds of women "in grand procession" with the striking shoemakers formed "an imposing spectacle."[156]

Other labor-saving inventions had been introduced in the industry in the years between 1845 and 1860, "rolling," "buffing," "splitting," and "racing" machines for preparing sole leather, the machines for cutting soles, tips, and heels, cable-wire nailers, sandpapering, heel-making, burnishing, and pegging machines; and with all of these the general substitution of steam for hand power.[157] No invention,

[156]See the account in Lewis and Newhall, "History of Lynn," 1865, p. 459.

[157]These inventions and others are enumerated in the 1905 "Census of Manu-

however, changed the work of men so completely as the sewing machine had changed the work of women. For binding and stitching had ceased to be a by-employment which women could carry on in as leisurely a fashion as they wished and earn a few cents a day in their own homes. Women who worked at the sewing of uppers were suddenly obliged to go to a factory and work regularly during a long working day.

An account of a Haverhill factory in 1860, after the introduction of the pegging machine, describes the various processes by which a shoe was then manufactured, all of which were carried on under one roof. The fourth story of one of the buildings was used as a stitching room "occupied by ladies who tend the stitching machines, which are also run by steam, thus saving them from what otherwise must prove a laborious and fatiguing operation"[158]

As the machine came to be more and more generally used, the piece-work rates for work done at home must have been greatly reduced, and binders who could not go into factories and continued to do hand work must have found their lot a very hard one. A Philadelphia shoebinder complained in 1862 that she was receiving only thirty-seven cents for work for which she had formerly been paid seventy-five cents.

The old system was not, of course, swept out of existence all at once, and the introduction in 1862 of the wonderful McKay machine for sewing uppers to soles greatly accelerated the movement toward the concentration of the industry in factories, and other inventions and improvements between 1860 and 1870 gave it a further impetus.

The McKay machine was introduced at a time when the industry was losing men on account of the war, and was said to do the work of the shoemakers who had gone to the front. This work of sewing uppers and soles together had always been done by men, but in the early experiments with the machine, women seem to have been tried as operators. One instance is given of a woman in Haverhill who for three years earned about eighteen dollars a week at the McKay machine shortly after its introduction.[159] The machine was, however, at first run by foot power, and operating it must have been heavy work. But the installation of power was not long delayed, and

factures," iii, 242.

[158] *Hunt's Merchants' Magazine*, liii, 471.
[159] See a pamphlet, "In the Matter of the Application of Lyman R. Blake," 1874, p. 42.

during this same decade, other improvements and inventions added new machines driven by power to those already in use.[160]

The factory system found its earliest and most complete development in Lynn. The report of the Massachusetts Bureau of Labor issued in 1872, said, in giving an account of the shoe operatives, that in Lynn, work in all departments was largely done by machinery and that each workman carried on one special process. At this time the work was confined to two seasons, each lasting about seventeen weeks. Women were given two to four days' work a week as the season began, with a gradual increase to full time during the rush season, which was followed again by a decrease. Wages during the busy season were very high for women, but it must not be forgotten that this was during the period of greenback inflation when everything was high. Wages were reported for 1,026 women in Lynn, and out of this number nearly half were earning more than ten dollars a week, 135 were earning from twelve to fifteen dollars, and 68 from fifteen to eighteen dollars.[161]

Two important strikes occurred in the industry during this year both of them "women's strikes." In Stoneham, three hundred of the "Daughters of Crispin Lodge,"[162] employed as machine operators in three different factories, struck for higher rates on a certain kind of piece work; they were out of work for about two weeks, when it became evident that their places could probably be filled without much difficulty, and the strike was declared off. The two leaders in the strike, however, according to a contemporary account, were not afterwards admitted to any of the shops, and were only able to obtain work of an inferior kind, which they were obliged to do at home.

The Lynn strike of the same year was a much more important

---

[160] For a full account of this period 1860-70, see Shaler, "United States of America," ii, 1855-57.

[161] "Third Annual Report of Massachusetts Bureau of Labor," p. 104. Under the shoemaking industry a report is given of women's wages in 1867 in the form of a classified wage table, with the following totals: 563 women at $8 a week, 408 at $9, 514 at from $10 to $12, 247 at from $12 to $15, 135 at from $15 to $18.

[162] Although no attempt is made in this or in any of these chapters to write the history of trade-unionism among women, strikes and labor difficulties are occasionally noted when they seem to throw light upon the relation of women to the industry. Early labor organizations among the shoemakers were called Lodges of the Knights of St. Crispin, and women, who often had lodges of their own, were "Daughters" or "Ladies of St. Crispin."

one. It began at first in one or two shoestitching shops, but finally extended throughout the city. It was caused by "an attempt of the boss stitchers [employers] to reduce the wages of those receiving the highest wages one seventh per cent and increasing the lowest paid as much, to establish more uniform prices." The women protested with great spirit "against any reduction of wages on any pretext whatever." The "boss stitchers" then agreed among themselves to compel every woman employed by one of their number to sign an agreement to give two weeks' notice before stopping, or to forfeit five dollars. The women shoe stitchers again acted with promptness and courage. At a meeting which was attended by about nine hundred of the women who were affected by the order, it was unanimously voted "that they would not comply with the resolution, nor submit to any rule or regulation binding them that did not likewise affect their employers." The resolutions which were passed at that meeting are of sufficient interest to be quoted at length, since they throw a good deal of light upon the character of the woman shoe operatives of this period.

"We, the Workingwomen, in convention assembled, do accept the following resolutions, as an earnest expression of our sentiments;

"Whereas, we have long been sensible of the need of protecting our rights and privileges, as free-born women, and are determined to defend them and our interests as workingwomen, to the fullest extent of our ability; therefore, be it

"*Resolved*, That we, the workingwomen of Lynn,

known as Upper Fitters and Finishers of Boots and Shoes, do enter a most solemn protest against any reduction of wages, on any pretext whatever; and that we will not submit to any rules binding us that do not equally affect our employers.

"*Resolved*, That we feel grateful to the shoemakers of Lynn for their interest and determination to stand by us in our time of need.

"*Resolved*, That we, the free women of Lynn, will submit to no rules or set of rules that tend to degrade and enslave us.

"*Resolved*, That we will accept no terms whatever, either with regard to a reduction of prices, notices to quit, or forfeiture of wages. That while we utterly ignore the spirit of selfishness and illiberality which prompted the late action of our would be oppressors, we will not hesitate to resist, in a proper manner, the unjust encroachments upon our rights.

"*Resolved*, That a copy of these resolutions be given to each one of the committee, to be by them presented to each girl in every shop, and her signature thereon obtained, that she will adhere to the terms of the resolutions; and should anyone of the employees of the shop be reduced in her wages, or ill treated, we will desist from our work until she has obtained her rights.

"*Resolved*, That a copy of the above be inserted in the Lynn papers, and a large surplus number be provided for distribution among the girls."

These resolutions were not only distributed in every shop in Lynn, but published in two of the leading newspapers as well. The "bosses" were afraid to carry on the contest in the face of such vigorous united action, and the shoe stitchers won the day. Their wages were unmolested, and the obnoxious certificates were never issued.[163]

Looking at the work done by women in the early seventies, after the application of machinery and the removal of the industry from shops and homes to the factories, it appears that the division of labor between men and women was altered very little if at all by these revolutionary changes. Men still did the cutting,[164] earning about three dollars a day in Lynn, and they continued to do the work of sewing uppers to soles, using the McKay machines instead of the old laborious hand sewing or pegging. For operating the new machine they received from twenty-five to forty dollars a week.[165] Women and girls were still almost exclusively engaged in fitting and sewing shoe uppers, earning at this time from seven to fourteen dollars a week. An employer from Stoughton reported that as fitters "girls and women of all ages from thirteen up" were employed, and were paid from fifty cents to three dollars a day.

The work of these fitters, however, was only a part of the work which the old binders had done, for the "fitter" as the name indicates, merely fitted or pasted linings to uppers and got the work ready to be stitched on the machine. "Lasting" in preparation for the sewing together of soles and uppers by the McKay machine was done by both men and women, the women earning from twelve to

---

[163]An account of these strikes is given in the "Third Annual Report of the Massachusetts Bureau of Labor" pp. 434-437.

[164]The following statements regarding work and wages are from re Blake, pp. 40-48. The quotations of wages are all from Lynn and Stoughton.

[165]The caution should be repeated with regard to quotations of wages that from 1861-79 we were on a "greenback" basis.

twenty dollars a week, the men from thirty-six to forty.[166] "Heeling" and "finishing" was done by men as it always had been,[167] and, at that time, for wages of three or four dollars a day.

It would seem, therefore, that in this early period immediately following the establishment of the machine system both men and women were doing much the same work as they had done before. The method of working had been radically changed, but this had not altered the line of delimitation which had of old been drawn between the work of the shoemaker and that of the shoebinder. Women were making uppers, stitching and binding by machine, and men were "bottoming," putting on soles, by machine. If either had encroached upon a field belonging to the other, it was not apparent at this time.

Attention should be called here, perhaps, to the fact that although the industry had become so generally a factory industry by 1870 the old hand processes had not altogether disappeared. In 1875 the state census of Massachusetts still reported 1,518 women in the boot and shoe manufacture employed in their own homes, and although 1,500 is quite insignificant compared with the 22,000 women who had been employed in this manner in 1850, just before the introduction of the sewing machine, it indicates that the hand industry had not altogether died out. There remained even after the introduction of machinery a considerable trade in hand-made goods, women's "buskins" and slippers and ankle ties for children. A manufacturer who produced such goods reported in 1872 that the work was done by both men and women. The women did the binding with leather, and the rest of the work was done by men, who were usually small farmers and who worked at shoemaking only part of the time. He found it impossible to estimate the earnings of either shoemakers or binders, because, he said, "they work at home and as and when they please."

The further question which concerns us is whether in the period of more than a quarter of a century which has followed the establishment of the machine system in the industry the further mechanical improvements which have taken place have resulted in changing the work done by women or in increasing the proportion of women em-

---

[166] Just how the work of men and women differed in this occupation, if there was a difference, it has not been possible to discover.

[167] There had been no heels on ladies' shoes from about 1830 to 1855, but after this time heels came back into fashion, and journeymen were employed to "heel" shoes, and "heeling" became a special process. See Johnson, p. 340.

ployed. A very interesting general statement on this point which is found in the report of the Commissioner of Labor, on "Hand and Machine Labor"[168] is as follows:

"As regards the displacement of males by females, it should also be noted that in the New England States there are comparatively few factories in the shoe industry where this has taken place, though in the shoe factories in other sections of the country it is not uncommon to find women and girls operating machines and doing work that was formerly done by men. On the other hand, in states west and south of New England, men and boys have for years been largely employed in the upper-stitching department, while in New England, and particularly in the province of women's shoes, this part of the work has always been done by females."

The census has commented upon this point from time to time. In 1880 the report of a manufacturer who had stated that the introduction of the sewing machine had greatly increased the number of women employed was declared to be perhaps "a correct statement so far as it applies to the manufactories directly, but . . . hardly a correct one if all the women employed under the old system are considered. Under the system in vogue before the introduction of the sewing machine, employment was given to large numbers of women at their homes. This method has almost entirely ceased with the introduction of machinery. More women are employed in the works than formerly, but many less outside."[169]

In 1900 the "twelfth census"' called attention to the fact that in the industry of boots and shoes from 1890 to 1900 there had been a remarkable increase in the number of women and children employed, while the number of men showed an actual decrease from 91,406 to 91,215. The explanation given by the census was that "women are largely taking the places of men in this industry in the operation of the lighter kind of machinery, and children are, to a considerable extent, succeeding to the places made vacant by women."[170] Part of this increase, however, was probably due to some changes in the preparation of leather which it seems fair to regard as indirectly connected with the industry. The census pointed out that in the tanning of leather, by reason of improved machinery, there had been a constantly decreasing demand for skilled workmen. "Women and

[168]"Thirteenth Annual Report" (1898), i, 122.
[169]"Tenth Census" (1880), xx, 15.
[170]"Twelfth Census (1900): Manufactures," i, cxxvii.

Table 18: Boots And Shoes, Factory Product. Number Of Persons Employed 1880-1905

Year.	Men.	Women.	Children under Sixteen	Per Cent of Women Employed.	Total Number of Employees.
1880	82,547	25,122	3,483	23	111,152
1890	91,406	39,849	2,435	30	133,690
1900	90,415	46,894	4,521	33	141,830
1905	95,257	49,535	5,132	33	149,924

girls are now performing the work of men."[171]

The census statistics showing the increase in the number of women employed during the last twenty-five years are presented in the following table[172] below.

Such statistical evidence as we have in this table shows quite plainly that, while there was a striking increase in the proportion of women employed from 1880 to 1890, since that time the movement, if it may be so called, has gradually died out. The increase was only three per cent from 1890 to 1900, and since 1900 there has been no change at all.

Perhaps the most satisfactory method of finding out how far the old lines of demarcation between men's work and women's work have been eliminated is to ascertain from the records of some individual factories the actual number of men and women employed today in the different processes. Such factory records are furnished us, without prejudice of choice, in one of the special reports of the Commissioner of Labor. While collected for another purpose, they[173] show clearly what the division of labor between men and women is at the present time.

An examination of these factory records shows that the large

---

[171] *Ibid.*, cxiv.

[172] Statistics from the earlier censuses are excluded from this table as not properly comparable with the data which are given. These data are for "boots and shoes — factory product," while in the census reports prior to 1880 data for "boots and shoes — factory product" and "boots and shoes — custom work and repairing" were so combined that the data cannot be correctly segregated. See the 1905 "Census of Manufactures," iii, 229.

[173] From "Eleventh Special Report Commissioner of Labor Regulation and Restriction of Output" (1904), pp. 592, 593.

Table 19: NUMBER OF MEN AND WOMEN EMPLOYED IN TWO SHOE FACTORIES IN 1904

	Union Factory.		Non-Union Factory.	
	Males.	Females.	Males.	Females.
Cutting Room, upper stock and trimming	239	5	205	10
Cutting Room, sole stock	148	15	176	25
Fitting and Stitching Room	101	351	117	309
Gang or Bottoming Rooms	620	...	807	...
Finishing Rooms	141	...	132	4
Dressing Rooms	98	35	110	52
Total	1,347	406	1,547	400

proportion of women employees, eighty-six per cent in one establishment and seventy-seven per cent in the other, are still engaged in the work of sewing uppers, which, although done with power machines, is essentially the same process that was carried on in the old days in fishermen's cottages and in country homes.

Moreover, it should be noted that work which was so exclusively done by women in the period preceding the establishment of the factory system is now shared with men. In one establishment twenty-seven per cent of the employees in the fitting and stitching room were men, and in the other twenty-two per cent were men. It is, of course, also significant that fourteen per cent of the women in one factory and twenty-three per cent in the other are engaged in other processes which were formerly carried on almost wholly by men. It seems clear, however, that the radical changes of the last twenty-five years in the place and in the method of work have altered only very slightly the old line of division between "men's work" and "women's work." The line is less distinct, possibly, but it is still drawn in much the same way.

Attention should be called to the fact that the factory records given above are very greatly simplified. The displacement of hand methods by machinery has resulted in the most elaborate division of processes within the six large groups which are indicated in the table. This can best be illustrated by giving as a concrete example, an account of the way in which the work in the stitching room, which corresponds to the "binding and sewing" done by women in the earlier period, is now subdivided. There are now forty-eight different occupations carried on in this room, and while an enumeration of them may be tedious, nothing short of this can indicate how minute this division of labor has become. The volume of the last census dealing with "Employees and Wages" gives the following list of the various classes of operatives employed in the stitching rooms:[174] Skivers, cementers, pasters, folders (these all employed in the work of preparation), upper stitchers, eyelet row stitchers, closers, seam rubbers, seam pounders, gore stitchers, gusset stitchers, lining stitchers, lining makers, liners, closers on, inseamers, vamp liners, facing stitchers, headers, top stitchers, corders, button-hole machine operators, button-hole finishers, button sewers, punchers (of holes for eyelets), gang punch operators, eyeleters, fastener setters, hookers, markers (of vamp tips), tip markers, tip stitchers, tippers, tip pasters, perforators, tip fixers, vamp closers, vampers, barrers, stayers, heel-stay stitchers, eyelet stay stitchers, fancy stitchers, foxing stitchers, tongue binders, tongue stitchers, strap makers, table workers and table hands.

It should be emphasized that this list includes only the operatives in one single department, the stitching room, and that the work which has been subdivided into these forty-nine processes was formerly a single process done by one woman in the days before the invention of the sewing machine. The same census volume from which this list was taken gives for the whole industry one hundred and twenty-six different classes of operatives. There is probably no industry today in which the subdivision of labor is more minute or in which the substitution of machine for hand labor has been more complete.

In the first part of this chapter certain points of contrast were noted between the manufacture of boots and shoes and the cotton industry, and it may be well to summarize these briefly: shoemaking had always been historically men's work, while the making of cloth had in large part been done by women; in the first half of the nineteenth century the industrial revolution was taking place in the cotton industry while boots and shoes continued to be made by the old hand processes; of the two industries, the cotton mills during this period offered greater inducements to women, while "boots and

---

[174]"Twelfth Census (1900): Special Report on Employees and Wages," by Davis R. Dewey, pp. 1198-1201.

shoes," with heavy skilled work demanding a regular apprenticeship, and offering high wages and independent conditions of employment, was more attractive to men. The cotton mills, therefore, continued through the first half of the nineteenth century to be a women's industry; shoemaking remained a men's trade although a system of division of labor had made it possible to employ large numbers of women for one of the intermediate processes.

In conclusion a further point of contrast between the two industries may be noted. Since 1850 one of the most striking changes that has occurred in the cotton industry has been the increase in the proportion of men employed. The number of men operatives has increased so rapidly that they now outnumber the women, and the last census has called attention to the fact that men are displacing women in the cotton mills. Moreover, few of the men who have been driving the women out of the mills are Americans. In round numbers, 28,000 of the 39,000 men employed as cotton operatives in Massachusetts during the taking of the most recent census were foreign born and nearly 9,000 more were the native-born sons of foreign-born parents.[175] The foreign element among the women operatives is quite as large. In brief, then, the tendency during the last half century has been toward the displacement of women operatives by men and toward the substitution of immigrant for American labor.

In the manufacture of boots and shoes, on the other hand, there has been an increase in the proportion of women employees, although not a large enough increase to indicate any tendency toward the driving out of the men operatives. Shoemaking remains a men's industry; and it remains at the same time predominantly American, with a large majority of both men and women operatives native born. A comparison of the data from the last census, showing the general nativity of the operatives of both industries, is of interest. Statistics[176] are given for Massachusetts, the State which, historically, took the lead in both industries.

These data show very clearly that while the great majority of cotton mill employees, both men and women, are foreign born, in the boot and shoe industry seventy-two per cent of the men and eighty-one per cent of the women are native born. There are, perhaps, two

---

[175]These data are from the "Twelfth Census (1900): Occupations." The census of manufactures does not give statistics relating to nationality.
[176]Statistics from "Twelfth Census (1900): Occupations."

Table 20: STATE OF MASSACHUSETTS

	Men.		Women.	
	Boots and Shoes.	Cotton Mill Operatives.	Boots and Shoes.	Cotton Mill Operatives.
NATIVE BORN:				
Native parents.	20,512	1,925	5,761	2,045
Foreign parents.	13,941	8,849	8,028	10,024
FOREIGN BORN:	14,016	28,092	3,181	25,843
Total	48,469	38,866	16,970	37,912

rather obvious reasons why immigrant labor has not been introduced to any great extent in the shoe factories. In spite of the fact that machinery has been applied to practically every minute process into which the making of shoes has been divided, the work continues to demand skilled and responsible operatives, and the level of wages has been kept so high that the industry continues to attract the more intelligent native-born working people.[177]

It is, of course, quite obvious that by the payment of high wages the boot and shoe industry has been able to hold its American working people as the cotton industry has not. There is, however, another possible explanation of this point in the fact that the shoe manufacture is one of the industries in which America has pioneered. In the cotton industry, immigrant operatives were quite likely to be equal or even superior to the native born in skill and training, but American methods in the making of shoes have been unique, and immigrant labor therefore has meant for this industry unskilled labor, only a limited amount of which could be utilized.

---

[177]The tables in Chapter XII, pp. 305, 307, make it clear that wages are in general much higher in the shoe factories than in the cotton mills. As long ago as 1872, an operative from a Massachusetts town which contained both cotton mills and shoe factories, in his testimony before the State Bureau of Labor, said, with regard to the frequent changes in the working force of the cotton mills: "There is shoemaking in town, for boys, and a great deal of stitching on machines, for girls. Their wages in the mill are very low — some ten to sixteen dollars a month — and as soon as the children are old enough they leave, the girls going to the stitching machines, the boys to shoemaking." — "Third Annual Report Massachusetts Bureau of Labor," p. 389.

Chapter IX - Cigarmaking

The increased employment of women in cigarmaking seems to indicate its tendency to develop into a "women's industry" and furnishes an interesting example of the industrial displacement of men by women. The history of the industry makes it of peculiar interest, because originally the women were displaced by the men, and they may perhaps in these later years be said to have come into their own again.

The manufacture of cigars in this country is an industry of nearly a century's growth[178] but it has not continuously throughout its history employed a large proportion of women. This is at first not easy to understand, for it has always been a trade for which women are seemingly better qualified than men. No part of the making of cigars is heavy work,[179] nor does it, like the manufacture of clothing, require great endurance. Skill depends upon manual dexterity, upon delicacy and sensitiveness of touch. A brief description of the three important processes in a cigar factory — "stripping," "making," and "packing" — will serve to make this quite clear.

---

[178]It is not mentioned in Hamilton's "Report on Manufacture" nor in Gallatin's later "Report on Manufactures" (1810).

[179]"Therefore the work of women is a more serious competitor than it is in the manufacture of clothing." — "Reports of the Industrial Commission," xv, 388. See also the "Eighth Annual Report of New York Bureau of Labor," p. 1024, where it is said that the trade has become open to the competition of young women "who find in cigarmaking a trade readily learned and with easier work than most other trades adopted by women"; and for a similar comment see the "Fifth Annual Report," p. 524.

The preliminary process of "stripping," which includes "booking," is the preparation of the leaf for the hands of the cigarmaker. The large midrib is stripped out, and, if the tobacco is of the quality for making wrappers, the leaves are also "booked" — smoothed tightly across the knee and rolled into a compact pad ready for the cigarmaker's table. Even in the stripping room there are different grades of work. Thus the stripping of the "filler" leaf for the inner "bunch" of the cigar is usually piece work, but the stripping of the wrapper and binder is likely to be time work, to avoid such haste as might tear the more expensive leaf. If a woman "books" her own wrappers, she gets higher pay than one who merely "strips"; and one who only "books" gets more than either, for this is much harder work and keeps the whole body in motion.[180] All of this work, however, is unskilled and all practically monopolized by women and girls.

Division of labor has been slow in making its way into cigar factories. The best cigar is still made by a single workman, who shapes his own bunch in his hand, binds it, and puts on the wrapper himself. The whole process demands a high degree of skill. Slightly inferior cigars, however, can be made by less skilled workmen, with "molds," which are blocks of wood in which a series of cigar-shaped hollows are carved. The bunches are placed in these and shaped under pressure. This makes it possible for inferior workmen to put on the wrapper.[181]

Packing cigars is called a "trade by itself." Those of like color must be packed together, and only the experienced eye can detect the varying shades of the leaf. Packers are the aristocrats of the trade in most places, and get better pay even than cigarmakers, though it is difficult to see that their work really requires more skill

---

[180]The scale of wages in a large union factory in Boston furnishes a measure of the supposed differences in these occupations: binder stripper, $6 a week; wrapper stripper who "books," $7 a week; filler-stripper, $6 to $10 a week. The lack of skill in any of this work is indicated by the fact that in places where the union requires a three years' apprenticeship for cigarmaking, two weeks is the rule for stripping, and competent forewomen say that "a bright girl can learn in a day." In England the situation in this occupation is rather different. "The work is well adapted for female hands, and in provincial factories they are largely employed in this department. In London, on the contrary, there seem to be not more than thirty women engaged as strippers." — Booth, "Life and Labour of the People," iv, 224.

[181]Machines which are now in use, and will be described later, and "teamwork," have simplified the process so that a still lower grade of labor has been made available.

or more training than "making."[182] The packer stands at his work, while the maker seldom leaves his seat.

Cigarmaking clearly seems to be a trade for which women are peculiarly adapted, and for a long time they have been very largely employed in the factories of Germany and England,[183] and almost exclusively employed in Austria and France,[184] where the tobacco industry is a government monopoly. The history of their employment in this country is of interest; for, on the hypothesis that women's labor is cheaper, and therefore will be substituted for men's wherever it can be profitably employed, the woman cigarmaker would always have controlled the trade.

The history of cigarmaking has received less attention than the industries which were of greater importance in the first part of the century; it is, for example, entirely neglected by Bishop in his "History of Manufactures," and, indeed, trustworthy accounts of it are difficult to trace. It is clear, however, that originally cigarmaking was one of the household industries,[185] and there is an interesting tradition to the effect that the first domestic cigars were made in 1801 by a woman, the wife of a Connecticut tobacco grower. In the early years of the century nearly the whole of the Connecticut tobacco crop was made by the farmers' wives and daughters into cigars known to the trade as "supers," "long nines," and "short

[182]In an article in *Tobacco*, iii, No. 19, on "The Boston Lockout," it is claimed that "too much pay is given cigar packers anyway. It is simply a matter of sharp eyesight, and men can make from $25 to $30 a week if they are able to detect the difference between a Madura, Colorado Madura, Colorado, Colorado Claro, or Claro cigar." Packing is the branch of the trade into which women have worked their way most slowly. There were, for example, in Boston a few years ago only two women packers. The wages of one averaged through the year about $31 a week (piece work). Her foreman said she was as good a workman as the men, who, however, objected "to having a woman around. The men smoke all the time, and they can't talk as free as if she weren't here."

[183]For the employment of women in Germany, see Frisch, "Die Organisationsbestrebungen der Arbeiter in der deutschen Tabak-Industrie," pp. 10, 264, 265; and E. Jaffé, "Hausindustrie und Fabrikbetrieb in der deutschen Cigarrenfabrikation," *Schriften des Vereina fur Socialpolitik*, lxxxvi, 286-299.

[184]The monopoly of the industry in Austria by women is evident from statistics in the "Bericht der K. K. Gewerbe-Inspektome ber ihre Amstätigkeit," 1900, pp. 507-538. For French statistics, see Mannheim, "De la condition dans les manufactures de l'état (tabacs-allumettes)," especially pp. 17, 18, 33-38.

[185]Trumbull, "Memorial History of Hartford County, Connecticut," i, 218 ff.; Morgan, "Connecticut as a Colony and a State," iii, 274; "Report of the New York Bureau of Labor," 1902, on "The Growth of Industry in New York," p. 153; special century edition of the *United States Tobacco Journal* (1900).

sixes." These cigars were sometimes peddled by the women, but more frequently they were bartered at the country stores, where they served as a substitute for currency. All of the groceries and dry goods used by the family during the year were often paid for in this way and represented the exchange value of the leisure hours of the farmer's wife. Although these were very inferior cigars, they were sold pretty generally throughout New England. The passing of this early "homestead industry" which existed in Pennsylvania and other tobacco-growing states as well as in Connecticut, was very gradual; for the transition to the factory system did not, in cigarmaking, involve the substitution of machine for hand work, and farmers' wives continued to roll cigars until the imposition of the internal revenue tax, — and even after that. Indeed, the making of cigars on the farm has lingered on even to the present day in Pennsylvania. In tobacco counties like York and Lancaster "the tobacco growers themselves with their families, occupy winter months and rainy days in making cigars."[186]

The early country cigars, however, did not compare favorably with the finer factory-made product, and as Connecticut tobacco grew in favor it became unprofitable to use it for the cheaper grades of work. Household industry, therefore, furnished a gradually decreasing proportion of the total manufactured product. But, unlike most work that left the home, cigarmaking had not finally passed into the factory; for it was to be established as a domestic industry on a much larger scale in the tenements of New York. Two questions are of interest at this point with regard to the history of the employment of women: Did they follow their work from the home to the factory? and, What was their part in the establishment of cigarmaking as one of the early tenement industries?

Women undoubtedly worked in the earliest factories. What was possibly the first cigar factory in this country was established at Suffield, Connecticut, in 1810, and employed only women. In 1832, the "Documents Relative to the Manufactures of the United States" contained returns from ten cigar factories in Massachusetts which together reported two hundred and thirty-eight women, forty-eight

---

[186]"Reports of the Industrial Commission," xv, 387. See also *United States Tobacco Journal*, century edition, p. 38. When the New York law was passed (1883) prohibiting tenementhouse cigar factories, one of the New York manufacturers said: "It will benefit the trade of New Jersey and Pennsylvania, where the farmers and their families can sit at home and make cigars." — *New York Tribune*, March 14, 1883.

men and nine children employed. The usual wages for women were forty or fifty cents a day, for men from a dollar to a dollar and a half a day. It was explained with reference to some of the tobacco factories that, in addition to the factory work, "many cigars" were made in families by women and boys. While there are few data showing the extent to which women worked as cigarmakers at this time, it is clear that this was not an uncommon occupation.

Just what their relation to the men in the trade was, it is not possible to say. The women were paid very much lower wages, but whether this means that they did a lower grade of work is not clear. In this connection, however, the following resolution, which was one of several passed in 1835 by the "Journeymen Segar Makers of Philadelphia," is of interest: "Resolved, that the present low wages hitherto received by the females engaged in segar making is far below a fair compensation for the labor rendered. Therefore, Resolved, that we recommend them in a body to strike with us and thereby make it a mutual interest with both parties to sustain each other in their rights."

It was estimated that one third of the persons employed at the trade in Connecticut in 1856 were women,[187] and the census of 1860 showed that seven hundred and forty women were employed in the country as a whole in that year. This was, however, but one ninth of the total number of employees and included the unskilled "strippers," so that the number of bona fide women cigarmakers in factories was probably very small, although it is impossible to say precisely what that number was. Mr. Adolph Strasser, for many years president of the International Union, said, in testifying before the Senate Committee on Labor and Capital, that there were not more than three hundred women in the whole trade at this time.

But if the displacement of the women cigarmaker is not easy to express statistically, the reason for it is not difficult to find. Cigarmaking, as has been pointed out, is a highly skilled trade, and it was early discovered that among our immigrants were men able to make cigars that could compete with those imported from Germany and Spain. These immigrant cigarmakers who proved to have the superior workmanship that was indispensable to the development of the industry took the places of the American women who had been formerly employed. The Cuban is said to have been the first male cigarmaker employed in this country, and as Spanish tobacco and

---

[187] *United States Tobacco Journal*, century edition, p. 34.

Spanish-made cigars were in high favor, a large market was found for the Spanish cigars made here by Cuban workmen. Later, expert workmen among immigrants from other countries became competitors of the Cuban, and among German immigrants especially were men of exceptional skill and experience in the trade. The woman cigarmaker almost disappeared during this time, and there are men, both cigarmakers and manufacturers, in New York, who say that there was "not a woman in the trade," except in the unskilled work of stripping, "back of the seventies"; and a recent report of the Commissioner of Labor[188] confirms this statement.

Before the close of the decade following 1860 there was a marked increase in the proportion of women employed. Statistics showing this increase and the increase for later decades are given in the census, and the table below has been prepared from these census data, and indicates also the percentage which women have formed of the total number of employees and the percentage increase during each decade.[189]

The number of women employed not only increased very rapidly after 1870, but the increase was greater proportionately than the increase in the number of men, and, indeed, since 1880 the percentage increase in the male population has been greater than the percentage increase in the number of men employed.

In the light, however, of the statistics in this table, which show that in 1905 the women constituted only forty-two per cent of all the employees, it may seem like hazarding a large guess to say that cigarmaking is becoming a "woman's industry." But it is not alone on the basis of the census statistics that this assertion r is made. It

---

[188]"Eleventh Special Report of the Commissioner of Labor," p. 575. "Formerly men only were engaged in cigarmaking, but since the introduction of machinery the proportion of female employees has become very large." This is obviously a superficial statement, for it disregards the employment of women in the early history of the industry, and is at variance with President Strasser's statement quoted *supra*.

[189]The table is compiled from statistics given for "cigars and cigarettes" in "Twelfth Census (1900): Manufactures," Pt. iii, 656. The numbers unfortunately do not form a basis for exact comparison. It appears that the enumeration included only cigars in 1860 and 1870, while for the other three years cigars and cigarettes are represented. It has already been pointed out that statistics for 1850 cannot be used because they refer to "tobacconists." Statistics in the "Twelfth Census: Occupations," for "cigars and tobacco," are, of course, unlike these data in the census of manufactures. See Appendix B for a discussion of general differences between the census of occupations and the census of manufactures.

Table 21: CIGARS AND CIGARETTES: NUMBER OF EMPLOYEES, 1860-1905

	1860	1870	1880	1890	1900	1905
Men	7,266	21,409	40,099	59,452	62,004	72,970
Women	731	2,615	9,108	24,214	37,740	57,174
Children under 16	...	2,025	4,090	3,334	3,531	5,274
Total number of employees	7,997	26,049	53,297	87,000	103,275	135,418
Percentage of women employed	9	10	17	28	37	42

will be shown later that there is a very great difference between the proportion of women among the employees in large factories where machinery is used and in those smaller or country establishments where it has not been introduced. Since the large machine factory is the factory of the future, the fact that it is being monopolized by women affords stronger evidence of the displacement of men than statistics for the industry as a whole would indicate. Testimony on this point will be given later; in the meantime an effort will be made to analyze the causes that have led to this displacement. The year 1869 begins a new period in the history of the industry. Since then three factors seem to have worked together to bring about a very rapid increase in the employment of women: (1) increased immigration from Bohemia, where women are exclusively employed in cigar factories; (2) the invention of machinery which has made the skilled workman less necessary; (3) a feeling on the part of employers that women are more docile than men, and that a large proportion of women among the employees would mean fewer strikes.

The immigration of Bohemian women cigarmakers began in 1869[190]

---

[190]Testimony in the "Report of the Ford Immigration Committee," p. 364. President Gompers, of the American Federation of Labor, who was at that time in the trade in New York, told me in 1906 that they were first brought over by employers to break the cigarmakers' strike of 1869. This is intimated also in the testimony referred to above. The Bohemian immigration movement was greatly furthered at this time by the effects of the disastrous Austro-Prussian War and the granting of the legal right to emigrate. See the account given by Josefa Humpal-Zeman in "Reports of the Industrial Commission," XV, 507, which makes special note of the settlement of cigarmakers in New York; and Balch, "Sources of Slav Immigration," *Charities*, xv, 598. It is noted in the latter article that a minor cause of immigration was a strike in the Bohemian tobacco factories in the seventies.

and meant the reestablishment of cigarmaking as a household industry — but this time under the commission rather than under the handicraft system. The home work which occupied the leisure of the Connecticut farmer's thrifty wife is clearly not to be compared with the home work of the Bohemian immigrant in the New York tenements. The New England women were independent producers. They owned. their raw material, the homes in which they worked, and the finished product, which they disposed of at their own convenience; the tenement women were helplessly dependent upon an employer who furnished the raw material, owned and marketed the product, and frequently charged them exorbitant rentals for the rooms in which they both lived and worked; they were merely hired wage earners working for a single employer in their own homes instead of in his factory. The explanation of the home work in both cases is found in the fact that cigarmaking is peculiarly adapted for household manufacture, and for this reason it still exists, not only as a domestic industry but as a lingering survival of handicraft.[191] When the only machine required is a pair of wooden molds, it is possible for the workman to own his own tools and a pair of molds, purchase his tobacco in small quantities, and, by disposing of the product quickly, carry on his trade as his own master and without having any capital.

By 1877, the year of the "great strike" which was meant to abolish it, cigarmaking as a tenement industry had become firmly established. It grew rapidly after 1869 and led to the first determined protest against unsanitary home work. The Cigarmakers Union in 1873 first called public attention to the dangers involved in carrying on the industry in tenements, and began a vigorous campaign against it. President Gompers, in testimony before the Ford Immigration Committee, said the effort to abolish tenement cigarmaking had been one of their "constant struggles."

The development of the tenement industry was due to Bohemian women who had worked in cigar factories in their own country. It is said that the customary method of Bohemian immigration was for the women to come first, leaving the men to work in the fields. Five or six wives would come over together, work at cigarmaking

---

[191]See, for example, Mrs. Kelley's account of the tenement worker in Chicago, who buys his own tobacco and disposes of his own product, and is in no way connected with a middleman or manufacturer ("Reports of the Industrial Commission" vii, 251).

as they did in Bohemia, and send money back for their husbands' passage, and then "the entire united family would take up the manufacture of cigars, emulating the industry of the mother."[192] These women cigarmakers were said to be more intelligent than their husbands, because of the fact that in Bohemia while the men worked alone in the fields, their wives were employed in factories. At this time, too, came the introduction of the team system — a division of labor by which one person prepares the bundles and another rolls them. In Bohemia the men had worked only in the fields, and their wives taught them cigarmaking at home after they came over. It was much easier, of course, for these men to learn the relatively unskilled work of "bunchmaking" while their wives did the rolling, than to learn how to make the whole cigar. "Team work" ultimately became an important means of furthering the employment of women, employers finding it easy to train young girls for the single process of bunchmaking or rolling, and cheaper to substitute them for skilled workmen who could make a complete cigar.

This decade, during which cigarmaking established itself as a tenement industry, was also the decade of greatest prosperity in the history of the trade. It was surely a decade of extraordinary exploitation of immigrant labor. Large manufacturers acquired blocks of tenements, for which they charged excessive rentals to their employees, who frequently, too, found themselves obliged to pay high prices for groceries and beer at stores owned by the employer. The expense of maintaining a factory, moreover, was thus made part of the employees' burden; and the wages of "strippers and bookers" were also saved to the manufacturer, for the tobacco was prepared in the homes by the workers themselves, or more often by their children.[193] The system also proved an effective coercive measure, and the eviction of the tenement strikers by the landlord manufacturers in 1877 was one of the distressing features of the strike.

It is difficult to make an exact statement either as to the extent

---

[192] New York *Tribune*, November 6, 1877, and see an article in the New York *Sun*, October 20, 1877. The testimony in the "Report of the Ford Immigration Committee," 1887, p. 381, was to the effect that the trade had been demoralized by the Bohemians who came over in large numbers, worked in tenement rooms, gradually brought over all their relations, and taught them the trade.

[193] There were numerous accounts of this system in the New York papers at the time of the strike in the fall of 1877. See, for example, the New York *Tribune*, July 10th, and the New York *Sun*, December 3d, of that year. See also "Report of the Ford Committee," pp. 396, 397, 376, 368.

of home work or as to the number of women employed. Writers
in the New York *Sun* estimated that a majority of the cigars made
in New York in 1877 were the product of tenement-house factories
and some estimates placed the proportion of tenement-made cigars
as high as four fifths of the entire New York product. So large was
the proportion of women employed in this work that the newspapers
and manufacturers referred to the strike, which was directed largely
against the home-work system, as an attack on the employment of
women and children. The manufacturers claimed that the strike was
"a movement on the part of the cigarmakers to throw out of business many women who could or would not work in shops." In 1882, a
circular issued by the union estimated that between 3,500 and 3,750
persons were employed at cigarmaking in tenement houses, and it
seems a fair estimate to say that during the decade from 1870 to
1880 between two and three thousand women had engaged in cigarmaking in their own homes.[194] Not only in tenement work, however,
but in factories as well, the number of women was increasing. Mr.
Adolph Strasser, then president of the union, said in 1883, in testimony before the Senate Committee on Labor and Capital, that
the gradual introduction of women into the industry was one of the
evils cigarmakers were facing, and he estimated that throughout the
country there were 10,000 women in the trade and the number, he
said, was increasing very rapidly, "increasing every year almost at
the rate of a thousand or more."

The increased employment of women as a result of the introduction of machinery belongs to the most recent stage in the history
of the industry. "Molds," which have already been described, and
which are more like tools than machines, were introduced from Germany in 1869, — the year in which production was also cheapened
by the coming of Bohemian women and the introduction of the team
system. Long after the mold came the long-filler bunching machine

---

[194]While it is not necessary in the present study to continue the history of
cigarmaking in tenements, it may be added, to make the accounts somewhat
more complete, that the law passed in 1883 abolishing this work was declared
unconstitutional in 1885 (98 New York Appeals, p. 98). The union, however,
continued its opposition and, owing in part to the use of its label and in part
to general public sentiment against tenement work, and more perhaps to the
development of the large machine factory, tenement cigarmaking has almost
disappeared. In 1901 there were in New York only 775 persons authorized to
make cigars in tenements, while 23,329 family workrooms were licensed in the
clothing industry.

and the suction table, both hand machines, the machines for strip-ping and booking, and the short-filler bunching machine operated by power.

So many unsuccessful machines were tried from time to time that it is not easy to fix any exact date as the period when machinery was first considered successful enough to be adopted on any scale worthy of note. By 1887, however, several of the large factories had begun to use machines, and in 1888 machines with women operators took the places of skilled cigarmakers who were on a strike in Philadelphia.[195] In 1895 a New York cigarmaker said, in describing the situation, "Colleagues that left New York ten or more years ago would be astonished if they returned now to find that hand work has almost entirely disappeared. . . . The suction tables, which are in reality nothing else than wrapper-cutting machines, are used ... as price cutters. More so, because there are only girls employed on them. . . . There are a few thousand of these tables in operation in this city, with the prospect of increasing the number daily."

In a recent report of the Commissioner of Labor,[196] it was pointed out that "for both machine operators, bunchmaking and rolling, a cheaper grade of labor may be employed. Formerly men only were engaged in cigarmaking, but since the introduction of machinery the proportion of female employees has been very large. In many factories only women and girls are employed on the bunchmaking machines and suction tables, and the number of females is as high as eighty per cent of the total number of employees." Statistics ob-tained in the investigation upon which this report was based show that in nine open or nonunion factories, which had more than 4,000 employees, and in all but one of which machinery was used, 73.1 per cent of the employees were women, while in eight union shops, which used no machinery and employed only 527 persons, the proportion of women employed was only 36.1 per cent. It is important to note that the machine, the large factory, and the increased employment of women go together. It is also significant that machinery is com-ing to be almost exclusively used in the manufacture of cheap cigars, and that the market for these cheap machine-made cigars is rapidly growing.[197]

Other available statistics add further testimony to show that

---

[195] *Cigarmakers' Official Journal*, May, 1888.
[196] "Eleventh Special Report of the Commissioner of Labor,"p. 575.
[197] "Eleventh Special Report of the Commissioner of Labor," pp. 574, 575.

there is a greater proportion of women employed in the large factories. In Professor Dewey's report on "Employees and Wages" for the last census, most of the data for cigarmaking are from relatively small factories, but in one of the larger ones 74.6 per cent, and in another 98 per cent of the employees were women; and in several others, where men are still more exclusively employed, it is noted among the changes in the establishment between 1890 and 1900 that "no females were employed in 1890."[198] In recent factory inspectors' reports there is some further evidence on this point. Statistics for the seven large factories in New York City, each of which employs more than two hundred men, show that 55.5 per cent, 60.5 per cent, 70.2 per cent, 73.3 per cent, 86.2 per cent, 88.3 per cent, and 91.3 per cent, respectively, of all the employees are women.[199] In Binghamton, an important cigarmaking center, reports from four factories, each of which employed more than one hundred women, showed that they constituted respectively 62.6 per cent, 62.9 per cent, 75.9 per cent, and 68.7 per cent of all employees. The report of the factory inspector of the State of Pennsylvania for 1902 showed that in the largest cigar factory in Philadelphia the 996 women who were employed were 97.3 per cent of the entire working force, and in a large Harrisburg factory the 993 women were 95 per cent of all the persons employed.

Similar factors that have helped to increase the employment of women have been the formation of the trust,[200] which has greatly furthered the movement toward large scale production; and the introduction of the "team system," which has already been described, and which, it is acknowledged, is used, not as a method of increasing the output, but because cheaper labor can be employed.

---

[198] "Twelfth Census (1900): Employees and Wages." These data are from the establishment comparison, not from the tables of totals; see pp. 1048, 1037, 1050, 1044, 1042, for the data from which these percentages were computed. It is noted as a "special feature" of one establishment that "in 1900 the wrapper classer was a woman receiving $6 per week. In 1890 the wrapper classer was a man receiving $12 a week" (p. 1046).

[199] "Fifteenth Annual Report of the Factory Inspector of the State of New York" (1900). See especially report of the Second District, Boroughs of Manhattan and Bronx.

[200] The union brings a bitter indictment against what it calls the "child-labor-employing trust." "The tobacco trust is its bitter foe and is probably the largest employer in the country of tenement-house sweatshops and child labor."—*Cigarmakers' Official Journal,* February 15, 1904. "We estimate that ninety per cent of the employees of the trust are females, and positively state that the great majority are minors." — *Ibid.,* November 15, 1902.

In discussing the tendency toward the increased employment of women as a means of avoiding or ending strikes, some account should also be given of the relation of the women to the Cigarmakers' International Union. It should perhaps be explained that the union admits only cigarmakers proper, bunchmakers and rollers, and packers, and that the latter are organized in separate "locals" Strippers and other unskilled and miscellaneous help are excluded, but in some cities the strippers have unions of their own. The union was organized in 1851, and in 1867 the constitution was so altered that women and negroes, hitherto excluded, became eligibly to membership.[201]

In 1877 women were employed in large numbers to break the strike of that year. Several hundred girls were taught the trade, and employers went so far as to call the strike "a blessing in disguise" since it "offered a new employment for women and secured workers whose services may be depended on at low wages."[202] According to an account in one of the New York papers, employers claimed an unusual sale for the bad cigars made by these untrained "strike breakers" because the boxes bore the legend: "These cigars were made by American girls." It is of interest that in this same year, the Cincinnati cigarmakers struck successfully for the removal of all women from the workshops[203] and in some other cities similar strikes were inaugurated but failed.

In 1879 the president of the union announced that one of its aims would be "the regulation of female labor"; and in 1881 he strongly advised the unions, in view of the fact that the employment of women was constantly increasing, "to extend the right hand of brotherhood to them"; and added: "Better to have them with us than against us. . . . They can effect a vast amount of mischief outside of our ranks as tools in the hands of the employer against us." The president of the New York local in 1886 complained that Bohemian women were doing work "that men were formerly employed to do. They have driven the American workmen from our trade altogether. They work for a price that an American could not work for." In 1894

---

[201] Strasser, "History of the Cigarmakers' Union" in McNeill, "The Labor Movement," p. 600.

[202] The New York *Sun*, November 26, 1877.

[203] *Cincinnati Daily Inquirer*, August 29, 30, and September 30, 1877. *The Inquirer*, in commenting on the situation, said: "The men say the women are killing the industry. It would seem that they hope to retaliate by killing the women."

the president of the international union said: "We are confronted with child and female labor to an alarming, extent"; and in 1901, at a meeting of the American Federation of Labor, the cigarmakers asked for the passage of resolutions expressing opposition to the use of machinery in their trade and to the employment of women and children. The hostility of the union to women is not difficult to understand. The women seemed to be lowering a standard wage that the men, through organization, were trying to uphold. They had, moreover, the workingman's belief in the old "lump of labor" fallacy, and for every woman who was employed they saw "a man without a job."

As in other industries, a much smaller proportion of the women than of the men in the trade are members of the union,[204] and the women seldom attend the meetings, and take small part in the proceedings when they do.[205] The union has, however, stood squarely for the same wage scale for both men and women, while in England the union maintains a women's scale that is twenty-five per cent lower than the men's. It is of interest too, that in England the women had a separate union for many years, and when they joined the men's union the question of how to reconcile the wage scales that had prevailed in the two unions caused great difficulty. To have raised the women's scale to the men's level would, it was felt, "have meant to drive the women from the trade and to alienate public sympathy."

Leaving the subject of labor displacement, it may be well to notice briefly certain other questions connected with the employment of women, which are of special interest with regard to women's work in the manufacture of cigars. These are: the effect of the work upon the health of women, the nationality and conjugal condition of the women employed, and their relative efficiency in comparison with men.

Conflicting testimony is found as to the effect of cigarmaking upon the health of women. Like all confining sedentary work, it must

---

[204]President Perkins, in a letter to the writer, estimated that less than fifteen per cent of the members of the union were women — obviously a very small percentage in view of the fact that women form so large a proportion of the total number of employees.

[205]This is almost invariably the rule when men and women are in one organization. It was said in the "Report of the Senate Committee on Education and Labor" ii, 809, that the women allowed the men to take the position of superiority that belonged to them.

be to some extent unhygienic; but much depends upon conditions in the factories themselves, which, of course, vary widely in regard to light, cleanliness, and ventilation. It has been pointed out that the work is for the most part very light, and certainly the strain on the nervous system is far less than in factories where there is the constant noise of heavy machinery. Although some physicians have claimed that all tobacco work is injurious to the women engaged in it,[206] a recent investigation in London, showed that the trade was not an unhealthful one for women,[207] and Dr. Oliver, after carefully weighing the testimony that has been given on both sides for the last twenty years, confirmed this conclusion. The annual report of the international union for 1901 showed that in 1890 forty-nine per cent, and in 1900 thirty-three per cent of their deceased members died of tuberculosis. The average age of deceased members had been raised during the same time from thirty-seven and one half to forty-three and one half years.[208] Aside from any question as to the effect of tobacco on the system of the worker, it is clear that shorter hours and improved conditions can do much to make the industry a more healthful one.

Statistics in the last census regarding the nationality of the women employed in cigar and tobacco factories show that 53.4 per cent are either foreign born or of foreign parentage; of these, 29.2 per cent are German and 20.8 per cent Austro-Hungarian. In New York the great factories are in the "Bohemian district," and Bohemian women are largely employed. The official journal of the union regularly contains articles and important notices in German and Bohemian as well as in English.

The percentage of married women employed in the manufacture of cigars and tobacco is larger than in any other industry in the list given under the manufacturing group, with the single exception of seamstresses; 11.8 per cent of the women in the whole group and 16.4 per cent of those in "cigars and tobacco" were married.[209]

---

[206]See Oliver, "Dangerous Trades" p. 793, and for a somewhat lengthy discussion of the whole subject see "Report of the New York Bureau of Labor," 1884, pp. 224-236. See also the testimony of Mr. Gompers and Mr. Strasser in "Report of the Senate Committee on Education and Labor," pp. 273, 274, 453.
[207]*Economic Journal*, x, 567.
[208]*Cigarmakers' Official Journal*, September, 1901.
[209]"Twelfth Census (1900): Occupations," p. ccxxii. This seems to contradict the statement that the average life of girls at the trade is five years (see "Eleventh Special Report of the Commissioner of Labor" p. 569). Census statistics as to

There are several reasons for this: Among the Bohemians there is less prejudice against the work of married women than among most other nationalities.[210] There is also the fact that cigarmaking is to some extent a home industry; and further, it is a skilled trade at which competent women can earn higher wages than they can in most other industries that are open to women. This is so true that many of them say it "pays" to go on with their work and "hire a cheaper woman" to do part of their housework and look after the children. A fore-woman once said, as if there were a superstition about the work: "It's a trade you always come back to. I don't know why, but it is!"[211]

The constant reference to women as a "cheap grade of labor" must not lead to the conclusion that women do not become as skilled cigarmakers as men and do not work on the higher grades of hand-made cigars. Undoubtedly there is a larger proportion of men than women among the most efficient workers in many factories, but some women who are "equal to any man" will be found in most of them, and foremen and manufacturers alike testify to the fact that the highest possible skill is often attained by their women employees.

In one of the reports of the Commissioner of Labor,[212] returns are given from nine establishments regarding the relative efficiency of men and women. In four, the men were said to be more efficient than the women; in one the women were more efficient than the men;

---

age show, however, that 69 per cent of the women in "tobacco and cigars" are below twenty-four, while only 54.1 per cent of all of the women in manufacturing pursuits are below this age (computations based on Table 4, "Twelfth Census, 1900, Occupations"). Since these figures are not for cigars alone, they are not largely significant. The same data show a very large increase for the decade in the number of girls employed and a very small increase in the number of boys.

[210]Testimony before the (Reinhard) "Committee on Female Labor," New York Assembly, 1896, p. 817.

[211]The employment of married women seems also to be common in other countries. In Germany there is in the union a confinement benefit for women (*Cigarmakers' Official Journal*, May 15, 1903), and in interesting contrast to this is Section 4 of the sick-benefit clause which was adopted by the American union at the convention of 1880: "Female members of any local union shall not be entitled to any sick benefit three weeks before or five weeks after confinement" (*Ibid.*, October, 1888). It is a curious bit of history that in Bremen as early as 1847 an exception to a law which prohibited women from working in cigar factories was made in favor of the wives of the men employed (Frisch, p. 12, n. 2).

[212]"Eleventh Annual Report" on "Work and Wages of Men, Women and Children," pp. 517-619.

in four, the men and women were equally efficient.[213] A London investigation showed that while there might be an exceptional woman who was "better than any man," yet, on the average, the men were faster workers than the women.

But in this as in all other trades, the ever-present possibility of marriage militates strongly against the woman worker's attaining her fullest efficiency. The few years that the woman who "marries and leaves" spends at the bench cannot be expected to develop the quality of workmanship that comes with life-long service. In anticipation, too, of her shorter "working life," a girl is often unwilling to serve the real apprenticeship so necessary in a skilled trade like cigarmaking, and more often still, her parents are not willing to undergo the sacrifices this may entail. In cities where the union is strong, and a long period of preliminary training is made a condition precedent to entering the trade, there are relatively fewer women employed.[214] The point must not be overlooked, however, that this condition is due in some measure to a feeling on the part of employers that boys are more profitable apprentices and that the work is not proper for girls. It is said, for example, that girls cannot carry tobacco and wait on the women and men at the benches as the boys do, but in England only girls are employed for this kind of work. Other employers say it is not worth while teaching a girl who is likely to leave the trade soon.[215] It is, however, clearly true that if the "aristocracy of male workers at the head" continues the apprenticeship situation will be one of the explanations.

It may be said, in conclusion, that while cigarmaking has in more recent years come to be a trade of lower grade employing less skilled workers at lower wages, this change is not to be attributed solely to

[213]Two minor advantages connected with the employment of women are noted by employers in discussing this question of relative efficiency. One is that the woman "is always here on Monday morning," as one employer tersely put it; the other is that a considerable saving is effected because the women do not smoke, for it is an unwritten law of the trade that the cigarmaker always "gets his smokes off the boss."

[214]In Boston, for example, where a three-years' apprenticeship is required, there was, in 1906, one girl to nearly 200 boys regularly apprenticed, and this one girl was serving in the small shop of a relative.

[215]Until recently a school has been conducted in New York to teach cigarmaking. The manager said he had in six years taught 3,000 persons, of whom eighty per cent were women and girls. There is no apprenticeship now in the New York trade, but in Boston it is practically impossible now for a girl to obtain a chance to "serve." In London, on the other hand, the large majority of apprentices are girls.

the increasing importance of women in the industry. For with women have come the mold, the team system, and machinery, all tending to diminish the demand for skilled workmen; and distinct, too, from the influence of women's work as such has been the deteriorating effect of cheap immigrant labor and the tenement system.

Chapter X - The Clothing Industry

Although the "sewing trades" are too important numerically from the point of view of the employment of women to be entirely neglected,[216] their history can be given here only in outline, partly because the clothing industry has become too complicated to make detailed treatment within the limits of a single chapter possible[217] and partly because of the fact that the employment of women in the making of clothing is less interesting than in the other industries which have been discussed. Sewing, needle-work of any kind except, perhaps, the making of men's garments, has always been regarded as within woman's "peculiar sphere"; and the point of interest is, therefore, not that so many women are employed in the sewing trade, but that so many men have come into the industry as their competitors.

Moreover, the problem of women's work in the making of clothing is much less interesting in itself than various other problems with which the industry is closely connected — the so-called " sweating

---

[216] According to the "Twelfth Census (1900): Manufactures" Ft. iii, 261, the clothing industry in 1900 employed 243,932 women, 138,654 men and 6,499 children.

[217] It should be explained here that there is no adequate treatment of the development of the clothing trades in this country. Reference should be made, however, to two rather elaborate special treatises on the subject, "The Employment of Women in the Clothing Trades" 1902, by Dr. Mabel Hurd Willett, and "The Clothing Industry in New York" 1905, by Prof. Jesse E. Pope. Both of these volumes are confined to the making of ready-made garments for men, except that Mr. Pope includes women's cloaks. Mrs. Willetts's study deals almost exclusively with conditions of employment today, and Mr. Pope's historical account is on the whole unsatisfactory.

system," restrictive legislation dealing with "home work," insanitary conditions of employment in homes, workshops, and factories, and finally the whole problem of the competition of immigrant labor. And, therefore, although any attempt to discuss the history of the employment of women in the clothing trades in brief compass must appear a superficial discussion in which the points of greatest interest are neglected, it will be necessary to limit the scope of the chapter to the history of women's work in connection with the manufacture of men's and women's ready-made clothing, and to make no attempt to deal with the work of the custom tailor, the dressmaker, or the household seamstress.

For purposes of classification, the manufacture of men's and of women's clothing may be called the two large divisions of the industry; each of these again is divided into the "ready-made" and the custom trade; and in the manufacture of ready-made garments for both men and women there are a large number of subdivisions; for the manufacture of a single kind of garment is often a distinct industry. Thus the making of overalls and of collars and cuffs are industries which are quite different in their method of organization, in the kind of labor employed, and in the places where they are carried on, from the making of men's outside garments; and the manufacture of women's underwear, or of shirt-waists, for example, is an industry quite distinct from the making of women's tailored suits.

We have to deal, then, not with a single industry but with a large and varied group of industries, in which the problem of the employment of women presents many different phases, from the work of the intelligent American-born women in the overall factories to the work of the Italian "pants" finisher who evades the law in her insanitary tenement.

Although the making of ready-made garments for men is as yet scarcely a century old, it has a much longer history than the manufacture of women's ready-made clothing. At the opening of the nineteenth century the finest and most expensive clothing for men was the work of skilled tailors who had served a long apprenticeship; but only the wealthy and fashionable could afford to wear garments made in this way, and the majority of men wore clothing which was made at home by their wives and daughters or perhaps by the village tailoress.

The first ready-for-sale garments were poor in quality and corresponded not to the fine work of the high-grade custom tailor, but rather to the inferior country product which had been made largely by women. It was only natural, therefore, for women to be employed in the early stages of the manufacture of the "ready-made" clothing; and in the second decade of the nineteenth century, when the making of such clothing for men began,[218] both men and women were found in the trade. An "Emigrant's Directory," in 1820, advised tailors who might come to this country that in New York their trade had been "much injured by the employment of women and boys, who work from twenty-five to fifty per cent cheaper than the men. A man that can cut out," it was specified, "will be occasionally very well paid, the women not being clever in this branch of the business, makes more men necessary. Trousers are all made by women."[219] Custom work and the making of ready-made garments were at first carried on together, for custom tailors found that during the slack seasons they could profitably employ their time making up a stock of clothing for the "ready-to-wear" trade. For this reason the women employed were most often the wife and daughters of the tailor himself, who found it profitable to give the lighter parts of the work to the women members of his family. But other women soon came into the trade in considerable numbers, and the making of trousers and waistcoats especially came to be quite exclusively women's work.[220]

Under the tariff of 1816 the duty on manufactured clothing was thirty per cent. This was raised to fifty per cent in 1828, and the imports consequently fell off nearly one third in the next six years.[221] By 1832 the "ready-made" was being manufactured in New York on a considerable scale, and in other large cities as well. Some of the manufacturers had an extensive business making clothing for shipment to the southern states and to some foreign parts, and a few establishments employed from 300 to 500 hands. , In 1832 the "Documents Relative to the Manufactures of the United States" reported that 300 men, 100 boys, and 1,300 women were employed in the tailor shops of Boston, and that the men were paid two dollars a day and the women and boys fifty cents. The comment upon these returns was: "The estimate of the tailoring business is founded on the best information which could be obtained. It has become usual

---

[218]See "Twelfth Census (1900): Manufactures," Pt. iii, 296.

[219]"View of the United States of America: A Complete Emigrant's Directory" (London, 1820), p. 371.

[220]Pope, pp. 15, 16.

[221]See the account of the clothing industry in the "Eighth Census (1860): Manufactures," p. lxiii.

in late years for most tailors to keep on hand a large stock of ready-made clothing."

The sewing machine was not invented until 1850 and ready-made garments of this early period were therefore entirely hand sewed. Large quantities of them, cut out at the dealer's place of business in the city, were sent to the country towns in the neighborhood of New York, Boston, and Philadelphia, where the wives and daughters of farmers and sailors made them in their own homes.

The Massachusetts "Tables of Industry" reported in 1837 nearly 2,500 women engaged in making clothing in Boston, and as many of the dealers there followed this custom of sending garments out to be "made up" on farms and in country villages, the total number of employees must have been much greater. In Groton alone, 11,000 garments were made annually and 245 women as well as three men were engaged in this work.[222] While none of the statements of the number of persons in the trade during this early period are more than approximately correct, they are interesting as evidence of the continuous employment of women in very considerable numbers from the time when the "ready-made" first began to be manufactured in this country.

The invention of the sewing machine made possible a much greater expansion of the industry than would have been possible under the old method. The machine was not altogether satisfactory until it had been perfected by the discovery of the lock stitch. The first machine stitching was so likely to rip that it was considered very unsafe, and hand-made garments were thought superior because they were firmer. "Women who could afford to purchase machines continued to work much as they had done before in their own homes; other women were obliged to seek employers who wanted "help" to run machines in their factories or workshops. Women had always been less frequently employed on the making of coats than in the manufacture of trousers and waistcoats, and after the invention of the machine, which was soon used with great success in the making of these garments, this work came to be done almost entirely by women.

Immigrants had already begun to come into the industry in large

---

[222]"Massachusetts Tables of Industry" (1837), p. 28. An interesting example of the way in which more primitive methods in the clothing industry have survived along with the evolution of the factory system is the fact that large quantities of clothing are still sent out to be made in the country districts of Pennsylvania and New England. See the "Reports of the Industrial Commission," vii, 194.

numbers, but how far the employment of women may have been effected it is not easy to say. English, Scotch, and, after 1840, large numbers of Irish immigrants were found in the trade. In 1848 and the years following, a great many Germans came, and in some accounts of the organization of the industry at this time the introduction of the "family home shop" and the first division of labor is attributed to them. "The German tailor took coats, vests, and pants to his home and was there assisted by his wife and daughters, the work being roughly divided into machine sewing, basting, and finishing. The family home shop in the clothing trade appearing among the Germans at that time is peculiar to the German people."[223] The employment of women as finishers and "foot-machine operators" on a considerable scale is also attributed to the Germans.

A larger proportion of women, however, were said to be employed in the inside shops[224] manufacturing "pants, vests, and cloaks" than under the family system, though the total number was large in either case.

An interesting account of the family system before and after the machine came into use was given by a German tailor in testimony before a Senate investigating committee. "Before we had sewing machines," he said, "we worked piece work with our own wives, and very often our children. We had no trouble with our neighbors, then, nor with the landlord, because it was a very still business, very quiet; but in 1854 or 1855, and later, the sewing machine was invented and introduced, and it stitched very nicely — nicer than the tailor could do; and the bosses said, "We want you to use a sewing machine; you have to buy one," Many of the tailors had a few dollars in the bank, and they took the money and bought machines. Many others had no money, but must help themselves; so they brought their stitching, the coat or vest, to the other tailors who had sewing machines, and paid them a few cents for the stitching. Later, when the money

---

[223]Willett, p. 33. See also "Reports of the Industrial Commission," xv, Chap. IX, in which the various modes of production which the different nationalities have introduced are discussed.

[224]The two prevailing systems of manufacture in the trade at that time were known as the "inside" and the "outside." In the former case, women were employed in the shop of the master tailor or manufacturer; in the latter they worked at home or in a room which they rented with fellow tailors or in some other place which they provided (see Pope, p. 15). In order to avoid as much as possible an account of technicalities relating to the organization of the industry, these terms have not been used.

was given out for the work, we found out that we could earn no more than we could without the machine; but the money for the machine was gone now, and we found that the machine was only for the profit of the bosses; that they got their work quicker and it was done nicer."[225]

A tailor's wages were then always the joint earnings of a man and his wife. In the words of the German witness again, "A tailor is nothing without a wife and very often a child."

In general it may be said that there was a new subdivision of occupations after the introduction of the machine; "operating," the term commonly used to describe the work of running the machine, became specialized as "cutting" had been; "finishing" and "pressing" also became distinct processes. A table of wages for 1860 published in one of the later reports of the Massachusetts Bureau of Labor furnishes some interesting evidence of the way in which these occupations were divided between women and men. According to this table in 1860, basters, machine operators, "finishers at home," "finishers in shop," custom finishers, and pantaloon and vest makers (custom work) were women.[226] Their wages ranged approximately from five to six dollars a week, while the men were paid from nine to nineteen dollars as overseers, cutters, trimmers, and pressers. These were, however, by no means exclusively men's occupations, for women seem to have been quite frequently employed as pressers[227] or "presswomen" as they were then called and there is some reason to think that they may have been cutters[228] as well; although it will

---

[225] "Report of Senate Committee on the Relations between Labor and Capital," 1885, i, 414.

[226] Average weekly wages, ready-made clothing, standard gold in the year 1860 ("Tenth Annual Report of the Massachusetts Bureau of Labor, 1879," p. 70): Overseers $19.45; Cutters $13.92; Trimmers $11 .06; Pressers $9.17; Basters (women) $6.32; Machine operators (women) $5.53; Finishers at home (women) $4.00; Finishers in shop (women) $4.56; Finishers, custom (women) $6.00; Pantaloon and vest makers, custom work (women) $5.58

[227] See the "Thirteenth Annual Report of the United States Bureau of Labor" on "Hand and Machine Labor" p. 266, in which it is said: "The ironing or pressing was done by hand under both methods, hand and machine, but a much better showing is made under the modern method. This is perhaps owing to the more skilled workmen (this work having been done by women under the hand method) and to better equipment as to appliances for heating under the modern method."

[228] With regard to this point, the statement is made in Pope, p. 28, that "in the early period of the industry women were often employed as cutters, in the manufacture of both men's and women's clothing." This statement, however, is

be remembered that even in 1820 women were said "not to be very clever in this line of business."

In 1872 another schedule of wages paid to women in the clothing industry was published by the same Bureau of Labor. According to this later list, more than a thousand women were employed in each of the women's occupations given in the first list except machine operatives, in which only 629 women were found. In addition, the later list reported sixty-two "presswomen" and seventy forewomen. No women, however, were reported as cutters or trimmers.[229]

A considerable expansion of the industry took place after the first year of the war, owing to the demand for army clothing, but no important changes in methods of production occurred until after 1870. In that year, knives which could cut a large number of thicknesses of cloth at one time first came into use, and since then a long series of mechanical improvements have been made from time to time, such as the invention of machines for cutting cloth, machines for cutting and making buttonholes, machines for sewing on buttons, pressing machines, and most important of all, the substitution of steam and electricity for foot power in running the sewing machine. How far these changes have affected the employment of women is an interesting question, but one difficult to answer.

In general, it is true that the proportion of women employed in the industry has declined in the last twenty-five years, but it will be pointed out that there have been causes in addition to the introduction of new machines and other inventions and improvements to explain the change. It is clear that women have not been extensively employed, unless in the very early years, either as pressers or operators, and that basting and finishing are the occupations in which the largest numbers have been found. Such inquires as have been made in the last decade indicate that their position as pressers and operators is much the same; they are found in both occupations, but it is the rare exception in the former and not common in the latter. An investigator in 1903 reported for New York: "There is perhaps

---

not altogether convincing, as no authority is given, and it contradicts the following statement from the "Report on Hand and Machine Labor": "The cutting was done by males under both methods (hand and machine), and the examining under the primitive method was also done by males. Under the modern method a number of girls were employed, and in most cases they worked side by side with women, thus indicating that in the machine work on these units they are as efficient as women."

[229] The list in detail will be found at the following table.

Table 22: WOMEN IN THE CLOTHING INDUSTRY (WHOLESALE) IN 1871-72

Occupation.	Total Number Employed.	Wages per Week. Average.
Coat basters	2,387	$5.84
Coat finishers	2,447	5.80
Pants basters	1,665	5.31
Pants finishers	1,777	5.53
Vest basters	11,783	5.44
Vest finishers	1,571	5.50
Forewomen	70	8.72
Machine operators	629	8.27
Buttonhole makers	25	7.68
Presswomen	62	7.35

From "*Third Annual Report of Massachusetts Bureau of Labor*, 1872", p. 86

no branch of the trade in which women are not to be found. Even in the pressing of coats, which is extremely heavy work, the exhausting effect of which is frequently noticeable on the men engaged in it, I have found women employed. But it is possible to visit hundreds of establishments without finding a woman doing this work."[230]

With regard to operating, the same investigator reported that if conditions in New York alone were considered "it would be natural to conclude either that machine operating and basting on men's clothing was, except in rare instances, beyond the physical strength of women, or that the skill demanded was such as they could acquire only with difficulty." In other cities, however, women were found doing this work except on the very heaviest grade of goods.

With regard to the basters, especially the basters on coats, there is an interesting example of the sacrifice of the woman wage earner to the increase in speed. Toward the close of the decade 1890-1900 men were gradually substituted for women basters in shops in which the task system prevailed because the women could not maintain the high speed demanded.

In one of the reports of the Industrial Commission in 1889, it

[230]Willett, p. 67.

was pointed out that the wages of women edge basters on coats had declined one fifth since the Jewish invasion and that women had been replaced by immigrant men who received about fifty per cent more a week than the women had formerly earned at the same piece-work rates, because of "the greater speed and endurance of the men". Attention was further called to the fact that the increased number of coats per task probably explained why, in the evolution of the trade, women could not hold their own as edge basters and finishers. "About 15,000 to 25,000 girls," it is said, "have been driven out and men have taken their places at wages fifty per cent higher. This is because the hours and the speed were increased continuously, so that women were physically unable to perform the task."[231]

Women are still employed, but chiefly by Germans, in basting vests and to some extent as operators in "pants and vest" shops. They are, however, exclusively employed on all kinds of garments for men in the lighter work of felling, tacking, and sewing on buttons. The conclusion drawn from a New York investigation is that "for this work no physical strength is necessary and practically no training, and consequently it is work readily resorted to by girls and unskilled women. Any man of ordinary strength finds day labor more remunerative than this work would be, even if he were as accustomed to sewing as a woman is. In this lightest grade of work, as in the heaviest, there is practically no competition between the sexes."[232]

The chief influence, however, which has tended to diminish the proportion of women employed has been the invasion of the industry by the Russian Jews, which began shortly before 1880. While a discussion of the effects of this movement on the industry would lead far afield into the problems connected with the sweating system and attempts to control it, it must be pointed out that immigration in general, and especially the coming of this particular race, has been an important factor in reducing the importance of the woman wage earner in the industry.

The clothing industry has been more affected than any other trade in this country by successive waves of immigration, and on the whole the women have felt keenly the pressure of immigrant competition in the low-grade unskilled work of the trade. The proportion of women employed is, therefore, noticeably lower in the large cities

---

[231]"Reports of the Industrial Commission," xv, 346, 368.
[232]Willett, p. 68. 229

than in the small towns, and it seems reasonable to assume that more women are employed in these towns because there are fewer immigrants than in the cities.[233] That the effect of Russian Jewish immigration, in particular, has meant a restriction of women's work in the trade is unmistakable. There is a larger proportion of men than women immigrants among the Russian Jews; there is, too, a general racial opposition to the employment of women ; and, finally, the pace set by the Jews in some branches of the trade has meant a rate of speed which it is said has been too great for women to maintain. Moreover, the general tendency of labor legislation since 1892 has been to aid in this movement by forcing work from the home into the outside shops. With the Jewish prejudice against the employment of women outside of the home, this has meant inevitably a proportionate decrease in the number of women in the trade.[234]

It seems to be clear, then, that the tendency of the last quarter century in the industry has been toward an increase in the proportion of men and a corresponding decrease in the proportion of women employed. The census report on the clothing industry in 1900 strangely enough implied that women were taking the places of men,[235] but

---

[233]The following data from Pope, pp. 57-58, are of interest in this connection.

"In the shops manufacturing pants, vests, coats, and cloaks inspected, the percentage of women to the total number employed was, in 1888, 40.7 per cent; in 1891, 27.5 per cent; in 1896, 26 per cent; and in 1900, 25.3 per cent. The following table shows the results of the Factory Inspector's investigations as to the percentage of women employed in the manufacture of cloaks, pants, coats, and vests, respectively, in New York City:"

Year	Cloaks	Pants	Coats	Vests
1888	45.5	62.4	28.3	63.6
1891	39.1	54.8	19.1	55.4
1896	29.0	25.0	20.6	42.8
1900	23.6	23.8	22.7	43.2
1902	In men's and boys' clothing 27.8 per cent.			

[234]In the shops connected with but technically separate from living rooms, the percentage of women workers remained high. "A condition was thus brought about just opposite to that which we should expect, namely that the smaller the shop, the higher the percentage of women." — Pope, p. 57.

[235]See "Twelfth Census 1900" Manufactures, iii, 262. The census says with regard to changes in employees and wages in this industry: "The total number of wage earners reported in 1900 showed a decrease of 23,976 or 16.5 per cent, and their wages decreased $5,570,059, or 10.9 per cent. The greatest decrease was in the number of men with 19,709, with a decrease in their wages of $5,968,327. This is partly due to a transfer of wages to 'contract' work under miscellaneous expenses. Besides, it can be explained partly by the substitution of women for

Table 23: MEN'S CLOTHING, FACTORY PRODUCT - NUMBER OF
EMPLOYEES

	1890	1900	1905
Men	67,786	48,070	58,759
Women	75,621	69,846	75,468
Children	1,519	3,011	2,963
Total number of employees	144,926	120,927	137,190
Percentage of women employed	52	58	55

the statistics of employment for the industry, which are given in the
following table[236], do not seem to justify the statement.

According to this table, fifty-two per cent of the total number
of persons employed in the manufacture of men's clothing in the
year 1890 were women; this percentage had increased to fifty-eight
in 1900, but had decreased to fifty-five in 1905, when the last census
of manufactures was taken. All of the statistics given in the census, however, are prefaced by a statement showing how impossible
it is to collect complete and accurate data for the industry. Existing conditions, particularly in the manufacture of men's clothing
made a complete canvas of the industry by the census office impossible.[237] Special agents and enumerators who collected the data
could not obtain information from a large number of places where
the manufacture was carried on. The majority of these places were in
tenements and small shops in the rear of dwellings and as a rule, the
men giving information were foreigners, without a knowledge of the
language and with "a prejudice against, and suspicion of, any person making inquiries about their business." Such men, it was said,
were not only not disposed to make any returns, but in general, were
not in the habit of keeping any books or accounts, and, therefore,
such information as they gave was for the most part "guesswork."
Moreover, it was added, "a part of the work is done by women in
their own homes; but it was impracticable to attempt to ascertain

---

men. The average number of women wage earners decreased 5,759, or 7.6 per
cent, but the total wages paid to women increased $131,649, or seven tenths of
1 per cent."

[236]The data for 1890-1900 are given in "Twelfth Census(1900): Manufactures"
Pt. iii, 261, and data for 1905 and again for 1900 are given in the 1905 "Census
of Manufactures," i, lxxviii.

[237]This is a statement condensed from the "Twelfth Census (1900): Manufactures," Pt. iii, 261.

Table 24: MEN'S CLOTHING, FACTORY PRODUCT AND CUSTOM WORK - 1850-1900

	1850	1860	1870	1880	1890	1900
Men	35,031	41,837	47,829	77,255	118,640	96,825
Women	61,500	72,963	59,019	80,994	95,400	89,395
Children	...	...	1,280	2,564	2,065	3,879
Total number of employees	96,551	114,800	108,128	160,813	216,105	190,099
Percentage of women employed	62	63	55	54	44	46

the number so employed."

It would seem, therefore, that conclusions of value could not be based on an increase of six per cent between 1890 and 1900 and a decrease of three per cent between 1900 and 1905, when the statistics upon which the percentages are computed are acknowledged to be incomplete and inaccurate. Moreover, it should be pointed out that the tendency particularly in the large cities toward a substitution of men for women which has been indicated in the preceding discussion seems to be borne out by such data as are available for a longer period of time. Thus, the following table[238] seems to indicate that the decline in the proportion of women employed has been going on for more than half a century.

While this table may seem clearly to indicate a decrease in the

---

[238]This table with the exception of data for 1890 and 1900, which have been changed as indicated below, are given in the "Twelfth Census (1900): Manufactures," Pt. iii, 261. The census explains that "the only comparison of any value that can be made is between the figures for 1890-1900," since the data for the two latter years are for the "factory product" only, while in the earlier census reports for the industry, statistics for custom-made and for factory-made clothing were not separated. If such a comparison is desired, however, the returns for custom and factory product may be easily combined for the later years. By adding the data for custom work which are given on p. 301 of the same volume to the data for the factory product which are given in the original table, and substituting these results for the factory product data in the table the objection to a comparison is, in part, done away with. In the table above, therefore, the data for 1890 and 1900 are not those given in the original census table, but they represent instead the sum of custom-made and factory-product data for each of these years. Data for 1905 are not included in this table, as those given in the 1905 "Census of Manufactures" are only for the factory product, and are given later.

proportion of women employed, yet it must again be said that for an industry in which reliable statistics cannot be gathered, the statistical method obviously cannot be relied upon alone. No conclusions, therefore, have been based solely upon these data which have, indeed, been presented as of interest in view of the fact that in the history of the industry causes have been found promoting such a decline.

There is another branch of the manufacture of men's clothing, the making of men's furnishing goods, which employs so many women that at least a brief account of it must be given. This is, indeed, no longer a single branch of the trade, but rather an aggregation of several distinct branches, some of which, such as, for example, the manufacture of shirts, of collars and cuffs, of neckwear, or of underwear, are really independent industries requiring specialized machinery and special skill in the manufacture. The census reported in 1900 a total of 56,357 women and 10,915 men engaged in making men's shirts and other "furnishing goods." That so large a number of women, should be employed in this work is not astonishing; in fact it is rather a matter of surprise that even one sixth of the employees are men. This is the kind of sewing that has always been considered "women's work," and the manufacture of "ready-made" articles of this class has always been in the hands of women. The industry of supplying ready-made "furnishings" for men began in the decade 1820-30, and by 1832 the manufacture of "custom-made" shirts had become an organized industry in New York, out of which the making of "stock shirts" soon developed. All of this work was done by seamstresses who worked in their own homes, and the factories established were merely places where the material was cut and the work given out and returned.

The making of detachable collars also began as a distinct industry before 1880. At one time shirts were made with collars attached, and it was a great innovation when a retired Methodist minister who kept a small dry goods store in Troy, New York, began a wholesale business in separate collars. These collars were at first all made by his wife and daughters at home, but he soon began to give out work to the women in the neighboring families, who received with each lot of collars a card carefully specifying: "In pay you buy my goods at my prices." The minister store keeper was not long the only collar manufacturer in the field, and Troy became the center of a great industry.[239]

The women who made collars, and later collars and cuffs, in the neighborhood of Troy, worked in their own comfortable homes, and were for the most part the wives and daughters of well-to-do and prosperous farmers and workingmen. In a striking contrast were the shirtmakers in the large cities, who in these early days were a notoriously oppressed class of working women. Prices for their work seem to have been from six to twelve cents for a shirt, most commonly eight or ten cents. As the ordinary steamstress working on coarse shirts could not make more than nine a week, her earnings were deplorably low.[240] These women often lived under the most distressing conditions in garrets and cellars. Indeed the life of the ordinary seamstress who made shirts by hand in the days before the invention of the sewing machine was one of great misery.

Matthew Carey, in a vehement protest in behalf of "those females who depend on their needles and live in their own apartments, in a situation almost too trying for human nature," declared that "neither skill, talent, nor industry [could] enable those poor creatures to earn more than a dollar and a quarter, or perhaps one out of ten a dollar and a half per week."[241] There were said to be thousands of women in Philadelphia earning these wages. It was estimated on the most careful inquiries that the number of women in Boston, New York, Philadelphia, and Baltimore who were self-supporting was from eighteen to twenty thousand; of these it was estimated that one third were "tayleresses, milliners, mantua-makers, colorists, attendants in shops, seamstresses in families, nurses, whitewashers and the like," who were said to be in general fairly well paid, but the other two thirds, seamstresses who worked in their own lodgings, spoolers, and shoe binders,[242] were reported to be working under intolerable conditions.

The federal government in its contracts for army clothing engaged in an early, and what seems to have been a very disgraceful, sweating system. The conditions among the women who did government work aroused so much indignation that, in the winter of 1829,

[239]For an interesting account of this industry, see "Twelfth Census (1900): Manufactures," Pt. iii, 310.

[240]M. Carey, "A Plea for the Poor" No. II, Philadelphia, December 26, 1831.

[241]*Ibid*, "Essays on the Public Charities of Philadelphia" Preface, fourth edition.

[242]An open letter "To the Ladies Who Have Undertaken to Establish a House of Industry in New York," M. Carey, "Miscellaneous Pamphlets."

a protest was sent to the Secretary of War, signed by one hundred and thirty-one "respectable citizens" of Philadelphia. It was claimed that the wages paid by the Government for making shirts of drilling were "utterly inadequate to enable the industrious females employed on them to pay rent and to procure a sufficient supply of clothing and the other necessaries of life." The Secretary replied that the Government did not wish to oppress the "indigent but meritorious females" employed in its service, yet, he said, "the subject is found to be one of so much delicacy and is so intimately connected with the manufacturing interests and the general prices of this kind of labor in the city of Philadelphia that the Department has not felt at liberty to interfere further than to address a letter to the Commissary General of Purchase"[243]

Women were also employed on a rather large scale during this period in the manufacture of men's stocks, the proper neckwear of the period, and suspenders. In two of the New England states more than 700 women were employed in this industry, and in many other

---

[243] A copy of the letter sent to the Commissary General is of sufficient interest to quote:

"DEPARTMENT OF WAR,

February 2, 1829.

Sir: — Communications, of which the enclosed are copies, signed by some fifty or sixty persons, who, as far as their names are known to this department, appear to be amongst the most respectable citizens of Philadelphia, have been received, complaining that the prices paid by you to the needy but industrious females whom you employ in making up clothes for the army, are too low— out of proportion to the compensation allowed to other branches of industry, and inadequate for their support.

While the Government highly commends the general spirit of economy and zealous regard to the public interest, displayed in your contracts, it cannot wish to impose terms that shall operate oppressively on any class of its citizens, and more especially on widows and other meritorious females employed in its service.

The difficulty, however, of correctly appreciating, at this place, the merits of the several suggestions contained in the communications of those gentlemen, and a want of sufficient knowledge of the effects which would be produced by acceding to their requests, not only on the particular interests of the Government, but on the prices of this species of labor generally throughout the large manufacturing city of Philadelphia, render it a subject of too much delicacy for the Department to interfere; and the whole must therefore be left, where it has been properly placed, in your sound discretion.

I have the honor, & etc.

(Signed)   P. B. PORTER.

parts of the country women were probably doing similar work. A single firm in Boston employed two men at $1.25 a day, one boy at 50 cents a day, and ninety women at $37\frac{1}{2}$ cents a day. In two establishments in Berlin, Connecticut, 225 women were employed in the making of suspenders alone.

There is, however, as has already been pointed out, nothing especially significant about the employment of women in this work. Needlework, except the heavy, highly skilled work of tailoring, was always accepted as peculiarly suitable for women. For the same reason little need be said about the making of women's ready-made garments, with perhaps the single exception of cloaks. No other garments for women were manufactured ready for sale, on any scale worthy of note, before 1860, and even until 1880 the women's ready-made clothing industry was pretty exclusively confined to cloakmaking. After this time women's tailored suits came into the market and formed a new branch of the industry which expanded rapidly. Later the making of shirtwaists, underwear, and similar products became another distinct trade within the industry, and at the present time all kinds of women's garments are manufactured ready for sale. Cloaks might, perhaps, because of their weight, seem to belong more properly with men's outside garments. They were, however, always made by women, and even the skilled work of cutting was done by a woman, usually by a French tailoress in the early days of the trade.[244]

In 1860, the first year when the census presented statistics for the industry, the returns showed that 889 men and 4,850 women were engaged in the manufacture of women's clothing; in 1905 the same industry employed more than 42,000 men and 72,000 women. Other data given by the census from decade to decade, are found in the following table:

It is of interest that the census in presenting these data speaks of

---

[244] An interesting contrast between the employment of women in cloakmaking and in other garmentmaking is found in Pope, p. 17: "The traditions behind men's clothing in the custom trade favored the skilled male workman, and the chief influence was English. In women's garments the tradition was that of the woman tailoress, and the chief influence was French. In the early years of the cloak industry the retailer employed a French tailoress to do the cutting and to have general supervision over the workers, who were largely women. The fact that the cloak industry had behind it a tradition of unskilled female labor, unprejudiced against the factory, coupled with the fact that many of the workers were young women who could not easily furnish their own workplace, accounts very largely for the making of cloaks in the inside shops."

Table 25: WOMEN'S CLOTHING, FACTORY PRODUCT

	1860	1870	1880	1890	1900	1905
Men	889	1,105	2,594	12,963	26,109	42,614
Women	4,850	10,247	22,253	25,913	56,866	72,242
Children	...	344	345	273	764	849
Total number of employees	5,739	11,696	25,192	39,149	83,739	115,705
Percentage of women employed	85	88	88	66	67	63

them as "more approximately correct" than those given in the table for men's ready-made clothing, and it is of interest that they show a constant decline since 1880 in the proportion of women employed and that the percentage of women employed in 1900 or 1905 is apparently very much lower than in 1860.[245]

In commenting on the change that had taken place between 1890 and 1900, the census pointed out that the development of the industry during the decade "was of such a nature that men were substituted for women in the manufacture of certain of the better grades of clothing, such as cloaks and ladies' suits, while the greatest number of women were added in the factories for shirtwaists and underwear." But whatever changes may have taken place in the last decade, it is clear that, if a longer period be considered, all of the men who are now employed in the manufacture of ready-made clothing for women are doing work that would have belonged to the dressy-makers and seamstresses of an earlier day, and the organization and development of the industry, therefore, has meant, to a considerable extent, the substitution of men for women.

In attempting a general summary for the clothing trades as a whole, it must again be pointed out that we are dealing with a complicated group of separate industries, some of which, such as the manufacture of women's shirtwaists and men's overalls,[246] are well

---

[245]The comment of the census on these data is as follows: "As the manufacture of women's ready-made clothing is not distributed over as many places as is that of men's, and as a large part of it is manufactured in large factories and in shops, the collection of statistics could be more accurately done, and the figures may be taken as more approximately correct." — "Twelfth Census (1900): Manufactures," Pt. iii, 283. Data for 1905 from the "Census of Manufactures" for that year, i, 6.

[246]The "overall" manufacture is a good example of one of the several minor

organized factory industries, while in others, like some branches of the "pants and vest" trade, a great deal of work is still done by the home finisher on the old domestic or commission system.

It is therefore impossible to present in clear outline a simplified account of the development of the industry as a whole. While all of the various branches had their origin alike in the work of the custom tailor, the dressmaker, or the seamstress, they became, at different stages in the evolution of the industry, distinct and unrelated trades.

A statistical outline of the industry in 1900 as presented in the census is given in the following table[247]. While this serves the purpose of giving an idea of the relative numbers of persons engaged in the manufacture of men's and of women's clothing, it fails to show all the special subdivisions of the industry, such as, for example, overalls, collars and cuffs, neckties, women's suits, cloaks, wrappers, aprons, shirtwaists, underwear, and other specialized branches of the trade.

So far as the employment of women is concerned, it may once more be pointed out that the line of descent of ready-made clothing for men is in part from the custom tailor and in part from the housewife or the country tailoress. In the earliest stage of the "ready-made" industry, however, the custom tailor employed women in the work, and although it is not possible to quote accurate statistics showing how far the proportion of men and women employees may have changed from time to time, there is evidence of the continuous

industries of which no special mention could be made. The census does not report statistics for the overall manufacture separately, but it is well known that the great majority of employees are women. In 1899, when the secretary of the United Garment Workers was testifying before the Industrial Commission, he said, in answer to the question "What part of the trade are the women members employed in?" that they were employed chiefly "in the overall branch and in the finishing work of the clothing trade." The overall operatives, he said, were largely American girls, who had had a common-school education and who represented the better class of working girls. See "Reports of the Industrial Commission," vii, 182 ,183, 194. Mrs. Willett devotes one chapter to overalls in her book on the clothing trade, and her statement as to the origin of the trade (p. 134) is of interest: "The manufacture of overalls and workingmen's garments is the branch of the clothing industry into which the factory system was first introduced, and in which it is now most largely employed. As early as 1871 there was in Wappinger's Falls, New York, the nucleus of the establishment that claims to have been the first overalls factory in the United States. By 1876 this factory had 256 employees, largely women, engaged in making overalls and workingmen's suits on machines run by steam power."

[247]From the "Twelfth Census (1900): Manufactures," Pt. iii, 301, 302.

Table 26: THE CLOTHING INDUSTRY IN 1900

	Men	Women	Children	Total Number of Employees	Percentage of Women.
MEN'S CLOTHING:					
Factory product	48,077	69,862	3,011	120,950	58
Custom work and repairing	48,748	19,533	868	69,149	28
Shirts	6,604	31,074	814	38,492	81
Furnishing good, men's	4,311	25,283	622	30,216	84
Buttonholes	426	479	39	944	51
Total men's	108,166	146,231	5,354	259,751	56
WOMEN'S CLOTHING:					
Factory product	26,109	56,866	764	83,739	68
Dressmaking	4,379	40,835	381	45,595	90
Total women's	30,488	97,701	1,145	129,334	76
Total miscellaneous	41,961	66,118	9,145	117,224	56

employment of large numbers of women in the trade from the early twenties of the last century down to the present day. And also it must be emphasized that in the manufacture of women's clothing nearly fifty thousand men are employed at work which would, under the more primitive system of the dressmaker and the seamstress, have been done entirely by women.

Chapter XI - Printing

In 1905 more than 37,000 women were employed in the printing trades in this country. The industry, however, is important from the point of view of women's work, not merely because so many women are engaged in it, but because it is one of the old skilled hand trades. Printing, like shoemaking, was one of the historic crafts and one which machinery has been very slow to change. As long as so many of the industrial occupations in which women are found are unskilled, their connection with a trade which requires training and skill is of special interest.

The employment of women in the industry known as "printing and publishing" has a long history. In the eighteenth century there were a great many women printers. The States of Massachusetts, Connecticut, Rhode Island, Pennsylvania, New York, Maryland, Virginia, and South Carolina each had one or more of them. These women worked as compositors as well as at the press.[248] Several colonial newspapers were published by women, and they printed books and pamphlets as well.

Margaret Draper of Massachusetts "printed" for the governor and council; in South Carolina a woman was appointed printer to the State after the close of the Revolutionary War; and Benjamin Franklin's sister-in-law at Newport, in Rhode Island, printed for the colony, supplied blanks for the public offices, published pamphlets, and in 1745 printed for the Government an edition of the laws, containing three hundred and forty folio pages. Her two daughters who assisted her in printing were said to have been "correct and quick

---

[248]That is, at setting type. See Isaiah Thomas, "History of Printing in America," i, *passim*.

compositors at case."

Although the number of women printers has always been small compared with the number of men in the trade, there has probably never been a time for more than a hundred years when women have not found employment in printing offices. Dr. Thomas, writing in 1815, called attention to the fact that women and girls were "not infrequently" employed as compositors; and at the same time he cited as an example of the kind of work they could do, that two women who were then working in a printing house in Philadelphia performed "their week's work with as much fidelity as most of the journeymen."

Although there is a good deal of indirect evidence[249] to show that women worked steadily in printing offices throughout the first half of the last century, very few data can be found relating to the number of women employed. Such statistics of employment as were collected in the first half century were, for the most part, got to show the progress our manufacturing industries were making and the need of protecting them ; and the printing and publishing trade was at that time of too little importance even to "foster." Some few data exist for 1832, but they relate chiefly to other branches of the printing trades. In Boston, for example, 15 bookbinders[250] in that year employed 60 men at $1.25 a day, 90 women at 50 cents, and 30 boys at the same wage. Ten manufacturers of blank books had 40 men, 20 women, and 20 boys at work at the same rates that were paid for bookbinding. Bookbinding, however, seems to have employed a larger proportion of women than other parts of the trade at this time. A few other data for 1831 bear out this statement. In New Haven, Conn., 16 men and 16 women were employed in bookbinding and 50 men and only 20 women in "publishing."

[249] Much of this is found in the records of the early printers' unions and will be discussed in connection with the attitude of the union to women's work. There are, of course, other statements, like the quotations from White, "Slater" (*supra*, p. 77) or the statement of Miss Martineau that typesetting was an occupation open to women when she visited America. See Chapter V, this volume.

[250] Just what processes women carried on in bookbinding is not altogether clear, but miscellaneous wages statistics for the decade 1830-40 in Massachusetts show that they were employed as collectors, folders, pasters, and sewers. Other data relating to wages in the following decade show that one establishment employed 21 women and 1 man as press feeders, and in the same occupation in the same establishment 14 women and 12 men were employed in 1891. See "Aldrich Report," II, 344. In Establishment Six (New York) women were also employed as press feeders and in Establishment Five (New York) as pressroom hands.

Two lithographing and 15 engraving establishments employed 16 men, 30 women, and 10 boys, the last probably apprentices. The type and stereotype founders employed 83 men at $1.50 a day, 55 women at from 42 to 50 cents, and 29 boys at 45 cents. The copperplate printers had 50 employees, all men and boys. Twenty publishers and booksellers employed a large number of hands, 400 men at $1.50 a day, 200 women at 40 cents, and 80 boys at 50 cents. No women were reported in the newspaper offices, where, altogether, 48 men and 36 boys were employed.[251] By way of summary, it may be said that the allied printing trades of Boston in 1831 together employed 687 men, most of whom were paid $1.50 a day, 395 women, most of whom were paid 50 cents a day; and 215 boys, who were paid in general at the same rate as the women.[252] Printing has, however, never been a trade which women have made their own. There are several reasons for this. It is, in the first place, a skilled trade in which a regular apprenticeship has always been required before a man could become a journeyman. Women, with the expectation of marriage before them, have not, as a general rule, entered trades which require a considerable time to learn. Moreover, the scarcity of male labor which was one of the reasons which led to the presence of women in large numbers in the early mills, did not affect skilled trades like printing, which offered inducements to men to enter them.

Another important factor affecting the employment of women in the trade has been the jealousy of the men . While women are sometimes excluded from occupations by reason of physical limitations, it also happens that a trade which is attractive to men and which is not too heavy for women is often quite effectually barred against them in other ways. It is amusing to find that in the decade 1830-40 Slater's biographer, a most zealous advocate of the employment of women in the mills, was publicly opposing their entering other industrial occupations. After a series of arguments to show the desirability of work in the cotton mills for women, he adds: "The attempt to introduce females into other employments, and especially into the

---

[251]In general, it may be pointed out here that women printers have never been employed to any extent on the great city newspapers where the work is, much of it, done under pressure and at night. In smaller towns women frequently set type for local papers, but in large cities their work is more strictly confined to "book and job" offices.

[252]The various data included in this summary were found in "Documents Relative to Manufactures" House Executive Documents, 1st session, 22d Congress, i and ii, (1832), i, 436, 458, 464.

printing office, is very properly reprobated."

It is also of great importance that the union policy in this trade, directed by the men, has always been hostile to the employment of women. As early as 1832 the Typographical Society of Philadelphia took action because it was rumored that a member of the society was planning to employ women compositors and to install a non-union printer as foreman over the women. The society protested so vigorously "that the member in question felt called upon to write a letter to be spread upon the minutes of the society denying that he had ever intended to employ women." This was by no means the last occasion upon which organized printers were to express officially their hostility to women in the trade. In 1835 a similar society in Washington called a special meeting to consider an alarming statement which had been published in a local paper "that girls were being employed as compositors in newspaper offices in Philadelphia to break a strike." Resolutions were adopted and embodied in a circular letter sent to the typographical societies of Philadelphia, Boston, New York, and Baltimore, asking if any girls were so employed, and if so, how many, and what action these societies "proposed to take to prevent the further progress of this evil." Unfortunately, if any replies were received, no record of them has been preserved.[253]

The records of the Boston Typographical Union give evidence of the same kind of hostility as late as 1856. In that year an unsuccessful attempt was made to carry the following resolution: "That this society discountenances any member working in any office that employs female compositors, and that any member found doing so be discharged from the society." Later, however, when the men had come to see that the women could not be driven from the trade and that their relation to the wage scale must be squarely faced as part of the problem with which the union had to deal, another resolution was passed :

"Whereas, The impression has gone abroad that this union discountenances the employment of female compositors. *Resolved*, That we recommend to the females employed in printing offices in this city to organize in such a manner as shall seem best to themselves, to prevent the present prices paid to them from being lowered, and that

---

[253]These statements and some later statements with regard to the relation of women to the various printers' societies are quoted from Mr. Ethelbert Stewart's valuable study of "Early Organizations of Printers" published in the "Bulletin of the U. S. Bureau of Labor," xi, 884.

in doing so they shall receive the cooperation of this union."[254]

The National Typographical Union also took action on the subject. "As early as 1854, the Union discussed the problem of the 'woman printer' and adopted a resolution that the Union would not "encourage by its act the employment of female compositors."[255] In 1855 the delegates to the national convention from Philadelphia were given special instructions "to oppose any recognition of the employment of females as compositors." After that year the subject of the woman printer was debated quite regularly at a long series of conventions, and most local unions were obliged to formulate some policy on the subject. The number of women printers was constantly increasing, and as they seemed unwilling to join the men's unions which were already formed it seemed for a time as if the best policy might be the formation of separate women's unions. In response to the petition from some women printers in New York the constitution of the union was so amended at the time of the national convention of 1869 as to permit "separate unions of female compositors." In 1870 "a union of women printers" was organized in New York City, but, in general, separate unions did not prove to be a success. A "committee on female labor" reported to the convention of 1872 that the result of the policy of having two unions was that the women were maintaining a lower wage scale. This was, of course, to make them much more dangerous as compositors, and in the following year, therefore, the problem of the woman printer was settled, so far as her relation to the union was concerned, by arrangements "for admitting women to full membership in local unions and demanding for their labor the same price paid to men." Since that time the union has made persistent efforts to establish everywhere the same scale for both men and women.

While women seem to have a secure position in the trade today, it is a most unsatisfactory one. They continue to be greatly handicapped by having no way of learning the trade properly. Printing is still a skilled trade, and while apprenticeships are nominally open to women, as a matter of fact no employer wants the trouble of having a girl apprentice when he can get so many more "odd jobs" out of

---

[254]See "Women Printers and the Typographical Union" in the "History of Trade Unionism Among Women in Boston," published by the Women's Trade Union League of Massachusetts, Boston, 1906.

[255]This comment on the "woman question" in the trade la quoted from Professor Barnett's careful study of the union. See Hollander and Bamett, "Studies in American Trade Unionism" p. 22.

a boy. The girl, therefore, in the language of the union, "steals the trade"; that is, she learns it without undergoing the same course of instruction that is prescribed for those who enter the trade properly, and she is, in consequence, imperfectly equipped. Few women are able to do any part of the work except "setting up straight matter," and although a woman may be quick and expert at this, she is very far from being an all-around efficient printer.

The president of the National Typographical Union testified as a witness before the Industrial Commission in 1899 that although, in Boston, the master printers employed all the women they could find, the tendency was to "keep a woman on straight composition, to make as much as possible an automaton of her," and not to permit her to reach high standards as a printer.[256]

In some localities there has been a special prejudice against the employment of women. For example, in the testimony just referred to, it was said that in Boston the master printers always claimed that a woman was a great inconvenience; that she needed a great amount of attention and assistance. She required boys to prepare her type, and a strongarmed man to lift her cases, and that, in general, she needed more supervision. It was charged, further, that large numbers of women were employed at wages from twenty to thirty per cent below the wages paid to men for the same kind of work. They were, more over, prevented by their employers from joining the printers' union by the threat of discharge if they demanded the "union scale" which was the standard wage rate for men.[257]

In New York, on the other hand, women printers were said to be dealt with very justly. Employers there followed the policy of refusing to employ a woman who was not able to "perform the work just as well as a man" One representative printer was quoted as saying that the women in his composing room were considered by the establishment as men, and that so long as they performed the work

---

[256] "Reports of the Industrial Commission" vii, 277 (testimony of Mr. Samuel B. Donnelly).

[257] "The typographical unions in New England have spent $5,000 in the last three years in endeavoring to secure a scale of wages for organized women, but their work has been circumvented and rendered abortive from the fact that the instant they secured any number of women in the establishment to join the organization, and it was known that they had attended the meetings, that instant the women were met by the employers, who said: "If you folks organize and demand a scale of wages we will discharge the whole of you and employ men; and to show that we mean it we will lay three or four of you off." — *Ibid.*, vii, 278.

in all its phases they would be employed; that he wanted competent printers who could be employed in any part of the composing room, and he would always pay them the same wages that he paid men; and, finally, that when he was compelled to reduce the wages for women, he would not employ women at all.

Printing is one of the trades in which the introduction of machinery was long delayed. As late as 1887, "typesetting was essentially the same art as in the sixteenth century. While other branches of the printing trade had been revolutionized, the compositor had not advanced in his processes beyond the point he had reached four hundred years before."[258] The invention of the linotype, however, meant that type was in the future to be set, not by hand, but by a machine, and for something more than a decade after the introduction of the linotype in 1887 the printers' union was actively engaged in trying to save its members from the disastrous effects of machine competition.

There was, of course, in the first stress of excitement over the impending change a very reasonable fear that unskilled labor might be successfully used on the machines, and this meant the possible substitution of women linotype operators for men printers. But while women have, in fact, found work to some extent as operators, their numbers have been small in comparison with the large numbers of men employed. There are perhaps two different reasons for this. President Donnelly of the Typographical union said that women learned the machine more readily than men but they had not the "endurance to maintain for any length of time the speed on a machine" that could be maintained by a man.

More important probably than the lack of endurance on the part of the women has been the policy of the union. With an unusual degree of intelligence and foresight, the printers took steps, as soon as it was realized that the machine had come to stay, to prevent as many men as possible from being thrown out of work. The union, therefore, demanded that machines should be operated only by "journeymen printers trained in the trade as a whole," and they were strong enough to enforce this demand very generally.[259] Since so few women were "journeymen printers," their chances for work were very much reduced.

[258]See Professor Barnett's interesting study of the "Introduction of the Linotype," *Yale Review*, xiii, 251.
[259]Barnett, in *Yale Review*, xiii, 257.

Table 27: PERSONS EMPLOYED IN BOOK AND JOB PRINTING, 1880-1905

	1880	1890	1900	1905
Men	45,890	40,010	52,311	65,748
Women	6,777	9,439	13,950	20,086
Children	5,839	1,412	2,127	2,489
Total number of employees	58,506	50,861	68,388	88,323
Percentage of women	12	19	20	23

Later the union established a requirement of a four years' apprenticeship as a prerequisite to becoming a linotype operator, a regulation which strengthened a policy unfavorable to the employment of women. But, from whatever cause, it is true that women have never been formidable competitors in the work of running the typesetting machines, and the percentage which women form of the total number of machine operators is very much smaller than the corresponding percentage of hand compositors.[260] The machine would seem, therefore, rather to have diminished than to have increased the opportunities of the woman printer.

How far the proportion of women in the trade as a whole may be increasing, it is not possible to say. Statistics for the industry, "printing and publishing," are not comparable except for very recent years. Such data, however, as are available for this purpose, are interesting. The following tables[261] show (1) the number of men, women, and children in the "book and job" branch of the trade, the only branch for which statistics were collected before 1890; and (2) the more recent data relating to the industry as a whole, which includes newspaper and periodical as well as book and job work.

These tables seem to indicate (1) that although women have been for so long identified with the trade, the men outnumber them four to one and printing is still pretty exclusively men's work; (2) that the proportion of women is increasing, but not at such an alarming

---

[260]Women formed only about five per cent of the total number of linotype operators in the United States and Canada in 1904. See Barnett, in *Yale Review*, xiii, 272.

[261]From Bulletin 70, 1905 "Census of Manufactures," p. 21; the table relating to the "Printing and Publishing" trade as a whole is from p. 10.

Table 28: PERSONS EMPLOYED IN "PRINTING AND PUBLISHING"

	1880	1890	1900	1905
Men	...	110,434	125,964	142,555
Women	...	19,026	28,765	37,614
Children	...	7,736	8,263	5,011
Total number of employees	...	137,196	162,992	185,180
Percentage of women	...	14	18	20

rate that the women can be said to be "driving out the men"; (3) that the proportion of women is larger in the "book and job" branch than in the trade as a whole, which includes newspaper work.

In general it may be said, by way of summary, that the history of the printing trade is of rather special interest from the point of view of the employment of women. Although it is a skilled trade, the work is light enough for it to be suitable for women. In fact, an official of the American Federation of Labor in testimony before the Industrial Commission in 1899 characterized the work of the printing trade as "peculiarly women's work." Typesetting, moreover, is work in which women were employed early in the eighteenth century and in which they have been employed ever since, but all of the time the men have treated it as a trade belonging especially to themselves. Officers of other trade unions frequently refer to the policy of the printers as an example of the way in which trade union control may be successful in checking or preventing the employment of women. The woman competitor, it is said, has been a comparatively slight problem in the printing trade.

It is not surprising, therefore, in the light of the organized hostility of the men, that while the women have more than held their own in the trade, their position remains a discouraging one. They are not as efficient as men, and at present there is no direct path to efficiency open to them. They are now admitted to the unions on the same terms as men, they pay the same dues, and receive the same benefits; but this is all done to protect the wage scale, not to encourage women to enter the trade. As a matter of fact, a comparatively small percentage of the women who work in printing offices belong to the union. A woman is not "worth as much" as a man who works as an "all-around" printer, and to join the union and demand the same rate of wages is to invite discharge. Most women consider it safer, therefore, to work in a nonunion shop where they will be allowed to take lower wages than the men. In the unions, the women form an insignificant minority; they seldom hold an office, and they have little influence in directing union policies.

Chapter XII - The Problem of Women's Wages

While some account of women's wages is needed to complete this discussion of the employment of women, no attempt will be made to write a history of women's wages in this country. Sufficient data for this purpose are not now available and it is doubtful if any will be discovered which will make possible a complete historical account. At the risk, however, of seeming to present a somewhat fragmentary account, an attempt will be made to give some idea (1) of what women were paid for their work at an earlier period, (2) of the relative rates of increase in women's wages and in men's wages, and (3) of the range of women's wages at the close of the last century in the five industries which have been specially studied, and in all of the industries for which returns were given in the special census report of 1900.

Women's wages during the colonial period may be disposed of briefly. It has already been explained that such industrial processes as were carried on by women at this time were for the most part domestic occupations. The work was done at home, and was, on the whole, so irregularly carried on as to make an estimate of wages, or regular earnings, impossible.

Examples have been given in an earlier chapter of the rates of payment for knitting, sewing, tailoring, spinning and weaving, and in particular the accounts of Mrs. Mary Avery and of Theodora Orcutt, which were quoted in detail, serve to show how considerable were the earnings of some of the women of the seventeenth and eighteenth centuries in connection with the cloth manufacture.

Some further information is available, however, regarding the wages of women who went into service, or, in the language of the day, were employed as "help." While this was not strictly speaking, an industrial occupation, it has been pointed out that the girl in service was often expected to do spinning, weaving, tailoring and similar work. The work of women servants, moreover, was for a more definite period and occupied a more regular portion of time than the more desultory employments which were carried on at home; and their wages were, therefore, more easily estimated. The wages of servants are further of interest as indicating the standard according to which women's work was valued and the earnings of women in service will, therefore, give some clue to what they earned in other occupations.

One of the earliest statements regarding the wages of women is found in Lechford's Notebook in 1639 to the effect that Elizabeth Evans of Bridgfield in the County of Glamorgan was to serve John Wheelwright, minister, for three years at "£3 per annum and passage paid."[262] Lechford also records the claim of John King and Mary, his wife, against the "worshipful John Humphrey, Esq.," their services being valued at the "rate of 6s. a weeke for the said John King and 3s. a weeke for his said wife."

In the "New Haven Colonial Records" in the year 1643, it is ordered that "Sister Preston shall sweep and dresse the meeting house every weeke, and have 1s. a weeke for her pains."

Similarly, the town of Dorchester, in 1667, paid "widow Mead" £3 for ringing the bell and keeping the meetinghouse through the year. An old Newbury account book shows that in 1667, a woman's wages were estimated to be £4-5 per annum, and a man's £10.[263] The old steward's book of Harvard College shows that the wages of a laundress between 1687-1719 were ten shillings a quarter.[264]

Wages were much the same in the South. In Virginia a maid was engaged by Sir Edward Plowden in 1643 at the rate of £4 per annum; about 1680 Pitzhugh, in writing to his agent, requested a

---

[262]"Notebook kept by Thomas Lechford, Esq., Lawyer," in "Transactions and Collections of the American Antiquarian Society," vii, 107.

[263]Coffin, "The History of Newbury, Newburyport, and West Newbury," p. 120.

[264]MS. records preserved in the library of Harvard University.

trained housekeeper and offered to pay her passage and £3 a year.[265] At the close of the century, they were nominally at least much higher in Pennsylvania where £6 to £10 a year was said to be the rate in 1689. Gabriel Thomas writing in that year said of women's work in general: "For the women who get their livelihood by their own industry, their labor is very dear, for I can buy in London a cheese cake for Two Pence bigger than theirs at that price, when at the same time their milk is as cheap as we can buy it in London, and their Flour cheaper by one half . . . another Reason why Women's Wages are so exorbitant; they are not yet very numerous which makes them stand upon high terms for their several services, in Sempstering, Washing, Spinning, Knitting and Sewing and in all other parts of their Imployments; for they have for Spinning either worsted or Linen, two shillings a pound, and commonly for Knitting a very Course pair of Yarn Stockings, they have half a Crown paid; moreover they are usually marry'd before they are twenty years of age."[266] Similarly in 1710, in an account of Philadelphia it was said: "All Women's Work is very dear there and that proceeds from the smallness of the Number and the Scarcity of the Workers; for even the meanest Single Women marry well there, and being above Want are above Work."[267]

In 1748 it was reported that a woman servant got £8 to £10 and a man servant £16 to £20, but this was in Philadelphia and wages were said to be less in the country.[268] During and immediately after the revolution, when prices were high as a result of the depreciation of the currency, women were, of course, paid more for their work, and in 1784, they earned £10 a year.[269]

Although teaching is not an industrial occupation and the wages of women who taught "dame's schools" need not be considered here it may be noted that such work was very much less remunerative

---

[265] Bruce, "Economic History of Virginia," ii, 48, 49.

[266] "An Account of Philadelphia and West New York," by Gabriel Thomas, pp. 43-45. Reprinted from the original edition of 1698 (Cleveland, 1903). "In general" he said, "Poor People (both Men and Women) of all kinds, can here get three times the Wages for Their Labour they can in England or Wales."

[267] See the narrative of "Richard Castelman, Gentleman," Hart, "American History Told by Contemporaries," ii, 76.

[268] Peter Kalm, "Travels into North America," i, 387. These wages were in addition to food.

[269] MacMaster, "History of the People of the United States," ii, 97; and see Willard, "History of Greenfield," p. 67, for an example of very high wages paid to women during the war.

than domestic service or spinning and weaving,[270] just as later, in the first quarter of the nineteenth century, teaching was much less remunerative than work in the cotton mills.[271] This was, of course, partly due, at both periods, to the fact that such schools as women were permitted to teach were kept only for a short time during the year while the other occupations meant much more regular employment.

Of much greater interest, however, than the earnings of women during the colonial period is the question of their wages in the early mills and factories. For those which were established in the eighteenth century, information concerning wages is not only difficult to obtain but of little value since so few persons were employed. In the early paper mills of Massachusetts, "ordinary workmen and girls were said to be paid the equivalent of seventy-five cents a week and their board";[272] and when Henry Wansey visited Dickson's factory at "Hell Gates" in New York, he said with regard to wages, "They give the women two dollars and find them in board and lodging."[273]

For the early nineteenth-century mills few data have ever been published, but some unique and interesting manuscript records have been found for two Massachusetts cotton mills which supply valuable information for the period from 1815 to 1825. These are a collec-

---

[270] For wages of "school dames," see Sewall, "History of Woburn," p. 51; Temple and Sheldon, "History of Northfield," pp. 162, 163; Barry, "History of Framingham," p. 76. In general, ten shillings seemed to have been the usual payment for this work. In 1686, when Widow Walker of Wobum was engaged to be "school dame," it was specified that she was to have ten shillings for her labor "as the other mistresses had before her." In 1673, however, Allen Connar's wife and Joseph Wright's wife, who together taught the school for Woburn, were given ten shillings to be divided equally between them for their year's work. Later, of course, wages were higher; see Samson, "History of Manchester" (p. 207), where it was noted on March 9, 1763, that one-half of the £50 for the support of a free school "be expended to support four School Dames to keep a free Schoole"; Blake, "History of Warwick" (p. 38), where it was noted in June, 1768, that Hannah Hanson be employed to keep school, and it was provided that "if the selectmen found any material objection against her, they should dismiss her, and she is to have four shillings and six pence per week for the time she keep, her father finding her board." (These last two references were kindly supplied by Dr. M. W. Jemegan of the University of Chicago).

[271] See Chapter VII, above, for extracts from Horace Mann's report calling attention to this fact.

[272] E. B. Crane, "Early Paper Mills in Massachusetts," "Collections Worcester Society of Antiquity," vii, 121, 127.

[273] Henry Wansey, "Journal of an Excursion to the United States" (1796), p. 107.

tion of books and papers which belonged to a small cotton mill at Lancaster, Massachusetts,[274] and an old wages book for the year 1821 which is still preserved in the mills of Waltham in the same state. While these data are all from Massachusetts, the Waltham mills were so much larger than those of Lancaster that the material relates to two different types of factories.

One of the earliest of these records is a memorandum made by the proprietor of the Lancaster mills on the 27th of January, 1815, as follows:

"Dennis Rier of Newbury Port has this day engaged to come with his family to work in our factory on the following conditions. He is to be here about the twentieth of next month and is to have the following wages per week:

Himself	$5.00
His son, Robert Rier, 10 years of age	0.83
Daughter Mary, 12 years of age	1.25
Son William, 13 years of age	1.50
Son Michael, 16 years of age	2.00
	$10.58

His sister, Abigail Smith	$2.33
Her daughter, Sally, 8 years of age	0.75
Son Samuel, 13 years of age	1.50
	$4.58

Reference has already been made to this document as an interesting evidence of the employment of families in the early mills. But it is further of interest here as showing that the sister Abigail Smith was paid only two dollars and thirty-three cents a week, while the "son Michael, 16 years of age" earned almost as much, and the wages of Dennis Rier were more than double that sum.

In the same collection of papers under date of February 13, 1817, is another memorandum of interest: "Aaron Jones has engaged that his daughter Almira shall work in our factory. We are to allow her one dollar per week and if she stays twelve months she is to have a gift of a pair of shoes or something equivalent." Almira's age is not given, but she was undoubtedly quite a young girl and it is possible that board was given in addition to her pay.

---

[274]The Poignaud and Plant papers in the Lancaster Town Library.

A more important item of information from these papers regarding wages is found in some correspondence of the year 1823. In answer to an inquiry regarding positions for girl weavers, the reply was: "I beg to inform you that our weavers average about two dollars per week and the person who takes care of our Dressing Machine can earn three dollars per week exclusive of board"; and it was added: "We don't admit any person to the care of our looms under twenty years of age."

In connection with their mill, the company maintained boarding houses both for men and girls.[275] The price of board for the girls was one dollar and eighteen cents a week, but this seems to have been paid for them by the company, so that the wages as indicated were clear of board. In this connection a memorandum of April 17, 1818, is of interest.

"This will serve to certify that I, Calvin Howe, of West Boylston, have this day engaged to take charge of Boarding the girls employed in the factory belonging to the Poignaud and Plant Company in Lancaster, and I will provide suitable provisions for such boarders and do their washing for seven shillings or one dollar and seventeen cents per week. This is to include board, washing, and lodging for each girl."

In 1819 the company paid one Willard Howe twenty-nine dollars for "boarding twenty-five girls one week at one dollar and sixteen cents"; and in 1820 the same Willard Howe engaged "to board the girls for one dollar and eight cents"; in 1827 one dollar and eighteen cents was paid.[276] There are other similar records.

---

[275]The rules and regulations for the girls' boarding house are given in Appendix C; and see Chapter VII of this book for an account of the corporation boarding-house system. The operatives in these early records are uniformly described as girls, never as women. In a still earlier period, when the machines were objects of wonder, the tenders were called "artists."

[276]These memoranda are, of course, all from the Poignaud and Plant papers. Another memorandum relating to this subject, dated February 5, 1827 (Document 281), is long, but interesting enough to quote:

"This will serve to certify that I, Isaac Whitney, of Harvard, have this day engaged to take charge of the Girl Boarding House belonging to the Lancaster Cotton Manufacturing Company's spinning Factory on the first day of April next, or sooner if necessary, and continue to manage the same for twelve months from said day, and that I will provide suitable provisions well cooked for all Boarders they may have occasion to send me and do their washing for one dollar and eighteen cents per week for each female Boarder. . . .

"The Beds and Bedding necessary for lodging the Boarders said Corporation may send to me is to be furnished by them without any charge, except for such

This payment of wages in addition to board was in contrast to the system in Lowell where, although the corporation owned the boarding houses, the operatives paid their own board. Even in Lowell, however, the corporations had, at first, paid part of the operatives' board directly to the boarding-house keepers. Later they withdrew this sum and the girls were obliged to pay an additional twenty-five cents a week for board. This was a virtual reduction of wages and caused the first strike among the Lowell operatives.[277]

Another point not to be overlooked in connection with wages is the fact that operatives were frequently not paid in money but in orders on a company store at which they were invariably overcharged for their purchases and frequently defrauded in other ways. Such a store was maintained by the Lancaster factory, and items like the following[278] in the accounts of the proprietors seem to indicate that the operatives were paid irregularly in goods at high prices.

Cash Mary Brooks	One Umberalla, one pair gloves	$4.63
" " "	One string heads	0.50
" Martha Bartlett	One Umberalla	3.50
	One Pocket-Book	0.50
Cash Betsey Raymond	One Bible	1.13
	One Hymn Book	0.63

Company stores were not a feature of the Lowell system but they were common enough in other parts of New England. Perhaps the most interesting illustration of the way in which the "store" was managed to the profit of the stockholders is found in the experience of Hannah Borden of Fall River.

Wages in the Fall River mills were never paid in money but always in goods from the company store. Accounts so invariably showed a balance in favor of the mill owners that the employees began to be much dissatisfied. Hannah Borden's position was a peculiarly independent one, not merely because she was a daughter of a stockholder, but because she was the best weaver in the city and the company could not afford to lose her. She felt that it was unfair that the operatives should not be allowed to see their accounts, and felt so certain that her own were not correct that she went to the agent

damage as may arise to the same from improper use."
[277] Robinson, "Loom and Spindle," p. 17.
[278] From Poignaud and Plant cash and time books, 1818;

and threatened to leave unless he would let her see the books. He ordered them sent up, and she found articles like suspenders and rum charged against her. She finally demanded money wages as the only condition on which she would remain in the mill, and the granting of her demand soon led the other hands to insist on the same treatment, and money wages for everyone became the rule.

To turn to the material referred to which was found in the Waltham mills, it must be again pointed out that these mills were very much larger and of much greater interest than those in Lancaster. Fortunately the wages book for 1821 which is still preserved at Waltham contains the most complete series of wages paid to cotton-mill operatives in the first quarter of the last century. In it are the signatures of the girl spinners and weavers and carders of the day, Everline Boutell, Joan Turner, Mindwell Smith, Hepsabeth Hunt, Roxy Shattuck, Prudence Barker, Relief Lovejoy, Alanson and Patience Crane, Marah Kimball, Asenath Haynes, Arbia Pratt, Arvilla Hopkins, who could only make her mark, and Polly Maynard, Balinda Clark, and Rhuane Nickles, who were similarly illiterate, and a host of Balindas, Clarindas, Malindas, Lucindas, Nancys, Pattys, Mercys, Roxanas, Dollys, and other girls with their old-fashioned New England names.[279]

Since an "average wage" fails to give any idea of the range of wages paid or of the number employed at either the highest or the lowest rates, and since the lists of actual rates are too long to be given in full,[280] it has seemed best to prepare some tables of wage groups, showing the exact numbers of women receiving wages within certain limits; that is, to show the number of women receiving less than $2 a week, the number receiving between $2 and $2.50 and so on up the scale; for it is just as interesting to know that some women were paid less than $2 and some more than $3.50 a week, as to know that the average wage was $2.25. Such tables have been prepared, therefore, for each of the important departments of the mill, carding, spinning, weaving, and dressing.

In the carding rooms of Waltham, sixty-two women were employed at the following weekly wages:

---

[279]In striking contrast are the wages lists of the same mill today, where French-Canadian, Italian, Armenian, and other equally foreign names are found.

[280]Data for this period are so rare that it has seemed worth while to reprint in full this unique record of the actual rates which were paid to these 317 Waltham operatives in 1821, and they have been collected, therefore, in Appendix.

Table 29: WEEKLY WAGES, CARDING — WALTHAM MILLS, 1821

	Number of Women.
Under $2	4
$2 and under $2.50	45
$2.50 and under $3	7
$3 and under $3.50	5
$3.50 and under $4	1
$4 or over	..
Total number	62

Table 30: WEEKLY WAGES, SPINNING — WALTHAM MILLS, 1821

	Number of Women.
Under $2	..
$2 and under $2.50	32
$2.50 and under $3	19
$3 and under $3.50	13
$3.50 and under $4	2
$4 or over	1
Total number	62

Wages were evidently low in the carding department since forty-nine out of sixty-two women were paid less than $2.50 a week. A comparison with the wages paid to men is interesting for twenty-two men and boys were also employed in this department, and although the wages of men were lower in this than in the other departments in the mills because of the employment of boys, they were higher considerably than the wages of the women. Thus the overseer was a man who earned $12 a week; the card coverer, who was also a man, earned $10 a week; five of the other men earned $6, five between $4 and $6, and ten, who were probably boys, less than $4. In comparison with the women's wages, it should be noted that eleven out of twenty-nine men were paid more than the highest wage given to any woman. No men or boys were paid less than $2, although four girls were under this wage, and while nearly three fourths of the women earned less than $2.50, only three of the men were paid so little.

Wages in the spinning rooms were higher, as the following table indicates:

In the spinning room no one earned less than $2 a week, but one

Table 31: WEEKLY WAGES, WEAVING — WALTHAM MILLS, 1821

	Number of Women.
Under $2	3
$2 and under $2.50	36
$2.50 and under $3	54
$3 and under $3.50	31
$3.50 and under $4	2
$4 or over	..
Total number	126

Table 32: WEEKLY WAGES, DRESSING — WALTHAM MILLS, 1821

	Number of Women.
Under $2	..
$2 and under $2.50	7
$2.50 and under $3	2
$3 and under $3.50	9
$3.50 and under $4	2
$4 or over	..
Total number	20

half of all the women in the department earned less than $2.50. The three men who were employed were, of course, paid higher wages than the women, one received $10.50 a week, another $10, and a third $7.

The rates for weaving, which are given below, show that this was, for women, a distinctly more profitable occupation.

In contrast to the rate of wages in the carding room where three fourths of the women and girls earned less than $2.50 a week and to the rates in the spinning rooms where one half received less than this sum, not one third of the girl weavers received such low wages. More than half of them, however, earned less than $3 a week and none earned as much as $4. The four men in the weaving room, who were probably overseers and assistant overseers, earned, of course, very much more, the latter $6.60 a week and the former $12.

In another important department of the mills, that in which the work of dressing or sizing the work was carried on, wages were still higher for women.

More than half of the women employed in the process of dressing

Table 33: WEEKLY WAGES, ALL OCCUPATIONS — WALTHAM MILLS, 1821

	Number of Women.	Number of Men.
Under $2	7	..
$2 and under $2.50	129	3
$2.50 and under $3	82	1
$3 and under $3.50	58	5
$3.50 and under $4	7	2
$4 or over	1	52*
Total number	284	63

*Of these 52 men, several were paid $12
a week, others $10.50, $10, etc.

earned more than three dollars a week; but the men in this as in the other departments got higher wages than the women. The "sizing" with which the yarn was "dressed" was made by a man who earned $7.50 a week; three other men were employed in the department, one at $7 a week, one at $9, and one at $10.

Of greater interest, perhaps, than the wages paid in the different departments are the rates for all of the occupations, that is, for the whole body of employees. A table, therefore, has been prepared in which are included not only the spinners, weavers, carders, dressers, and overseers, whose wages have already been given, but other employees such as cloth-room hands, warpers, drawers, machinists, and other operatives, of whom few were employed in the same work.

Of the 284 women and girls 136 were paid less than $2.50 a week, and while only 11 of the 52 men employed were paid less than $4 a week, but one of all the 284 women was paid as much as $4. These rates were exclusive of board and it must be noted that rates of board in the corporation boarding houses were generally higher for men than women. It has already been shown that the Poignaud and Plant Company paid $1.16 a week for each girl boarder; the rates for men in the boarding house kept by the same company were $2; and in Lowell, where the women paid $1.25, the rate for men was $1.75.

Wages in Lowell, during this period, seem to have corresponded quite closely to the Waltham rates. Tables of wages for the Merrimack Mills, which were established in 1823, show the following

Table 34: WEEKLY WAGES IN THE MERRIMACK MILLS (LOWELL), 1824

WOMEN.		MEN.	
Doffers	$2.25	Strippers, etc. (card-	
Drawers-in (card-room)	2.25	room)	$4.50
Speeders	2.25	Grinders (card-room)	6.00
Dressers	2.25	Second-hands (dressing)	6.00
Drawers-in (dressing)	3.00	Second-hands (carding)	7.50
Spinners	3.36	Second-hands (spinning)	7.50
Weavers	4.00	Second-hands (weaving)	7.50
		Overseers (dressing)	9.00
		Overseers (spinning)	10.50
		Overseers (carding)	12.00
		Overseers (weaving)	12.00

rates[281] for the year 1824:

This table is less interesting than those for Waltham because average wages are quoted here instead of actual rates, and because the number of employees is not given. It is, however, significant that here the lowest wage for men is higher than the highest wage for women. Moreover, this highest rate paid to women, $4 a week for weaving, was probably an accidental rate which does not represent the normal wages for such work, since the same mills reported $3 a week as the rate for the same occupation in 1840. Moreover a high rate in 1824 is easily explained. An account has already been given of the beginnings of power-loom weaving in Massachusetts and it need only be recalled here that when the first power-loom weaving was done in Lowell, a Deborah Skinner was induced to leave Waltham to teach the Lowell girls how to run their looms. The Waltham wages book for 1821 shows that Deborah Skinner was one of the best weavers there, where she was earning $3.12 a week. Undoubtedly higher wages were offered in Lowell to induce her and perhaps other experienced weavers, as well, to leave.

"Average wages" for two other Massachusetts mills for the year

---

[281]From the collection of wage statistics in the "Tenth Census" (1880), XX, 349. The rates have been changed from daily to weekly wages and the rates for the bleacheries, print works, etc., which employed no women, are omitted. The rates, therefore, are only for the departments in which women were found, and for those departments rates are given for both men and women.

1828, which were computed for a later census report, show not only a very much lower rate for weavers than that of the Merrimack mills, but a lower rate for other occupations as well. Women in the carding room were said to get on the average $2.55 a week, in the spinning room $2.58, for weaving $2.61, and for dressing $2.82.[282] Average wages are not very illuminating, but the comment of Colonel Wright, who computed these averages, that the rates did not vary much for several years and that in 1836 the rates were below those of 1828 is of interest. In both years, board for operatives was $1.25 a week.[283]

For the decade 1830-40, there are very few interesting estimates of the rates of wages paid in the mills. One statement which is found in the Poignaud and Plant papers is that "girl spinners" were paid $2.75 a week, girl carders $2.75, and warpers $3.75. Unfortunately the rate for weavers is not given.[284]

These rates, which seem to have been estimated on the basis of the operatives paying their own board, were certainly very low, especially low for carders and spinners. The Poignaud and Plant factory, however, was typical of the small country mills and wages were lower in them than in the larger manufacturing centers. It is indicative, too, of the comparatively low rates of wages paid in Lancaster that, after straw braiding became an established industry and the women and girls of the neighborhood could get work to do at home, it was very hard to get operatives enough to run the mill

---

[282]From Carroll D. Wright's "Report on the Factory System," in "Tenth Census" (1880), ii, 576.

[283]The rates quoted (Carroll D. Wright's "Report on the Factory System," ii, 576) for 1836 are as follows: Drawers $1.87; Weavers 2.05; Filling spinners 2.13; Warp spinners 2 .21; Warpers 2.43; Speeders 2.44; Dressers 3.11.

[284]The table in the Poignaud and Plant papers, entitled "An estimate of wages for 25 looms and preparation," is:

One overlooker, carding room	$8.00
One stripper	5.00
One picker	5.00
Five girls @ $2.75 a week	13.75
One overlooker, spinning, dressing and covering room	6.00
Three girls, spinners, @ $2.75 a week	8.25
One girl warper @ $3.75 a week	3.75
One mule spinner — 500 spindles	8.00
Two boy piecers	4.00
One spare man	5.00
One dresser	6.00
One picker	2.25
One measurer	2.50

Table 35: WOMEN'S WAGES PER WEEK IN THE COTTON MILLS IN
1836

	$3.60
Drawing-frame tenders	2.50
Dressers	3.80
Speeders $3 and	3.60
Spinners	3.00
Spoolers	2.72
Warpers $2.97 and high	3.51
Weavers (two looms)	3.78

and the proprietors were obliged to return to their earlier methods
of getting "help" from a distance by sending their agents up into the
states north "to hunt up girls." It is of interest that this method of
obtaining hands when operatives were scarce was adopted by various
corporations. A long, low, black wagon was employed in making
regular trips to the northern part of Massachusetts and around in
Vermont and New Hampshire; and the man having the team in
charge was paid "a dollar a head" for all the girls he secured. It was
charged that these men frequently misrepresented conditions to the
girls whom they engaged, that they said the wages were very high,
the work so neat that the "help" could dress in silks and so light
that they could spend half the time reading!

Another interesting estimate of the rates of wages paid to women
operatives during this decade was made by James Montgomery in
his treatise on the cotton manufacture in this country. He reported
in 1836 that the "average wages" of women in Lowell were $2 a week
besides their board and the average wages of men in the same place
$4.50 or $4.75 besides board. Montgomery was a practical manufacturer himself with experience in operating mills in this country as
well as in England, so that his observations are on the whole valuable. He also gave in addition to this general estimate, a statement
regarding wages in specific occupations as follows:

It is of interest that the rates given by Montgomery are rather
higher than those which have been quoted from other sources, for
Montgomery thought that the general rate of wages was higher in
the United States than in Great Britain, and this was, he believed,
particularly true of "the wages of females employed in the factories.
The greater part of these," he said, "are farmers' daughters, who

go into the factories only for a short time until they make a little money and then "clear out," as it is called; so that there is continual changing amongst them and in all places I have visited, they are generally scarce. On that account manufacturers are under the necessity of paying high wages as an inducement for girls to prefer working in the factories to home work; and while this state of things continues, it is not to be expected that wages in this country will be so low as in Great Britain" He added further: "The price of living here is higher and the hours of labor longer; besides the greater part of the factory workers being connected with farming whenever wages become reduced so low as to cease to operate as an inducement to prefer factory labor above any other — then factories must stop. Stagnation sends people back to farms." Attention was also called to the fact that by these girls the financial crisis of 1837 was not looked upon as a disaster because they regarded the time during which they were unemployed as a period of needed recreation.

While there are no other estimates of wages for this period prior to 1840 which. are of sufficient interest and value to quote,[285] some further comment regarding Lowell wages is necessary. Mrs. Robinson, who, it will be remembered, worked in the Lowell mills during the decades 1830-40 and 1840-50, said with regard to wages, that "the agents were paid only fair salaries, the overseers generally $2 a day and the help all earned good wages." Many of the girls, she said, made from $6 to $10 a week. This is, of course, much more than the rates which have been quoted and while it is perhaps true that occasionally wages of $6 and even of $10 were paid, these must have been quite exceptional. That the rate for the vast majority of girls was very much lower than this is indicated not only by the quotations of wages which have been given but by several contemporary accounts of the Lowell mills and operatives.

Scoresby, the English traveler, who was there in 1844 and whose description is a most favorable one, estimated that $1,75 a week,

---

[285]Some data were collected by the Massachusetts Bureau of Labor for this period, but they seem to have been taken from a considerable number of different mills; part of the quotations are stated to be averages and part actual rates, so that the results are too confusing to be of value. For 1831, a general average wage for men, women, and children in each state and in the country as a whole is given in the "Report of the Committee on Cotton," in the "Addresses of the Convention of the Friends of Domestic Industry in New York," p. 112. According to this table "average wages" for women ranged from $1.58 estimated for Virginia to $2.60 for New Hampshire; for men, $2.73 in Virginia to $7 in Massachusetts.

"clear of board," at a time when board was $1.25 a week, was the ordinary rate for the girls employed there; and that $4.90 a week, with board $1.75, was the common rate for men.[286]

In 1846 Henry Miles, a Lowell minister, who published a favorable account of the city of Lowell, made some interesting comments regarding wages. Girls who had just come in from the country, he said, were first employed as spare hands and were paid 55 cents a week and board;[287] but it was not long before they were earning $1.50 a week. The average pay of all women operatives, however, was said to be "a little below two dollars a week, clear of board, but if we include their earnings on extra work, it would be more than that sum."[288] Occasionally, he said, $3 or $4 a week might be earned and on a single pay roll in the year 1846, there were the names of twenty-four girls who had received $4.75 and board without extra hours or extra work; this, however, was mentioned "as an unusual case"[289]

As an example of what were considered unusual earnings, a statement contributed by a Lowell girl to one of the Boston papers in the autumn of 1844 may be quoted: "In May, 1842, the last month before the reduction of wages, I tended two looms, running at the rate of 140 beats of the lathe per minute. In twenty-four days I earned $14.52. In the next month, June, when speed and prices had both been reduced, I tended forty-one looms at a speed of 100 and earned in twenty-four days $13.52 and I certainly, after the first few days, had a easier task than with two looms, at the high rate of speed. I increased my earnings every month a little, by the gradual increase of the speed, as I grew accustomed to it. In January, 1843, the speed was raised to about 418 and the price reduced still lower. I earned in that month in twenty-four days, on three looms, $14.60 and my work was in no degree harder. The , speed was raised as fast as we could bear it, and I often almost always at our own request, because in the increase of speed our pay increased. In June, 1843, I still

---

[286] Scoresby, "American Factories and their Female Operatives," p. 30.

[287] Miles, "Lowell as It Was and as It Is," p. 112.

[288] *Ibid.*, p. 183. The "average pay" of male operatives was estimated to be about 85 cents a day "clear of board."

[289] *Ibid.*, p. 113. The comment was added: "It will hereafter be seen how frequently the prospect of greater gain draws young women who have kept country schools to working in the mills in Lowell. As another evidence of their great earnings, it may be stated that it is estimated that the factory girls of this city have, in round numbers, $100,000 in the Lowell Institution for Savings."

tended three looms, and in twenty-four days earned $15.40, and in June, 1844, feeling able to tend four looms at a speed of about 120, I received $16.92 in pay for twenty-four days' work. I affirm that I have not in any of these, or other months, overworked myself. I have kept gaining in ability and skill and as fast as I did so I was allowed to make more money, by the accommodation of the speed of the looms to my capacity."

This contribution is an interesting one, indicating as it does that the maximum wage earned in a year by this girl, who considered herself "better than the average [weaver], but not better than the best," was $4.23 a week.

Higher wages, however, were undoubtedly sometimes earned. Quotations in the original exhibits of the "Aldrich Report" show that in one Massachusetts establishment in 1842, out of forty-one women weavers, two earned $7.50 a week and five $5.40; in the same establishment, during one month in 1843, one woman earned $7.50, four $6.96, and three $6. These were, however, very high rates, indeed, considerably higher than any that were paid again in those mills until after the Civil War.

This collection of wage statistics, known as the "Aldrich Report,"[290] contains some valuable data relating to women's wages from 1842 to 1891. Unfortunately the report presents not separate wage tables for men and women, but merely tables for all employees averaged together. Bates of women's wages must be sought, therefore, in the original data from which the tables were computed. The old tables must be discarded and new ones constructed.

The data in the report, however, relate only to two of the five industries studied in this volume, the cotton industry and printing and publishing; and for the latter the data are too meager to be significant, so that only the data relating to the cotton industry have been used. Such tables as have been prepared , for this period, therefore, are for this one industry only.[291]

The first of these, Table36, which is given on the next page shows for each year from 1840 to 1891, the number of women in each of sixteen different wage groups in two establishments which had preserved continuous records throughout this period.

---

[290]Senate Report No. 1394 on "Wholesale Prices, Wages and Transportation" (1893).

[291]See Appendix C for a further note on the "Aldrich Report" data and the tables prepared from them.

The method of reading this table is easily explained. In the year 1840, for example, only one operative earned less than $2 a week, four earned from $2 to $2.49, thirteen from $2.50 to $2.99, twelve from $3 to $3.49, and only one from $3.50 to $3.99.

This table of classified wage groups is a good substitute for a list of actual rates, for it shows the range of wages, and the exact number of operatives in the lower as well as in the higher groups as an average wage cannot show.

Some comments and explanations with regard to this table are necessary. The comparatively small number of operatives in the first two years is due to the fact that the records for the second establishment did not begin until 1842; the increases, therefore, in the rate of wages or in the total number of persons employed should be calculated not from 1840 but from 1842. Wages for the period from 1861-79 are in greenbacks, not in gold, so the unusual rise in wages during and after the war is explained in large part by the depreciation of the currency. It is clear, however, that although wages were reduced somewhat after the return to a gold basis in 1879, there has been on the whole an unmistakable upward movement in women's wages.

During the whole of the decade 1840-50 and the greater part of the decade 1850-60, half or more than half of all the operatives earned less than three dollars a week. In 1890 only two out of 313 women, and in 1891 only one out of 355 earned wages as low as this. This advance is made more clear by the following list of medians. For in order to quote a single significant term for each year the median wage was computed as superior to an "average." The "median" is the wage of the operative who stands just halfway up the scale; that is, half of the operatives are paid more and half are paid less, and there are as many earning more than the median rate as there are earning less. The median for each year is given with the table but, for convenience, the following list is given of median rates for each five-year period during the period from 1840 to 1890.

The increase indicated by median rates is also shown in the advance in weekly wages for specific occupations. A series of tables of weighted averages has been prepared showing weekly wages for the period 1840- 91, in each occupation in which women were employed, in three different establishments. These tables are published in detail in the Appendix, but the rates in the most important occupation for each five-year period between these dates are given below.

Table 36: RATES OF WAGES FOR WOMEN OPERATIVES, ALL OC-
CUPATIONS, IN TWO MASSACHUSETTS COTTON MILLS

NUMBER OF WOMEN EMPLOYED.

Year	Less than $2	$2.00-$2.49	$2.50-$2.99	$3.00-$3.49	$3.50-$3.99	$4.00-$4.49	$4.50-$4.99	$5.00-$5.49	$5.50-$5.99	$6.00-$6.49	$6.50-$6.99	$7.00-$7.49	$7.50-$7.99	$8.00-$8.49	$8.50-$9.00	More than $9	Total No.	Median Wage
1840	1	4	13	12	1	..	..	..	..	..	..	..	..	..	..	..	31	2.91
1841	1	7	16	15	1	..	..	..	..	..	..	..	..	..	..	..	43	2.92
1842	1	26	62	82	10	..	..	9	..	..	..	..	2	..	..	..	142	2.84
1843	6	18	80	3	..	..	..	8	..	3	4	..	1	..	..	..	123	2.73
1844	4	39	80	5	..	1	..	..	..	..	..	..	..	..	..	..	129	2.63
1845	..	25	70	10	..	..	..	..	..	..	..	..	..	..	..	..	105	2.69
1846	..	42	66	21	..	..	..	..	..	..	..	..	..	..	..	..	129	2.66
1847	2	32	77	22	..	1	1	..	..	..	..	..	..	..	..	..	135	2.71
1848	..	23	74	32	2	2	..	..	..	..	..	..	..	..	..	..	183	2.79
1849	..	13	61	28	3	4	..	..	..	..	..	..	..	..	..	..	109	2.83
1850	2	24	45	27	..	1	..	..	..	..	..	..	..	..	..	..	99	2.76
1851	4	18	35	27	2	..	..	..	..	..	..	..	..	..	..	..	88	2.79
1852	9	39	49	28	4	1	..	..	..	..	..	..	..	..	..	..	130	2.68
1853	5	17	32	82	4	3	1	..	..	..	..	..	..	..	..	..	94	2.88
1854	5	15	30	88	6	4	1	..	..	..	..	..	..	..	..	..	96	2.96
1855	3	20	25	81	6	2	1	..	..	..	..	..	..	..	..	..	93	2.87
1856	..	2	17	18	1	..	..	..	..	..	..	..	..	..	..	..	38	2.99
1857	5	4	18	25	8	..	1	..	..	6	1	..	1	..	..	..	64	3.09
1858	7	19	31	48	9	9	3	3	..	4	..	..	..	..	..	..	153	2.99
1859	3	20	34	58	12	9	4	1	..	3	1	..	..	..	..	..	140	3.11
1860	8	17	35	36	11	8	1	2	..	2	5	1	..	..	..	..	126	3.03
1861	11	23	25	38	16	6	5	1	..	2	2	2	2	..	..	..	131	3.09
1862	8	22	33	33	11	6	3	3	..	..	..	..	..	..	..	..	116	2.96
1863	7	14	18	27	12	5	2	..	..	..	..	..	..	..	..	..	88	3.06
1864	7	10	8	40	81	26	18	4	1	2	..	..	..	1	..	1	149	3.65
1865	7	11	18	44	83	29	31	5	..	1	1	..	4	..	1	2	187	3.70
1866	..	8	13	29	17	21	43	34	12	29	2	1	5	..	..	3	218	4.73
1867	..	4	15	35	21	23	45	31	7	27	8	1	9	..	..	5	231	4.69
1868	..	..	15	22	23	12	59	38	21	14	6	1	4	1	..	5	222	4.82
1869	..	..	6	26	13	39	40	31	15	15	8	2	18	11	2	13	233	4.90
1870	..	..	8	33	21	24	43	71	8	58	3	1	4	10	..	12	291	5.11

Continued overleaf

Table 37: RATES OF WAGES FOR WOMEN OPERATIVES, ALL OC-
CUPATIONS, IN TWO MASSACHUSETTS COTTON MILLS - *Continued*

Year	Less than $2	$2.00-$2.49	$2.50-$2.99	$3.00-$3.49	$3.50-$3.99	$4.00-$4.49	$4.50-$4.99	$5.00-$5.49	$5.50-$5.99	$6.00-$6.49	$6.50-$6.99	$7.00-$7.49	$7.50-$7.99	$8.00-$8.49	$8.50-$9.00	More than $9	Total No.	Median Wage
1871	..	..	..	23	11	12	50	71	18	86	24	4	29	24	14	8	328	5.48
1872	..	1	..	21	6	9	43	74	12	67	23	4	15	31	14	1	321	5.78
1873	..	3	..	8	13	29	25	59	6	72	16	6	18	19	4	10	293	5.49
1874	2	4	..	16	34	15	49	55	13	35	10	1	10	1	5	1	261	5.07
1875	..	4	1	22	74	23	48	38	11	22	3	8	3	5	7	1	279	4.57
1876	5	4	4	26	53	18	44	28	13	12	3	8	6	17	..	..	246	4.52
1877	2	7	6	23	73	24	40	34	1	23	10	..	10	..	..	..	253	4.32
1878	4	7	1	45	60	30	28	38	8	18	8	..	12	..	22	..	276	4.34
1879	1	18	12	12	54	56	21	49	14	22	1	..	15	6	9	..	290	4.42
1880	1	16	..	26	33	55	32	46	15	57	1	1	18	10	7	..	318	4.93
1881	1	30	..	19	42	47	27	57	25	66	2	1	22	6	9	..	354	5.09
1882	1	13	19	16	39	48	58	42	28	51	5	1	11	13	9	1	363	4.90
1883	1	21	12	16	22	31	59	47	32	95	1	3	22	3	9	1	376	5.27
1884	..	11	10	17	17	18	83	24	25	75	..	11	18	7	8	..	317	5.05
1885	..	9	9	17	14	33	69	19	36	77	2	2	16	11	7	..	321	5.25
1886	..	3	5	9	22	41	72	32	24	56	11	1	15	25	4	6	325	5.16
1887	..	1	9	19	29	28	71	39	15	40	28	3	15	4	27	11	334	5.18
1888	..	2	4	19	21	16	78	37	7	40	8	5	23	16	21	4	298	5.18
1889	..	2	1	31	14	13	79	42	7	50	6	11	29	11	12	3	301	5.24
1890	..	2	..	26	10	33	72	32	10	45	6	18	36	16	8	4	313	5.21
1891	..	1	..	24	21	84	53	46	10	67	11	9	37	26	10	8	355	5.48

Table 38: MEDIAN WEEKLY WAGE FOR WOMEN FROM TABLE 36

1840........	$2.91		1870........	$5.11
1845........	2.69		1875........	4.57
1850........	2.76		1880........	4.93
1855........	2.87		1885........	5.25
1860........	3.03		1890........	5.21
1865........	3.70			

Table 39: AVERAGE WEEKLY WAGE FOR WOMEN, 1840-1890.
ESTABLISHMENT 39, ALDRICH REPORT

YEARS	Spinners	Warpers	Weavers
1840	...	...	...
1845	$2.64	$3.00	$2.67
1850	2.61	3.51	2.58
1855	2.55	3.36	2.76
1860	2.85	3.57	2.85
1865	3.36	3.48	3.87
1870	6.42	5.49	5.91
1875	5.43	5.22	3.96
1880	6.06	5.25	6.39
1885	6.21	4.95	6.30
1890	7.05	6.39	6.36

Table 40: AVERAGE WEEKLY WAGE FOR WOMEN, 1840-1890.
ESTABLISHMENT 40, ALDRICH REPORT

YEARS	Spinners	Warpers	Weavers*
1840	...	...	...
1845	...	$2.40	...
1850	...	...	...
1855	...	...	...
1860	...	4.14	...
1865	$4.65	4.50	...
1870	4.95	5.97	...
1875	4.97	8.10	...
1880	4.23	5.73	...
1885	4.50	6.51	...
1890	4.68	6.00	...

*In this establishment only piece-
work rates are given for weavers

Table 41: AVERAGE WEEKLY WAGE FOR WOMEN, 1840-1890.
ESTABLISHMENT 43, ALDRICH REPORT

YEARS	Spinners	Warpers	Weavers
1840	...	...	...
1845	...	...	...
1850	$4.32	$5.40	$5.28
1855	3.36	4.98	4.05
1860	3.36	4.38	4.32
1865	4.80	4.80	5.79
1870	6.00	7.20	7.74
1875	6.30	9.48	7.80
1880	6.00	6.90	7.08
1885	4.20	5.76	6.30
1890	5.10	7.80	7.02

The movement of women's wages in the cotton mills indicated by the table of classified wage groups and by the list of medians is further confirmed by these lists of wages in various occupations.

No attempt, however, can be made on the basis of these tables to estimate the exact percentage increase in women's wages. In table 36, only two establishments were considered; in the lists just given, only three; moreover, all of these mills were located in Massachusetts, so that the data are not only meager but extremely local in character. On the other hand, they are in a sense unique, since they relate to the same establishments for the whole period under consideration. And it must not be forgotten that these data relate to what was, throughout the entire period, the most important industry in the country from the view of women's work, aid, although local, they also relate to what was likewise, throughout the entire period, the state in which this industry was carried on most extensively.

Without computing a single statistical expression of the rate of increase from 1840 to 1890, it may be pointed out that a very considerable advance is unmistakable. It is clear, too, that, in general, women's wages followed the trend of wages in general, sharing, as one authority has described it, in the great upward movement culminating in the early 70's, in the great downward movement culminating in the late 70's, advancing in 1880 and ending with a considerably higher wage level in 1890.

Granting, however, that women's wages have increased, the question that follows inevitably is how this increase compares with the increase in the wages of men.

Such a comparison between the rates of increase for women and for men has fortunately been made possible as one of the results of a remarkable attempt[292] to make the valuable data in the exhibits of the "Aldrich Report" of greater service. A great deal of the material has been recently retabulated by Prof. Wesley C. Mitchell, in order to correct certain important errors of method which have thrown doubt on the trustworthiness of the original tables which were published with the report. In the retabulation, the wages of men and women were kept distinct, so that the new Mitchell tables show the difference between rates of increase for men and rates of increase for women.

Four of these Mitchell tables, therefore, are reprinted here in order that the change in the relative wages of men and women may be followed from year to year. It must, however, be explained that these are tables, not of money wages, but so-called index numbers or percentages, in which the wage for 1860 is taken as 100 and the wage for each following year is represented as a percentage of the wage in 1860.

Separate tables[293][294] are given here for cotton goods and ginghams, and a table is added for all of the industries in which both men and women were employed. Although the original report presented data for twenty-one industries, it was found that the majority of these had no women employees, and that it was only in the textile industries that the number of women was large enough to be significant. But in Part III of the table which follows, all of the industries

---

[292]See the elaborate collection of tables in "Gold Wages and Prices, 1860-80," by Prof. Wesley C. Blitchell, of the University of California. In a chapter dealing with wages in his earlier "History of the Greenbacks" (Chicago, 1904), Dr. Mitchell began the retabulation of the "Aldrich Report" data, which he has carried on in this later volume to the year 1880. It is a pleasure to be able to put some of his tables to a new service here.

[293]Data obtained from the exhibits of the Aldrich Report.

[294]From Mitchell, "Gold, Prices and Wages," p. 122. The relative rates are computed from arithmetic means of the money rates for the years specified. In the original tables rates are given both for January and July, but only one rate a year is quoted here, that for January. A table for woolen goods which is also given with the other tables in the Mitchell volume and omitted here, since it did not deal with one of the industries specially studied in this volume, is of interest as confirming the conclusions drawn (Number of Series: Men, 51; Women, 11. Average No. Employees: Men, 212; Women, 71.)

which reported any women employees are included; these are cotton goods, ginghams, and woolen goods, which together had 43 series for women and 773 women employees, and "books and newspapers," leather, and paper, which together had but seven series for women and only 64 women employees.

Before discussing these tables, it must be emphasized that they afford a means of comparing, not women's wages with men's wages, but the rate of increase in women's wages with the rate of increase in men's wages in the same establishments over a considerable period of years. The tables show, then, that the median wage for women in the cotton industry in 1880 was 172 as compared with 100 which represented the wage in 1860 ; for men the 1880 rate was only 136 as compared with the 1860 rate of 100. Similarly in ginghams which might properly be classed with cotton goods, wages for women had advanced from 100 in 1860 to 167 in 1880, while the wages of men had reached only 140; for all industries the relative wage for women was 165, for men only 139. The percentage increase, therefore, in women's wages between 1860 and 1880 was greater than the percentage increase in men's wages during the same period; but again it must be said that this does not mean that women's wages became higher than men's. Women's wages were very much lower than men's in the beginning, and they were very much lower in the end; the tables merely show that relative wages for women in 1880 as compared with 1860 were higher than relative wages for men in the later, as compared with the earlier year.

Year	Men	Women	Year	Men	Women
1860	100	100	1865	146	130
1861	106	108	1866	152	143
1862	107	112	1867	149	148
1863	121	117	1868	140	145
1864	122	120	1869	147	154

Year	Men	Women	Year	Men	Women
1870	140	150	1875	147	158
1871	146	154	1876	144	157
1872	146	156	1877	135	150
1873	146	155	1878	140	156
1874	142	153	1879	137	156
			1880	139	153

186

Table 42: MITCHELL TABLES OF RELATIVE RATES OF WAGES FOR MEN AND WOMEN EMPLOYEES IN VARIOUS INDUSTRIES, 1860-1880

| YEAR | RELATIVE WAGES | | | | | |
| | I. Cotton Goods | | II. Ginghams | | III. All industries | |
	Men	Women	Men	Women	Men	Women
1860	100	100	100	100	100	100
1861	96	98	100	104	99	102
1862	98	97	99	109	100	104
1863	107	106	101	113	110	109
1864	127	115	104	109	120	112
1865	144	125	128	133	142	128
1866	159	159	158	161	156	156
1867	167	164	164	174	160	166
1868	166	160	160	176	160	164
1869	168	161	162	177	162	166
1870	166	167	164	176	161	168
1871	170	182	175	199	166	185
1872	178	190	183	210	170	193
1873	173	180	180	211	168	190
1874	162	165	172	201	159	178
1875	150	150	165	186	155	167
1876	142	146	165	185	152	165
1877	137	145	147	162	142	155
1878	134	157	149	168	142	162
1879	130	157	143	166	137	159
1880	135	171	139	167	137	164
Av. No. of Employees	419	296	301	406	1,049	837

Professor Mitchell's comment on these tables is that "during the years of large enlistments in the army, wages of men advanced more rapidly than those of women — a rule to which one establishment manufacturing gingham affords a doubtful exception. But after 1869 the relative wages of women almost always stand higher, and by the end of that period the differences in favor of women are wide in all industries." [295]

The account which was given in an early chapter of the difficulty of finding women operatives for the New England mills in the latter part of the war decade, undoubtedly throws some light on the relatively higher rates of increase in women's wages at this time and very soon after. The "unusual scarcity of female operatives" which, it was said, had not been remedied by a large advance in wages, was without doubt the cause of the relatively higher rate of increase in women's wages. The tendency for educated women to leave the mills, which had been noticeable before the war, became more marked during its progress, when women were wanted to fill teaching posts and other professional positions left vacant by men who had "gone to the front"; and after the war, when the westward expansion created new and attractive openings for women in teaching and other occupations superior to those in the mills, considerable inducements were necessary to keep the more efficient operatives. This point has already been discussed in greater detail,[296] but it seemed important here in connection with these tables as an explanation of the higher

---

[295]Mitchell, p. 121; see also pp. 103-104, in which the following comment is made regarding another table containing relative wages for both men and women: "The columns for number of series and of employees show that the data for males are much more abundant. In the majority of the twenty-one industries, indeed, no female employees are reported; it is only in the textile industries that their numbers are important. For the present, it is sufficient to notice that from 1863 to 1865 men had their rates of pay increased decidedly faster. From 1865 to 1870 the relations are irregular; sometimes men, sometimes women are in the lead; sometimes the differences are small, sometimes large. But after 1870 women uniformly have higher relative wages."

[296]See Chapter VII of this volume. In the collection of wage statistics in the "Tenth Census" (1880), xx, 361, a New Hampshire cotton factory made the following report concerning the decrease in the efficiency of labor after 1865: "The mills here were formerly operated by native American labor, supplied principally from the interior and surrounding farming communities, and nearly all had the advantages of the New England common schools. It was then thought no disgrace for a farmer's daughter to run the loom and spindle. Since the late war other and more congenial pursuits have attracted this class of labor, and in their place we have the poorest of the European and Canadian population with little or no education."

Table 43: NUMBER OF EMPLOYEES RECEIVING LESS THAN A DOLLAR A DAY IN 1860

	Group I. 25-49 cents	Group II. 50-74 cents	Group II. 75-99 cents	Total Earnings Less than a Dollar a Day
Number of men	96	105	1,600	1,801
Number of women	195	550	17	762

relative rates for women which prevailed after the war.

Attention has already been called to the fact that; women received very much lower wages than men in all industries, both at the beginning and at the end of the period under discussion. Interesting proof of this fact is found in some of Professor Mitchell's other tables. In attempting to classify wage earners, not according to industries or occupations, but on the basis of the rates of wages received, all of the wage earners were arranged in five groups, those who received less than a dollar a day in January, 1860, which meant from 25 cents to 99 cents a day, those receiving from $1 to $1.49, from $1.50 to $1.99, from $2 to $2.49, and $2.50 and over. It was found in arranging such a distribution that the lowest group, that of persons earning 25 to 99 cents a day, included all but two of the series given for women in 1860 and, therefore, it was not necessary to prepare separate tables for men and women except for the lowest group;[297] that is, substantially all of the women but less than one fourth of the men were in this lowest wage group.

A further investigation brought out the fact that the women were not merely in the lowest group but in the lowest half of the lowest group. All wage earners, both men and women, who received less than a dollar a day were subdivided into three smaller groups, (1) those receiving from 25 to 49 cents, (2) those receiving from 50 to 74 cents, and (3) those receiving from 75 to 99 cents. The result of this reclassification is seen in the table[298] below:

On the basis of the classification into the five groups which were first given, the tables of relative wages which are given below[299] were

---

[297]Mitchell, pp. 145 and 153.

[298]This table is prepared from data in Mitchell tables 44, 45, pp. 166-168.

[299]Data obtained from the exhibits of the Aldrich Report. Initial wages from Mitchell, "Gold, Prices and Wages," p. 166. The initial wage for these tables was that of January, 1860.

prepared for each group for the period 1860-80.[300] Although rates for the three higher groups in which no women were reported may not seem to be of special interest here, they are given for purposes of comparison.

Two interesting conclusions are drawn from these tables.[301] The first is that in comparing the relative rates for men and for women, here, as in the previous tables, "men have higher relative wages during the war; the relations vary for the next few years; women are always in the lead after 1870." The second conclusion is a more general one relating to the effect of the increase in prices during the war that "the lower the actual wages of a group, the greater was the relative increase in the rates of pay." The single exception that the rates in the lowest wage group, in which all of the women are found, did not advance so rapidly as in the next group above is explained by the supposition that "the family responsibilities of the lowest paid workers were on the average less than those of men earning a dollar or more a day," and for this reason they felt the pressure of the increased cost of living less than those. in the group above.[302] It is of special interest in this connection that women's wages during the war increased less rapidly than the wages of the men in any of the groups. Professor Mitchell's explanation of this fact was that workingwomen in general had fewer family responsibilities than workingmen and would, therefore, fall behind even the men in Group I, as the men in Group I fell behind the men in Group II.[303] A further explanation, however, which arises from the fact that all of the women were in this group, would seem to be that the effect of the war diminished very greatly the supply of men and caused a relatively greater increase in their wages.[304]

---

[300] Professor Mitchell's explanation of his purpose in computing such tables is of interest: "The classification of wage earners according to the actual wages received at some period is less common in making tables of relative wages than the classification according to industries or occupations. But it has quite as much significance as either of these other classifications; for persons earning low wages form an economic group differing in important respects from persons receiving high wages" (p. 145).

[301] See Professor Mitchell's comments, *ibid.*, pp. 165, 167.

[302] A detailed explanation of this point is given in Mitchell, "History of the Greenbacks," pp. 305, 306, and again more briefly in "Gold, Wages and Prices," p, 165.

[303] Mitchell, "History of the Greenbacks," p. 307.

[304] Professor Mitchell has also computed the relative wages for the groups within the "less than one dollar" group. For men in the group 25-49 cents, the rate was

Table 44: MITCHELL TABLES OF RELATIVE RATES OF WAGES OF ALL EMPLOYEES IN ALL INDUSTRIES, CLASSIFIED ACCORDING TO SEX AND INITIAL WAGES

Year	Daily Wages Less than $1		$1.00-$1.49	$1.50-$1.99	$2.00-$2.49	$2.50 and over
	Men	Women	Men	Men	Men	Men
1860	100	100	100	100	100	100
1861	101	102	102	102	100	99
1862	102	104	101	105	99	100
1863	114	110	119	116	103	98
1864	120	112	140	127	117	106
1865	150	130	161	150	142	123
1866	166	150	167	157	150	126
1867	173	169	170	161	161	131
1868	169	168	190	165	160	133
1869	179	170	181	166	186	132
1870	184	172	188	167	188	131
1871	180	191	187	176	181	131
1872	179	201	181	166	181	131
1873	178	197	183	169	182	132
1874	172	184	183	164	181	130
1875	160	170	177	157	166	131
1876	157	169	169	154	165	128
1877	142	156	150	141	144	130
1878	143	162	143	137	138	124
1889	137	162	138	135	137	119
1880	138	165	138	135	140	119
Av. No. of persons	1,039	762	2,358	990	423	65

Table 45: MITCHELL TABLES, RELATIVE WAGES IN 1860 AND 1891

YEAR	ALL INDUSTRIES		COTTON GOODS.		COTTON GOODS (GINGHAMS)		WOOLEN GOODS	
	Men	Women	Men	Women	Men	Women	Men	Women
1860	100	100	100	100	100	100	100	100
1891	155	173	161	181	150	174	158	164

The Mitchell tables, however, afford, finally, a comparison be-tween relative rates for 1860 and for 1891, although the detailed tables are not brought down to the latter date. Relative rates for the two years in the cotton industry, and in all industries in which both men and women were employed, are given as follows[305] :

More interesting, however, than the fact that women's wages were higher in 1890 than during the fifty years preceding is the ques-tion of what women really earned in the last decade of the nineteenth century. To answer this question, resort must be had to a different collection of data — the report on "Employees and Wages" which was prepared by Professor Davis R. Dewey for the Twelfth Census. From this report it is possible to obtain tables showing the weekly median wage for women and for men, not only in the cotton mills, but in each of the other four industries studied. These tables,[306] un-like those which have just been given from the Mitchell collection, are tables of money wages, and, along with the rates, the number of men and women employed is given.

There are several comments to be made with regard to this table. The rates are, in the first place, slightly higher for New England than for the country as a whole, but since the earlier data related exclusively to this section, it seemed best here to quote the table

---

171 compared with 163 for the women in the same group; for men in the group 50-74 cents, it was 155 for men and 159 for women. In 1880 the rate for men in the 25-49 cent group was 168 and for women 177, in the 50-74 cent group 135 for men and 160 for women. Although Professor Mitchell believes that a fairer comparison results by taking the smaller wage groups, the 25-49 cent group can hardly be considered significant in connection with women's wages, since the employees in this group must have been quite young girls and boys.

[305]These are from Mitchell's weighted averages, "Gold, Prices and Wages," p. 173.

[306]From the Dewey Report, "Employed and Wages," p. xxxiii. In this and in the other tables from the Dewey Report, "all occupations" does not represent a series of totals for the lists as given here since those occupations in the original list which were not peculiar to the industries selected have been omitted.

Table 46: WEEKLY MEDIAN WAGE IN NEW ENGLAND COTTON MILLS, 1890-1900

OCCUPATIONS	NUMBER OF EMPLOYEES				WAGES PER WEEK			
	Men		Women		Men		Women	
	1890	1900	1890	1900	1890	1900	1890	1900
Back tenders	52	51	...	...	$3.50	$4.50	...	...
Beamers and slasher tenders	104	187	321	296	9.50	10.50	$5.00	$5.50
Bobbin boys, banders and carlers	41	49	...	...	4.50	6.50	...	...
Card hands	78	90	...	...	6.00	7.00	...	...
Doffers	22	27	...	...	4.50	6.00	4.00	5.50
Drawing-frame tenders	23	27	...	...	4.50	5.50	...	...
Drawers-in	...	...	61	64	...	...	5.00	5.50
Dye-house hands	50	82	...	...	9.00	6.50	...	...
Foremen and overseers	66	70	...	...	20.00	21.00	...	...
Loom-fixers	108	132	...	...	11.00	12.00	...	...
Roving-frame tenders	...	...	245	240	...	...	6.00	7.00
Second and section hands	98	123	...	...	11.00	12.00	...	...
Spinners	75	93	399	447	9.50	11.50	5.50	6.00
Weavers	83	186	1,083	913	8.50	9.00	6.50	7.50
All other occupations peculiar to cotton mills	224	258	285	529	7.00	7.50	5.00	5.00
All occupations	1,688	2,182	2,640	2,653	8.00	8.50	5.50	6.00

Table 47: WEEKLY MEDIAN WAGE IN THE "BOOTS AND SHOES"
INDUSTRY, 1890-1900

| | NUMBER OF EMPLOYEES | | | | WAGES PER WEEK | | | |
| OCCUPATIONS | Men | | Women | | Men | | Women | |
	1890	1900	1890	1900	1890	1900	1890	1900
Bottomers	101	209	...	...	$10.00	$12.00	...	...
Bottom finishers	41	99	...	...	9.00	8.50	...	...
Cutters, soler leather	142	190	...	...	9.50	12.00	...	...
Cutters, upper	378	556	...	...	12.00	13.50	...	...
Edgers	62	64	...	...	15.00	15.00	...	....
Foremen	90	101	...	...	18.00	20.00	...	...
Lasters	85	76	...	...	11.00	13.00	...	...
Stichers, upper	...	...	165	106	...	...	6.00	5.50
Stock fitters	46	53	...	...	10.00	10.50	...	...
All other occupations	246	477	118	252	12.50	11.50	6.00	5.50
All occupations								

for New England rates here. It is, in the second place, to be noted
that women's wages in specific occupations and in the industry as a
whole are uniformly lower than men's wages. That is, in 1900 the
median wage for 2,653 women was $6 a week, for 2,182 men, $8.50 a
week; for beamers and slasher tenders, the median wage for women
was $5.50 and for men $10.50. In other occupations, although the
difference is not so marked, it is, nevertheless, always there.

The next table[307], is for the manufacture of shoes, and the rates
are for the country as a whole and not for any one section.

The same comment as to the difference between the wages of
women and men that was made with regard to the preceding table
can be made here. The median wage for women was uniformly $6
in 1890 and 1900. While the corresponding wage for men was $11
in 1890 and $11.50 in 1900.

That the men so largely outnumber the women is also a point of
interest here since it adds further testimony to that which has been
given in an earlier chapter to show that this still remains a men's
industry.

Wages in cigarmaking, according to table 48 [308], show an even

---

[307] From the Dewey Report on "Employees and Wages," p. xcii.
[308] From the Dewey Report on "Employes and Wages," p. lxxiv.

Table 48: WEEKLY MEDIAN WAGE FOR CIGARMAKING, 1890-1900

| OCCUPATIONS | NUMBER OF EMPLOYEES | | | | WAGES PER WEEK | | | |
| | Men | | Women | | Men | | Women | |
	1890	1900	1890	1900	1890	1900	1890	1900
Packers	32	47	15	30	$16.50	$18.50	$7.50	$8.00
Cigarmakers or rollers*	457	691	61	186	13.00	13.00	5.50	6.00
Strippers	57	68	132	188	5.00	5.50	5.50	6.00
All other occupations	117	172	15	96	7.50	6.50	5.50	3.00
All occupations	697	1,065	254	573	11.00	11.50	6.00	5.50

*As the men are called "cigarmakers" instead of "rollers" it is probable that
the wages given above do not represent the same work for women as for men.

greater difference in favor of men.

Cigarmaking is one of the few industries in which men and women compete directly, and the difference in their wages is, therefore, of special interest.

In the occupation of "packing" the wage for women is $8, while it is $18.50 for men; in cigarmaking, $6 for women and $13 for men, but in this occupation the women are described as "cigarrollers" so that their work is probably rolling or wrapping machine-made bunches, and is not really like that of the men. That the women "strippers" earn more than the men is explained by the fact that very capable women are found in this occupation, but ordinarily none but very old men who are no longer competent to earn a "man's wage" at anything. In general, it is not, of course, easy to say just how much of an injustice the women's lower wage may indicate, for the work is largely "piece work," and the women may have been slower, or they may not have worked at the same rate and on the same kind of cigars. The difference, however, between the median wage of $5.50 for women and $11.50 for men seems quite too great not to contain some measure of discrimination. It is, moreover, of interest that in the report of the commissioner of labor on "Work and Wages of Men, Women, and Children," in which the efficiency and wages of the employees are both reported, the returns from all of the cigar factories showed, with a single exception, that women were receiving less pay than men for equally efficient work. It has already been pointed out that in union factories the women receive the same rate of wages as the men.

In the clothing industry, the discrepancy between the wages of

Table 49: WEEKLY MEDIAN WAGE IN THE CLOTHING INDUSTRY, 1890-1900

	Wages per Week				Number of Employees			
	Women		Men		Women		Men	
Occupations	1900	1890	1900	1890	1900	1890	1900	1890
Basters	$5.00	$5.00	…	…	33	27	…	…
Bushelers	…	…	$10.00	$10.00	…	…	84	71
Cutters	…	…	17.00	18.00	…	…	312	248
Finishers	4.50	4.00	…	…	43	52	…	…
Foremen	…	…	25.00	24.00	…	…	41	33
Seamers	5.50	5.50	…	…	63	55	…	…
Sewing-machine operators	4.00	4.00	7.00	8.00	1,488	863	185	108
All other occupations peculiar to clothing	6.00	6.00	11.00	11.00	139	119	166	121
All occupations	4.00	4.50	10.00	11.50	2,051	1,263	1,094	737

women and men is even more marked as the next table[309] indicates.

This is an interesting table, not merely because the median wage was $4.50 for women and, in contrast, $11.50 for men in 1890, and $4 for women and $10 for men in 1900, but because so good an example is offered of the fact that men and women seldom do the same work, and that the highly paid work is invariably done by men. The cutters, earning $18 a week in 1890 and $17 in 1900, are all men; the finishers, earning $4 in 1890 and $4.50 in 1900, are all women; the bushelers, who earned $10 in both years, are all

---

[309] From the Dewey Report on "Employees and Wages," p. lxxvii.

Table 50: WEEKLY MEDIAN WAGE - PRINTING, 1890-1900

OCCUPATIONS	NUMBER OF EMPLOYEES				WAGES PER WEEK			
	Men 1890	Men 1900	Women 1890	Women 1900	Men 1890	Men 1900	Women 1890	Women 1900
Apprentices	86	86	..	..	$4.00	$6.00	..	..
Binders	164	207	251	409	14.00	15.00	$4.50	$5.00
Compositors hand	1,513	878	..	..	19.00	18.00	..	..
Compositors machine	56	42	..	..	25.00	30.00	..	..
Electrotypers	36	47	..	..	15.00	18.00	..	..
Engravers	37	65	..	..	18.00	18.00	..	..
Foremen	139	160	..	..	25.00	25.00	..	..
Foremen, assistant	48	58	..	..	22.00	25.00	..	..
Pressmen	278	370	..	..	15.00	15.00	..	..
Stereotypers	57	81	..	..	15.00	19.50	..	..
All other occupations	90	115	27	36	12.00	13.00	9.00	9.00
All occupations	3,082	3,033	374	572	16.00	15.00	5.00	5.00

men, and the basters who earned $5 in both years, are all women. Machine operating is the only occupation for which both men and women are reported, and here the wages of men were $8 in 1890 and $7 in 1900, while women were paid but $6 in both years.

Table 50[310], for the printing trade, is less satisfactory than any of the others, since the wages of women are reported only for a single occupation.

This table shows again that men's wages are very much higher than women's. In all occupations, the median wage was $16 for men in 1890 and $15 in 1900, and for women $5 in both years, and again, in the number of employees returned there is evidence of the fact

---

[310]From the Dewey Report on "Employees and Wages," p. lxxxvii.

Table 51: RATES OF WAGES FOR MEN AND WOMEN OVER SIXTEEN
YEARS OF AGE IN 1900

	Lower Quartile	Median	Upper Quartile
Men	$8.31	$10.55	$13.93
Women	4.49	5.64	6.86

that the trade still belongs to men. In the one occupation for which both men and women employees are given, it is quite impossible that they can be doing the same work; with the wages of men binders at $14 in 1890 and $15 in 1900 and the wages of women $4.50 and $5 in the same years, so great a difference can be explained only on the ground of different work.

Of greater interest, however, than the rates in any of these special industries is the summary of all the data published in the Dewey report for the year 1900. From the returns published for 156,569 men 16 years old and over, from 22 important manufacturing industries and from returns for 16,724 women, also 16 years or over, who were employed in 13 different industries, certain rates of wages, found on table 51 [311], were computed.

The use of the terms upper and lower quartile needs some comment. The median has already been explained as the wage received by the employee half the way up the wage scale, the lower quartile is the wage of the employee who is one quarter the way up, the upper quartile, the wage of the employee who is three fourths of the way up. That is, one fourth of the men were below $8.31 a week, one fourth of the women below $4.49; one half of the men below $10.55, one half of the women below $5.64; three fourths of the men below $13.93, three fourths of the women below $6.86. The rates for women are, then, on the whole slightly more than one half of the men's rates.

By way of summary, then, it may be pointed out that the median rates given in the Dewey report show that in "all industries" the median rate for women is fifty-three per cent of the rate for men; that in the tables which have been given for the different industries, the women's median wage is uniformly lower than the men's, varying,

---

[311]Data from the Dewey Report, "Employees and Wages." This interesting computation was made in the statistical laboratory of Columbia University under the direction of Prof. Henry R. Seager, and the results were published in "Publications of the American Statistical Association," ix, 142, 143.

in fact, from one third in the printing trade to approximately three fourths (seventy per cent) in the cotton industry. In the manufacture of clothing, the median wage for women is forty per cent of the wage for men; in cigarmaking forty-seven per cent; in "boots and shoes" fifty-two per cent.

No stress need be laid here, however, upon the fact that women earn so much less than men. The general inferiority of woman's wages has not only been acquiesced in as a custom in England and on the Continent through six centuries of economic development, but it has long been a subject of public comment in this country.[312]

It is further of interest that not only the tables which have been given here, but the discussion in the preceding chapters contribute additional evidence in support of the fact that, in general, the low wages of women in industrial occupations is not unequal pay for equal work, but unequal pay for different and probably inferior work. As long ago as 1891 Mr. Sidney Webb pointed out that, in manual work, it is impossible to discover more than a very few instances in which men and women do precisely similar work, in the same place and at the same epoch,[313] and that the frequent inferiority of women's earnings in manual work is due, in the main, to a general but not invariable inferiority of productive power, usually in quantity, sometimes in quality, and nearly always in net advantageousness to the employer. It has become apparent, in the preceding discussion, that for the most part, women not only do the low-paid, but the unskilled work. The work of women in the cotton industry might seem to furnish an exception, and that it does, to some extent, is evidenced by the fact that in this, more nearly than in any other industry, women's wages approximate the wages of men. But even here, where at one time women dressers and weavers were among the skilled and well-paid operatives, the work of dressing is now done by men, and mechanical improvements in the looms have tended to make men weavers superior to women. In the discussion of the manufacture of boots and shoes, it appeared that there was a quite strongly marked line of delimitation between women's work and men's work, and that the cutters and the Goodyear and McKay stitchers or bottomers, all highly skilled operatives, were men, while

---

[312]For an interesting discussion of the history of women's wages, see J. Shield Nicholson, "Principles of Political Economy" iii, 158-166.

[313]See an article on "The Alleged Difference in the Wages Paid to Men and to Women for Similar Work," *Economic Journal*, i, 635.

the women did work which was in general of a lower grade. In the manufacture of men's clothing, cutters, pressors, and powermachine operatives, the most skilled workers in the trade are alike men; and quite recently the call for greater speed and endurance has given the man an advantage over the woman baster. With regard to cigarmaking, it was pointed out that a girl rarely obtains an apprenticeship, and that the woman cigarmaker, who, occasionally may be "more efficient than any man" is, in general, a less skilled worker. Similarly, in the printing trades, the woman who is obliged to "steal the trade" becomes inferior to the all-around printer who has not only had the chance to "serve his time" but has been required to do so.

All of this is, therefore, further testimony in support of Mr. Webb's theory that the woman is poorly paid, in part at least, because she is inefficient and is doing work which is less skilled than that done by men.

To discuss the causes which lie back of the woman's lack of efficiency, — how far it is due to her exclusion from the occupations which demand higher skill and in turn offer larger remuneration, or to a restriction of opportunity by which she is denied proper training for her trade, — would be of interest, but such an inquiry is clearly beyond the scope of this study. Nor can account be taken here of other causes of low wages with which the economist might be concerned. The influence of custom and tradition, of the woman's "lower standard of life," of her expectation of marriage and her consequent "shorter working life," of the lack of organization among women, of the narrow field of employment open to them and the resulting oversupply of labor within that field, — of these and other causes of women's low wages there can be no discussion here. Nor will it be possible here to attempt to ascertain how far the wage of the workingwoman is really a subsistence wage or whether "if the wages of virtue be dust," the community should not be called upon to make some attempt at regulation.

It must not, however, be overlooked that there are factors in the present industrial situation which will ultimately lead to an improvement in women's wages. The growing class consciousness among women which is bringing them into the labor movement, the influence of the trade union which demands the same wage scale for women as for men, the effect of the piece-work system, by which women, in so far as they work with men, are almost invariably paid at the same rate, and, in the long future, the effects of the "woman

movement," which by the removal of their political and social disabilities, should do away with influence of custom and tradition which
have had so depressing an effect on their economic condition.

Chapter XIII - Public Opinion and the Working Woman

An attempt has been made in the preceding chapters to apply the historical rather than the statistical method to the problem of the employment of women. It is only within the last few decades that statistics of employment have been comparable from one decade to another and sufficiently complete to make it possible to draw any conclusions of value from them. To ascertain, therefore, how far women have been employed in the work of manufacturing in early years, evidence was collected which, if less direct than statistics, is more reliable.

In a study of our economic development it becomes clear that women have been from the beginning of our history an important factor in American industry. In the early days of the factory system they were an indispensable factor. Any theory, therefore, that women are a new element in our industrial life, or that they are doing "men's work," or that they have "driven out the men," is a theory unsupported by facts.

In order to avoid the vagueness which might come from generalizations dealing with our industrial system as a whole, an attempt has been made to review the history of the employment of women in several different industries. In this way, it has been possible to ascertain what work women were doing before and after the establishment of the factory system, and to show in what occupations and in what proportions women have been substituted for men, or men for women. A study of the five industries which employ today the largest numbers of women has furnished some interesting illustrations of the way in which the introduction of machinery and the establishment of the factory system have made necessary a readjustment of the work both of men and of women, and in the long run it has meant the breaking down of old customary lines of delimitation between women's work and men's work.

In the cotton manufacture and in the clothing trades, it was found that occupations such as spining, weaving, and sewing, which historically had been pretty exclusively women's work in this country, are today not only shared with men but are in process of being taken over by men. On the other hand, printing and shoemaking are examples of skilled trades which may be said on the whole to have belonged to men in the colonial period, but which are now employing large numbers of women. Printing required very little physical strength, and women, therefore, became printers long before they entered the shoemaker's trade, which was too heavy to be carried on by women until a system of division of labor made it possible to give them lighter portions of the work. Cigarmaking, although it is an industry which has no history in the seventeenth and eighteenth centuries, has been carried on at different times both by men and by women, and furnishes an interesting example of the way in which work that was done originally by women but later taken over by men, may come to be women's work again.

In the cotton industry and in the clothing trades, therefore, men are doing work which for the most part was once done by women. In the printing trade and in the manufacture of boots and shoes, women are doing the work which would a century ago have been done by men. It should, however, be noted as a point of interest, that today the men's share in the two women's industries is much greater than the share of women in the two men's industries. That is, nearly 250,000 men, approximately one half of the total number of persons employed in the cotton and clothing industries, are men, while the number of women in "printing" and "boots and shoes" is, in round numbers, but 70,000 or not quite one third of the total number in those trades.[314] It would appear, therefore, that men have gained more than women by this readjustment of work. But it may be again repeated that in all of these five industries, women have been employed for more than a hundred years, and it is now

---

[314]See table 52.

Table 52: NUMBER OF PERSONS EMPLOYED IN 1905

	Women	Men
In the cotton mills	128,163	147,283
In the clothing industry	147,710	101,373
Total	275,873	248,656
In "boots and shoes"	49,535	95,257
In printing and publishing	19,975	65,293
Total	69,510	160,550

too late to look upon them as entering a new field of employment in which they have no right. It should be especially emphasized too, that during all of these years, women not only were industrially employed in large numbers, but that they were liberally encouraged by the public opinion of an earlier day to enter these occupations. Throughout the colonial period, and for more than half a century after the establishment of our Republic, the attitude not only of the statesman but of the public moralist was that of rigid insistence on the gainful employment of women, either in the home, or as the household industries grew decreasingly profitable, away from it. In the seventeenth and eighteenth centuries court orders directed that the women of the various towns should be kept employed, and Puritan ministers warned them of the dangers of idle living. Spinning schools were founded to assist women in earning their own maintenance; and when the first cotton factories were established, they were welcomed as a means of enriching the country by women's labor. The same confident approval of every means of providing gainful occupations for women, particularly poor women, is to be found in the discussion which centered about the policy of encouraging and protecting our infant industries after the present government had been established.

Looking back at the change in the domestic economy of the household which was being wrought at this time, we see the carding, spinning, weaving, dyeing — the old historic occupations of women in the home, being taken away from them; a great demand for hands to police the new machines; and the women quietly following their work from the home to the factory. This was not only the natural thing for them to do but it was demanded of them by the public opinion of their day, and there was no voice lifted then to remind

204

them that woman's proper place was at home.

It is clear that it was primarily as an economic problem, and in relation to other economic problems that Hamilton, Trench Coxe, Gallatin, Matthew Carey, Hezekiah Niles, H. C. Carey, and the minor pamphleteers who followed in their wake, concerned themselves with women's work. Here was a fund of labor from which a larger return could be obtained if it were employed in manufacturing industries, and they made precise computations as to just how much that gain would be. More than that, here was also a defensive argument sustaining an important measure of public policy and suggesting a solution for one of the economic problems of the time. Unfortunately the employment of women was not considered on its own merits, and how far it would have met condemnation instead of encouragement if it had not fitted into the scheme of a contemporary policy it is impossible to say.

It has become something of a public habit to speak of the women who work in factories today as if they were invaders threatening to take over work which belongs to men by custom and prior right of occupation. This mistake is due to the fact that there has been an increase in gainful employment among women, and although attention is frequently called to this fact, it is not pointed out that this increase is not equally distributed in all groups of occupations. Tables from the data furnished by the last census, which have already been given, show that this increase is disproportionate only in the group, trade and transportation, and that in the manufactures group men are increasing more rapidly than women. In this connection, attention may be called once more to the fact that the "woman movement" of the last century belongs most exclusively to educated women. So far as industrial employments are concerned, they were considered especially suited to women at a time when men did not regard such work as profitable enough for themselves. By prior right of occupation, and by the invitation of early philanthropists and statesmen, the workingwoman holds a place of her own in this field. In the days when the earliest factories were calling for operatives the public moralist denounced her for "eating the bread of idleness," if she refused to obey the call. Now that there is some fear lest profuse immigration may give us an oversupply of labor, and that there may not be work enough for the men, it is the public moralist again who finds that her proper place is at home and that the world of industry was created for men. The woman of the working classes was self-supporting and was expected to be self-supporting more than three quarters of a century ago, and even long before that she was reproached for "eating the bread of idleness." The efforts of the professional woman to realize a new ideal of pecuniary independence, which have taken her out of the home and into new and varied occupations, belong to recent, if not contemporary history. But this history, for her, covers a social revolution, and the world she faces is a new one. The woman of the working classes finds it, so far as her measure of opportunity goes, very much as her great grandmother left it.

Appendices and Index

Appendix A - Child Labor in America Before 1870

It has been pointed out from time to time in the preceding chapters that the early conditions which led to the employment of women led also to the employment of children. The same economic necessity, — the scarcity and high cost of male labor in this country, which caused early manufacturers to rely upon women's labor, led them also to depend on children. The social philosophy which encouraged one, encouraged the other. The colonial tradition which believed in the virtue of industry was handed down to promote the employment of little children as well as women.

The introduction of children into our early factories was a natural consequence of the colonial attitude toward child labor, of the provisions of the early poor laws and of philanthropic efforts to prevent children from becoming a public charge, and, above all, of the Puritan belief in the virtue of industry and the sin of idleness. Industry by compulsion, if not by faith, was the gospel preached to the young as well as to the old, and quite frequently to the children of the rich as well as the poor.

Thus we find Higginson rejoicing over the "New England Plantation" because "little children here by setting of corn may earne much more than their owne maintenance;[315] and less than a decade later Johnson was commending the industrious people of Rowley who

---

[315] "Collections Massachusetts Historical Society," First Series, i, 118 (1629).

"built a fulling mill and caused their little ones to be very diligent in spinning cotton wool."[316]

Throughout the seventeenth and eighteenth centuries, the court records and province laws give evidence of the serious attempt made to prevent idleness among children. In 1640 an order of the Great and General Court of Massachusetts required the magistrates of the several towns to see "what course may be taken for teaching the boyes and girles in all towns the spinning of the yarne." And in 1641 "it is desired and will be expected that all masters of families should see that their children and servants should be industriously implied so as the mornings and evenings and other seasons may not bee lost as formerly they have bene."

In the following year more definite orders are given. For a child to "keep cattle" alone is not to be industrious in the Puritan sense, and it is decreed that such children as have this for their occupation shall also "bee set to some other impliment withall as spinning upon the rock, knitting, weveing tape, etc." In 1656 a consideration of the advisability of promoting the manufacture of cloth led to the order that "all hands not necessarily imployed on other occasions, as woemen, girles, and boys, shall and hereby are enjoyned to spin according to their skill and abilitee and that the selectmen in every towne doe consider the condition and capacitie of every family and accordingly assess them as one or more spinners." In the same year Hull recorded in his diary that "twenty persons, or about such a number did agree to raise a stock to procure a house and materials to improve the children and youth of the town of Boston (which want employment) in the several manufactures." In short there is no lack of evidence to show that it was regarded as a public duty in the colony of Massachusetts to provide for the training of children not only in learning but in "labor and other employments which may bee profitable to the Commonwealth."

The belief in the necessity and propriety of keeping little children at work may also be read in the early poor law provisions. In dealing with dependent children, as in so many other methods of providing for the poor, the colonies were much influenced by the practice of the mother country. In England, the Elizabethan poor law had provided for the apprenticing of the pauper child, and in the eighteenth, and even in the latter part of the seventeenth century, the "philanthropic

---

[316]"Wonder-Working Providence," "Collections Massachusetts Historical Society," Second Series, vii, 13 (1638).

device of employing cheap child labor" was much approved. Spinning schools were established and houses of industry founded in order to provide for the employment of children.[317]

Much the same policy was followed in the colonies with regard to the children of the poor. In Plymouth, in 1641, it was ordered "that those that have reliefe from the townes and have children and doe not ymploy them that then it shal be lawfull for the Towneship to take order that those children shal be put to worke in fitting ymployment according to their strength and abilities or placed out by the Townes." The Town of Boston in 1672 notifies a list of persons to "dispose of their severall children . . . abroad for servants, to serve by Indentures accordinge to their ages and capacities," and if they neglect this "the selectmen will take their said children from them and place them with such masters as they shall provide accordinge as the law directs. "The children are both girls and boys, for eight years old up. In 1682 the rebuilding of an almshouse and workhouse in Boston was recommended in order that children who "shamefully spend their time in the streets" and other idlers might be put to work "at ye charge of ye Town." The Province Laws also provide for the binding out of the children of the poor, and the records of many towns give evidence that the practice was widespread. In some places where the custom of bidding off the poor prevailed, children were put to live "with some suitable person" until they were fourteen; at that age they were to be bound until they became free by law, with the special provision "if boys, put . . . to some useful trade."[318]

In Connecticut the system of dealing with the children of the poor was similar to that of Massachusetts. If their parents allowed them "to live idly or misspend their time in loitering," they were to be bound out, "a man child until he shall come to the age of 21 years; and a woman child to the age of 18 years or time of marriage."[319]

---

[317]B. Kirkman Gray, "History of English Philanthropy," pp. 101-103. Mr. Gray notes the shifting of attention from the parent to the child during the period subsequent to the Restoration, and points out that "whereas in the early years of the seventeenth century the philanthropic policy was to find employment for adults, at the close this had given place to the working of little children." This point is also discussed in Hutchins and Harrison, "Factory Legislation," pp. 2, 3, and in Cunningham, "English Industry and Commerce," ii, p. 52.

[318]Marvin, "History of Winchenden," p. 268.

[319]E. W. Capen, "Historical Development of the Poor Law of Connecticut" p. 55. See also pp. 94, 95, for later laws continuing the same policy in 1750 and 1784. The law of 1750 expressly provided that not only should the "children of paupers or poor people who could not or did not "provide competently" for

Information as to the exact character of these early apprentice-ships is meager. That the work was in some cases very heavy, and the treatment severe and unkind, there is little reason to doubt,[320] although conditions varied greatly according to the character of the master and his home. It should be noted further, that the binding out of poor children as apprentices did not necessarily mean teaching them a trade, and it is often expressly stated that the person who takes a child oft the town shall have him "to be his servant until he comes of age."[321]

It is not to be assumed that the work of these apprenticed chil-dren was as great an evil as child labor in a modern factory. In many cases they were employed in the open air and their tasks were only properly disciplinary.[322] The point which is to be emphasized is that child labor was believed in as a righteous institution, and when the transition to the factory system was made it was almost inevitable that this attitude toward children's work should be car-ried over without any question as to whether circumstances might not have changed.

There are also records of the employment of children in some

them" be bound out, but also "any poor children in any town, belonging to such town, that live idly or are exposed to want and distress, provided there are none to care for them" (p. 95).

[320]See, for example, the Connecticut case of the charges brought against one Phineas Cook for his ill-treatment of "one Robert Cromwell, a poor, helpless, decrepid boy, an apprentice to the said Phineas for a term not yet expired," "New Haven Colonial Records," xi, p. 138 (referred to in Capen, *op. cit.*). And this law of the Great and General Court of Massachusetts in 1634 tells its own story: "It is ordered that if any boy (that hath bene whipt for running from his maister) be taken in any other plantacon, not having a note from his maister to testifie his business there, it sh(al be) lawfull for the constable of the said plantacon to whip him and send him home" ("Massachusetts Bay Records," i, 115). In 1653 a law is needed to provide that "no apprentice or servant is in any way lyable to answer his master's debts, or become servant to any other than his master, but by assignment according to lawe, and that the said apprentice, being deserted by his master is thereby released from his apprenticeship" (*ibid*, iv, Part i, 150).

[321]See, for example, in "Dorchester Town Records," p. 150, the binding of Francis Tree.

[322]It is probably true that in this country as in England children were very much overworked before the days of the factory system. In domestic industries on isolated farms, much less would be known about their condition than when they were gathered together m large factories. The judgment of some very fair investigators as to England is probably true of America. "Whether children were really worked harder in the early factories than under the domestic system, it is not easy to say" (Hutchins and Harrison, "History of Factory Legislation" p. 5).

colonies outside of New England. Like the Puritan, the Quaker believed that children should be taught to work at an early age, and the Great Law of the Province of Pennsylvania provides that all children "of the age of twelve years shall be taught some useful trade or skill, to the end none may be idle, but the poor may work to live and the rich if they become poor may not want."[323] In Virginia the employment of children was as distinctly for purposes of gain as it has been in the past century. The London Company was not engaged in teaching moral precepts and its records indicate that child labor was accepted without any question as one way of developing the colony. There is the record of the acknowledgment of the General Court in 1819 of the arrival of the one hundred children sent over, "save such as dyed in the waie," and it is prayed that one hundred more, twelve years old or over, may be sent the following spring.[324] In 1621 the adventurers of Martin's Hundred sent over "twelve lustie youths";[325] a letter from England in 1627 relates that "there are many ships going to Virginia and with them fourteen or fifteen hundred children";[326] a few years later the City of London is requested to send over "one hundred friendless boys and girls"; and it is held out as an inducement to the prospective immigrant laborer that "if he have a family, his wife and children will be able to beare part in that labor, . . ."[327]

Virginia also looked after the employment of the children of the poor. In 1646 two houses were erected in Jamestown for manufacturing linen. The different counties were respectively requested to send two poor boys or girls at least seven or eight years old "to be instructed in the art of carding, knitting and spinning."[328]

The Virginia emphasis on the commercial side of child labor became pretty general in the other colonies in the eighteenth century, particularly in the latter half of it when attention began to be di-

[323]"Duke of York's Book of Laws" (Harrisburg, 1879), pp. 102, 142.

[324]"Our desire is that we may have them 12 yeares old and up-ward. . . . They shall be apprentizes; the boyes till they come to 21 years of age; the girles till like age or till they be marryed" (Neill, "Extracts from Manuscript Transactions of the Virginia Company of London").

[325]Neill, "Extracts from Manuscript Transactions of the Virginia Company of London," p. 23.

[326]These children were "gathered up in divers places," the victims of the once dreaded "Spirits" (Neill, "Virginia Carolorum," p. 46. For the work of the "Spirits" see p. 277.)

[327]*Ibid.*, p. 77.

[328]Bruce, "Economic History of Virginia," ii, p. 455.

rected to the importance of developing domestic manufactures; and we find that the policy of keeping children at work becomes less and less a question of moral principle, even in New England. It is not so much the virtue of industry about which men are concerned but the fact that child labor is a national asset which may be used to further the material greatness of America.

The experiment in Boston, of which John Hull made record in 1656, was the prototype of many attempts in the following century to make children useful in developing the cloth manufacture. In 1720 the same town appointed a committee to consider the establishment of spinning schools "for the instruction of the children of this Town in spinning," and one of the committee's recommendations is a suggestion that twenty spinning wheels be provided "for such children as should be sent from the almshouse"; while a generous philanthropist of the time erected at his own expense the "Spinning School House" which ten years later he bequeathed to the town "for the education of the children of the poor."[329]

In the latter half of the eighteenth century, when more persistent efforts were made to further the cloth-making industry, there is much interest in the possibility of making children useful to this end. Two Boston newspapers in 1750 announce that it is proposed "to open several spinning schools in this Town where children may be taught *gratis*"[330] Reference has already been made to the organization in the following year of the "Society for Encouraging Industry and Employing the Poor," which was formed with the double purpose of promoting the manufacture of woolen and other cloth, and of employing "our own women and children who are now in a great measure idle."[331]

The province laws of the session of 1753-64 provide for a tax on carriages for the support of a linen manufactory which it is hoped will provide employment for the poor — "especially women and children" and lessen the burden of caring for them.[332] Although this

---

[329] Bagnall, "Textile Industries of the United States," i, 18, 19.

[330] *Boston Evening Post and Post Boy*, quoted in Bagnall, p. 30. The latter half of the advertisement adds, "and it is hoped that all Well-wishers to their Country will send their children that are suitable for such schools, to learn the useful and necessary Art of Spinning."

[331] Bagnall, p. 33.

[332] The preamble recites that the "number of poor is greatly increased . . . and many persons, especially women and children, are destitute of employment and in danger of becoming a public charge" ("Acts and Resolves," iii, pp. 680, 681).

scheme did not realize all the hopes of its promoters, the policy was not abandoned. In 1770 Mr. William Molineux, of Boston, petitions the legislature to assist him in his plan for "manufacturing the children's labour into wearing apparel" and "employing young females from eight years old and upward in earning their own support" ; and public opinion commends him because, owing to his efforts, "the female children of this Town . . . are not only useful to the community, but the poorer sort are able in some measure to assist their parents in getting a livelihood."[333]

As domestic industries became increasingly important, children were not only employed in the various processes of manufacture carried on in the household but it was considered a subject for public congratulation that they could be so employed. The report of the Governor of New York declares that in his province "every home swarms with children, who are set to spin and card."[334] In 1789 the New York Linen "Manufactory" advertises that "the Directors are disposed to take young boys as apprentices to the linen and cotton branches" and notifies parents to make application for their children.[335] An account has already been given of the sail duck manufactory in Boston where Washington found fourteen girls "spinning with both hands, the flax being fastened to the waist," and with children (girls) to turn the wheels for them; that children should be employed at work of this kind seems to have been regarded without any misgivings. Bagnall's history of the textile industries in this country gives many instances of the employment of children in these early "manufactories." Thus an establishment in Bethlehem, Connecticut, advertised for boys and girls from the age of ten to fourteen; and another in the same state "having made and making additions to the factory" wanted "a number of lively boys from eight to eighteen"; in the Globe Mills of Philadelphia at this time, the labor was chiefly performed by boys; and other examples have already been given in the chapter dealing with this period.

It has already been pointed out that with the establishment of the factory system a new and pressing demand for operatives was created which was met by the employment of women and children.

---

[333] *Boston News Letter*, March 1, 1770, quoted in Bagnall, p. 59.

[334] Governor Moore to Lords of Trade, January 12, 1767, in "Documentary History of New York," i.

[335] Bagnall, p. 123. A cotton factory in Worcester, Mass, similarly advertised for "three or four healthy boys as apprentices," ibid,, p. 129.

The petition for the "first cotton factory" in Massachusetts has been quoted and Samuel Slater's first time list, which contained the names of Ann and Eunice Arnold and other children, has been referred to.

The reliance of early protectionists upon the argument for employing women and children; the encouragement given to such arguments by early philanthropists, and the efforts of early inventors to discover new means of using children's labor, have already been discussed.

It is true that the absolute number of children employed in our early mills was not appalling, but the absolute number of all employees in our manufacturing industries was small. It seems clear, however, that children formed a very large proportion of the total number of employees and that the utilization of children's labor was commended almost with unanimity. Such protests as one meets come, for the most part, from foreigners. A French traveler before the close of the eighteenth century writes that he finds "manufactures are much boasted of because children rare employed therein from their most tender age."[336] An Englishwoman in 1829 addressed an American audience in terms of reproach : "In your manufacturing districts you have children worked for twelve hours a day and . . . you will soon have them as in England, *worked to death.* . . ."[337] Now and then a free-trader comes in with a word of opposition. Condy Raguet, finding it hard to deny that manufactures make it possible to get large profits out of children's labor, fell back upon the argument that farm work was better for both boys and girls than factory work, and that girls were more likely to become good wives if they worked in kitchens instead of factories.[338]

An American manufacturer called as a witness before the English Factory Commission, was asked, "Have any complaints been made in the United States as to the propriety of such extent of labour for children?"[339] His reply was: "There have been newspaper com-

---

[336]Brissot de Warville, "New Travels in U.S.A.," p. 126. He adds, "that is to say, that men congratulate themselves upon making early martyrs of these innocent creatures, for is it not a torment to these poor little beings . . . to be a whole day and almost every day of their lives employed at the same work, in an obscure and infected prison?"

[337]Frances Wright, "Lecture on Existing Evils" (pamphlet, New York, 1829), p. 13.

[338]"Free Trade Advocate" (Philadelphia, 1829), i, p. 4.

[339]He had pointed out that no difference was made on account of age ("We have a great many between nine and twelve"), and that children as well as adults worked from ten to fourteen hours according to the season. Testimony of

plaints originating probably from the workmen who came from this country to the United States, but among our workmen there is no desire to have the hours of labor shortened, since they see that it will necessarily be accompanied by a reduction of wages."

Unfortunately there are no available statistics showing the extent of child labor in the first half of the nineteenth century. From time to time, however, estimates are recorded which, in the absence of accurate data, are of considerable interest. The Committee on Manufactures in 1816 reports vaguely 24,000 "boys under seventeen" and 66,000 "women and girls" out of an estimated 100,000 cotton mill employees. John Quincy Adams in his *Digest of Manufactures* gives statistics which show that in the various manufactures of cotton more than fifty per cent of the total number of persons employed are children, but again the age limit for "children" is not given and the *Digest* itself was considered unreliable for many reasons. There are other estimates for the first quarter of the century for individual towns and mills, but all alike give only the classification "women and children" or "girls and boys," and although they uniformly show an extremely small percentage of men employed, they do not answer the question. How many children were at work and of what age were they?

But documents like the memorandum which was quoted in the chapter on wages of the hiring out of Dennis Rier and his little children, and of his sister and her "daughter Sally, 8 years of age" and "son Samuel 13 years of age," are of very great interest and significance.

The employment of children varied not only from state to state but from district to district. Child labor was much less extensive in Massachusetts than in Rhode Island. Samuel Slater had established in Providence and its vicinity the plan of employing families in his mills — a transplanting of the system with which he had been familiar in England. The factory village of the Rhode Island type, therefore, was composed of families entirely descendent upon their labor in the mills, and the mill children lived at home with their parents. On the other hand, in towns like Lowell and Waltham in Massachusetts,[340] the operatives were almost entirely farmers'

James Kempson, "First Report of Factories Inquiry Commission" (1833), E, p. 21.

[340]Hon. H. R. Oliver, "Massachusetts Senate Document 21" (1868), points out that the "English or family system" of hiring whole families was not so desirable

daughters, who, being away from their own homes, were cared for in corporation boarding houses. The result was, that since the cost of their board was more than a child could earn, the employment of children was not profitable Kirk Boott's estimate for Lowell in 1827 was that, in six milk employing 1,200 persons, nine tenths of the operatives were females and only twenty were from twelve to fourteen years of age. But that children were often employed very young, even in so-called model places like, Waltham and Lowell, cannot be questioned. Mrs. Robinson, who gives us a delightful if somewhat optimistic account of the early mill girls, was only ten years old when she went to work in the Tremont Mills, and Lucy Larcom was only eleven when she became a little doffer on the Lawrence Corporation.

The New Hampshire factories were more like those of Eastern Massachusetts,[341] but Connecticut[342] and the southern and western parts of Massachusetts[343] were more like Rhode Island, where the tendency was all along toward the "family system." Smith Wilkinson

as the Lowell system of hiring individual operatives (pp. 24, 25).

[341] See the account in White's "Slater, "p. 134, of a New Hampshire factory which employed 250 girls, 5 boys, and 20 overseers; 9 of the girls were under 15, 6 of the girls and 3 of the boys under 14; the comment is, "the relative number of children employed in this establishment, it is believed, will correspond without much variation with the proportion to be found in most of the factories east of Providence and its vicinity; in the latter district, the manufactories were established at an earlier period, and still give employment to a large proportion of children."

[342] Smith Wilkinson's letter from Pomfret, Conn. ("Documents Relative to the Manufactures of the United States," 1832, i, p. 1046), contains an interesting statement regarding Connecticut: "We usually hire poor families from the farming business of from four to six children, and from a knowledge of their former income, being only the labor of the man, say $180-$200, the wages of the family is usually increased by the addition of the children to from $450-$600."

[343] The document relating to Dennis Rier which is referred to *supra* is an illustration of this. And the situation in Fall River was described by the superintendent of public schools as follows: "The operatives are for the most part families, and do the work in the mills by the piece, taking in their children to assist. . . . The families are large . . . and the mill owners are not willing to fill up their houses with families averaging perhaps ten members and get no more than two of all the number in the mill. The families are also, in most instances, so poor that the town would have to aid them, if the children were taken from their work. . . . I do not think the English system of family help is found in other places to any great extent. It gives a great number of children, compared with the whole number of operatives, and their labor could not be dispensed with in the mills nor could we accommodate them in our schools" ("Mass. Senate Doc. 21" (1868), p. 46). By 1875 ("Mass. Senate Doc. 50," p. 27) it was clearly stated that "men with growing families" is the standard demand in many of our manufacturing centers.

writes from Pomfret, Connecticut:

"In collecting our help, we are obliged to employ poor families, and generally those having the greatest number of children;" and the company's real estate investments are explained as an attempt "to give the men employment on the lands while the children are employed in factory."[344]

But Connecticut's point of view with regard to Rhode Island was distinctly Pharisaical, and a Connecticut official in 1842 gave the following account of the situation:

"The English factory system was introduced into Rhode Island by Slater, and along with it, many of the evils of that system as it was before a more enlightened public opinion and beneficial legislation had improved it. There is a much larger proportion of children among the factory laborers in Rhode Island than in Connecticut or Massachusetts."[345]

The contrast between Rhode Island and the other cotton manufacturing states in respect to child labor is made clear by the table accompanying the "Report on Cotton" at the Convention of the Friends of Industry in 1831. The total number of children under twelve employed in cotton factories in 1831 was 4,691 (excluding printeries which employed 430 more). Of this number 3,472 were from Rhode Island, 484 from New York, 439 from Connecticut, 217 from New Jersey, 60 from New Hampshire, 19 from Vermont, and none from Massachusetts.[346]

The Committee on Education of the Massachusetts Senate reported in 1825 that there was no necessity for legislative interference on the subject, and concluded that "this is a subject always deserving the parental care of a vigilant government. It appears, however, that the time of employment is generally twelve or thirteen hours

---

[344]White's "Memoir of Slater" (Philadelphia, 1836), p. 127.

[345]Pamphlet on "Legal Provision Respecting the Education and Employment of Children in Factories" etc. (Hartford, 1842).

[346]"Report of the Committee on Cotton," "Proceedings of the Friends of Domestic Industry at New York" (Baltimore, 1831), p. 112. These figures are clearly the result of an underestimate taken from special reports by employers, who, then as now, were not overanxious to report the employment of young children. It is shown, e.g., in "Documents Relating to Manufactures" (1832), *op. cit.* ii, 59, that 323 boys twelve to sixteen, and 406 under twelve were employed in New York; i.e., nearly as many boys under twelve according to this report as children under twelve according to the above report.

each day, excepting the Sabbath."[347] But a report from the House Committee on Education from the same state in 1836 is of considerable length and of a somewhat different tenor, as the following extracts sufficiently indicate:

"According to an estimate made by an intelligent friend of manufactories . . . there were employed in 1830, in the various manufacturing establishments in the United States, no less than 200,000 females. If the number has increased in other parts of the country since the estimate was made, as it has in this state, it must at the present time amount to more than half a million! . . . These are females alone, and most of them of young and tender years. . . . Labor being dearer in this country than it is in any other with which we are brought in competition in manufacturing, operates as a constant inducement to manufacturers to employ female labor, and the labor of children, to the exclusion of men's labor, because they can be had cheaper . . . [With the increase of numerous and indigent families in manufacturing districts] there is a strong interest and an urgent motive to seek constant employment for their children at a very early age, if the wages obtained can aid them even but little in bearing the burden of their support . . . [Causes] are operating, silently perhaps but steadily and powerfully, to deprive young females particularly, and young children of both sexes in a large and increasing class in the community, of those means and opportunities of mental and moral improvement . . . essential to their becoming . . . good citizens . . .

"In four large manufacturing towns, not however including the largest, containing by the last census a population of little less than 20,000, there appear to be 1,896 children between the ages of four and sixteen who do not attend the common schools any portion of the year. . . . If full and accurate answers were given by all the towns in this Commonwealth, . . . it is believed there would be developed a state of facts which would at once arrest the attention of the legislature and not only justify but loudly demand legislative

---

[347] *Archives*, 8,074. Some documents appear with the report, one containing statements from a considerable number of firms as to the number of children under sixteen employed, their hours of labor and their annual school attendance. As the statements are so incomplete the report seems of slight value. A total of 978 children under sixteen is given, the number of hours varying from ten to fourteen per day, the school privileges from none at all to four months. I am indebted to Mr. C. E. Persons, of Harvard University, for the use of notes on this report.

action upon the subject."[348]

Turning from the extent of child labor to the conditions under which children worked, there is also much variation from state to state; but this variation is due rather to standards set by different manufacturing centers than to the interference of state laws. For child labor was practically unregulated in this country until after the Civil War. A few laws had been passed, but they remained on the statute books as so many dead letters. In Massachusetts a ten hour law for children under twelve years was ineffectual,[349] and not only in Massachusetts but in Connecticut and Rhode Island, laws which provided a low minimum of "schooling" went unenforced.[350] The inevitable result of this lack of regulation was not only that very young children were worked, but that they were worked long hours, overtime, and at night. Even in Lowell, where conditions were

---

[348]Report of the Committee on Education on "Whether any or what provision ought to be made for the better education of children employed in manufacturing industries in Massachusetts" (1836), "House Document No. 49." The first paragraph quoted is from p.8, the second from p. 10, the third, p. 11, and the last, pp. 13, 14.

[349]Act of 1842, chap. 60. The act was ineffective owing to a clause which penalized only those who "knowingly" violated it (Whittelsey, "Massachusetts Labor Legislation," pp. 113 and 9, 10).

[350]Regarding the situation in Rhode Island, the superintendent of public schools in Providence wrote: "But this law (requiring some school attendance) is, so far as I can learn, a dead letter. There has never been a complaint although it has been violated constantly. The employment of minors now depends upon the necessities and cupidity of parents and the interests of manufacturers. The manufacturing interests are now a controlling power in the state, and it will be extremely difficult to enforce a law against their wishes." Quoted in "Mass. Senate Doc. (1869), No. 44," p. 37. In Connecticut, the school report of 1839 stated that "in the manufacturing villages . . . the precise number of children of very tender age, who should have been in school but are thus consigned to excessive and premature bodily labor to the utter neglect of their moral and intellectual training, I cannot give. But the returns from the districts in these villages show that nearly two thirds of those enumerated have not been in school. The law which was passed many years since, to secure a certain amount of instruction to this class of children is a dead letter in nearly if not every town in the state" ("Second Annual Report of Board of Commissioners of Common Schools in Connecticut" [Hartford, 1839], p. 24; see also "Third Annual Report," p. 21). As to the ineffectiveness of the Massachusetts laws, see Whittelsey, *op. cit.*„ pp. 9, 10. A somewhat inflammatory writer in the last state charged that the law which prohibited a child under fifteen working more than nine months in a factory without passing the other three in school "is evaded by the cruel and mercenary owners of the children who keep them nine months in one factory and then take them directly to another with a lie in their mouths." Denied in Bartlett, "Vindication of the Females in the Lowell Mills" (Lowell, 1841), p. 16.

particularly favorable, little mites of ten were on duty nearly fourteen hours a day, and then did household tasks and went to evening school.[351] The testimony quoted in the special report of the committee of the Massachusetts legislature in 1866[352] throws much light on all of these points. It was claimed that at that time overseers in need of "small help" went about and systematically canvassed for children.[353] There is an increasing amount of testimony that many were employed very young. Witnesses from New Bedford and Fall River testified that in both places children of seven were employed. In answer to the question: "Is there any limit on the part of the employers as to the age when they take children? " the reply was, "They'll take them at any age they can get them, if they are old enough to stand. . . . I guess the youngest is about seven. There are some that's younger, but very little.[354] From Lawrence it was

---

[351]Robinson, "Loom and Spindle," pp. 36-40. Mrs. Robinson says: "Except for the terribly long hours there was no great hardship." Lucy Larcom's story is much the same, early rising and long hours being the great grievances ("New England Girlhood" pp. 153, 154). The testimony of "an agent" in the "Report of the Massachusetts Bureau of Labor" in 1871 contains interesting information on this point (p. 500): "We run our mills sixty-six hours per week. When I began as a boy in a mill, I worked fifteen hours a day. I used to go in at a quarter past four in the morning and work till quarter to eight at night, having thirty minutes for breakfast and the same for dinner, drinking tea after ringing out at night. But I took breakfast and dinner in the mill as the time was too short to go home, so that I was sixteen hours in the mill. This I did for eleven years, 1837-48. The help was all American. . . . In 1848 we dropped to fourteen hours. In 1850 or '51 we went down to twelve hours."

[352]"House Document No. 98" (February, 1866), "Report of the Special Committee on the Hours of Labor and the Condition and Prospects of the Industrial Classes."

[353]"Small help is scarce; a great deal of the machinery has been stopped for want of small help, so the overseers have been going round to draw the small children from the schools into the mills; the same as a draft in the army."

"Q. Do I understand that agents go about to take children out of the schools and put them into the mills?

"A, They go round to the parents and canvass them. This produces nothing but misery and crime. . . . The boys and girls are mixed up together from seven years up to thirteen and are entirely demoralized." (Testimony T. J. Kidd, of Fall River, ibid., p. 6.)

[354]"House Document No.98." Rpt. Spec. Com. of Mass. Legislature (1866), p. 7. Testimony of John Wild (Fall River). Other parts of this testimony are also interesting:

"Q. How old are the children?

"A. Seven and eight.

"Q. Have you a child of seven working in the mills?

"A. Yes, I have. . . .

reported that "a great number of children from twelve to fifteen" were working at night. "The majority of those who do night work are under eighteen years of age."[355] There were no laws requiring the fencing of machinery nor prohibitions regarding the care of dangerous machinery by children, and accidents were common enough.[356] While there seems to have been no such gross and widespread brutality as the earlier English investigations revealed, cases of corporal chastisement were not unknown.[357]

It may seem that much of this is the testimony of *ex-parte* witnesses and to be discounted as such, but in the absence of disinterested official investigations, no unimpeachable evidence exists. Such information as is furnished by the state reports has been utilized

---

"Q. Does he get any schooling now?

"A. When he gets done the mill he is ready to go to bed. He has to be in the mill ten minutes before we start up, to wind spindles. Then he starts about his own work and keeps on till dinner time. Then he goes home, starts again at one and works till seven. When he's done he's tired enough to go to bed. Some days he has to clean and help scour during dinner hour. . . . Some days he has to clean spindles. Saturdays he's in all day."

[355] *Ibid.*, p. 6. See also testimony of an overlooker of seventeen years' experience in "Report Massachusetts Bureau of Labor" (1870), p. 126: "Six years ago I ran night work from 6:45 P.M. to 6 A.M. with forty-five minutes for meals, eating in the room. The children were drowsy and sleepy; have known them to fall asleep standing up at their work. I have had to sprinkle water in their faces to arouse them after having spoken to them till hoarse; this was done gently without any intention of hurting them." It is recorded (pp. 155-158) that children worked all night after working all day, but this seems to have been most exceptional. See also "Senate Document No. 21" (1868), p. 14. In this report Mr. Oliver says that wherever children had been kept at work during entire nights they were not the same set that had been employed during the day, the day set resting at night. "This night work, so far as I can learn, has been of limited extent."

[356] See "Report Massachusetts Bureau of Labor" (1871), p. 483; also p. 58.

[357] "A witness described to us an instrument for whipping children at a factory in Rhode Island, consisting of a leather strap, eighteen inches long, with tacks driven through the striking end." "Report Massachusetts Bureau of Labor" (1870), note, p. 107. See also *ibid.*, Report for 1871, p. 489. Seth Luther, an agitator of the early thirties, gave an inflammatory account of cotton-mill children being driven "with the cow-hide or the well-seasoned strap of 'American Manufacture.'" He said he had seen "many females who have had corporal punishment inflicted upon them; one girl of eleven years of age who had a leg broken with a billet of wood; another who had a board split over her head by a heartless monster in the shape of an overseer." But he pointed out in a footnote that of course all overseers are not so cruel. He added, however, that foreign overseers were frequently placed over American women and children. See "An Address to the Working Men of New England," by Seth Luther (2d ed.. New York, 1833), p. 20. See also *ibid,*. Appendix F, p. 35, for further illustrations of ill treatment of factory children in America.

but few of them are thorough or satisfactory. The old method of sending out "questionnaires" to employers who found it along the line of least resistance to disregard them, made such inquiries so incomplete as to be fruitless. General Oliver of Massachusetts in one of his reports explains that he is obliged to qualify his statements by saying " 'so far as I can learn,' because in some cases answers to this query were not given, and such declining can have only one cause; and that not unreasonably may be assumed to be that children had been so employed but it was thought preferable not to refer to it"[358] A further difficulty in attempting to ascertain the extent of child labor was that parents were allowed to take young children into the mills as their assistants, and by this means they were able to tend a larger number of looms. The names of such children did not, of course, appear upon the company's books and their work was paid for only as an increase of their parents' earnings.[359]

In conclusion it may be said that although data do not exist for accurately estimating the extent of child labor before 1870, it has seemed worth while to bring together whatever available material on the subject there may be, with the hope that, even if fragmentary, it may throw some light on the origin and growth of one of our modern problems of poverty. It has been assumed by reformers both within and without the labor movement that child labor is a social sin of the present day. Mrs. Kelley dates its growth from 1870,[360] and among labor agitators it has been considered a result of deterioration in working-class conditions which has necessitated an increase in the family earnings by the employment of children.[361]

These statements may be true in part. Child labor has undoubtedly increased greatly since 1870 and the workingman may be right

---

[358]"Massachusetts Senate Document No. 21" (1868), "Report of Henry K. Oliver on the Enforcement of the Laws Regulating the Employment of Children in Manufacturing and Mechanical Establishments" pp. 14, 20, from which it appears that only 19 per cent of the establishments applied to sent replies; i.e., only 100 out of 519 circulars were returned.

[359]*Ibid.*, p. 26.

[360]"Ethical Gains in Legislation," p. 33. Mrs. Kelley may be right in saying that although child labor existed before, it "reached no large dimensions in the United States before 1870." Absolutely the number may not have been large, but singly evidence is not lacking to show that in the textile industries, a relatively larger number of children were employed than are employed today.

[361]See "Report of Massachusetts Bureau of Labor"' (1870), p. 108, where it is intimated that women and children have come into factories because conditions have changed and "low pay compels all to help."

in thinking that this has been in some measure due to a social injustice which has not preserved a proper balance between his wages and the cost of his standard of living. The late veteran labor leader, George E. McNeill, in an argument before a committee of the Massachusetts legislature, declared that the poor man had been unable to subsist on the "pauper wages" of the cotton industry, and as a result the wife, mother, and child had been dragged "from the sanctity of the home, and had become the prey of this devouring monster [the cotton mill]."[362] Mr. McNeill was probably right as to the insufficiency of the man's wages, but the presence of women and children in the mills was certainly as much cause as effect. Ample evidence certainly exists to show that both women and children were employed in the earliest factories, and in the early part of the nineteenth century they were the most numerous class of operatives.

The history of the employment of children in industry is an interesting chapter in the story of our economic development. Looked at through an historical perspective our modern child-labor problem seems to have been inherited from the industrial and social life of the colonies, as well as from the industrial revolution and the establishment of the factory system. The having "all hands employed" was a part of the Puritan idea of virtue, and although the employment of children tended to become more and more for commercial purposes rather than for moral righteousness, the old moral arguments were used and are still used to support the commercialized system. It is clear and unmistakable that the colonial policy of promoting thrift and industry was skillfully used in the early part of the nineteenth century by the "friends of industry" who saw in child labor a useful instrument for the development of our national resources. Such documents as Samuel Slater's time list for his first group of operatives, all children, the memorandum of the hiring out of Dennis Rier and his family of little children from Newburyport, or Lucy Larcom's "strange story of a little child earning its living"[363] all point to a general acceptance of the propriety of children's labor in the early

---

[362]"Argument of George E. McNeill" (pamphlet, n.d., but probably 1871-75, Boston Public Library).

[363]Lucy Larcom, "An Idyl of Work" (Boston, 1875), p. 50. This poem of Miss Larcom's which she describes in her preface as a "truthful sketch of factory life drawn from the memory of it during the time about thirty years since, when the work of the mills was done almost entirely by young girls from various parts of New England," is very interesting. The words of one of the two little doffers (aged eleven and thirteen years) are worth quoting as an illustration of Lucy Larcom's own attitude toward the work:

days of the factory system. That so little interest was taken in the subject until the last two decades is due, perhaps, to the fact that our social reform movement belongs to recent, if not contemporary, history. A consciousness of our social sins today does not mean that they are of sudden growth, but rather that public opinion has slowly become enlightened enough to take cognizance of them.

"We must learn,
While we are children, how to do hard things,
And that will toughen us, so Mother says;
And she has worked hard always. When I first
Learned to doff bobbins, I just thought it play.
But when you do the same thing twenty times —
A hundred times a day, it is so dull." (p. 49.)

226

Appendix B - Concerning the Census Statistics of Industrial Employment

BEGINNING with the "Seventh Census" (1860), statistics showing the number of women employed in our manufacturing industries have been published for each succeeding decade. But so many difficulties arise in attempting to make comparisons from one census to another that it has seemed worth while to make a more detailed statement regarding these statistics than could properly be made within the limits of any one chapter.

It is necessary to explain, at the outset, that data regarding the number of persons employed in manufacturing pursuits are collected through two different schedules: first, in taking the population census, the occupation of every person over ten years of age is reported and the results tabulated from the population schedules and published under the head of "Occupations" in a special section or volume; second, another schedule which is used in collecting information regarding our manufacturing industries reports the number of persons employed in them. These two sets of returns present many seeming discrepancies which result from the different methods of collection. In the "Twelfth Census," for example, tables in the "Occupations" volume for "manufacturing and mechanical pursuits" showed 120,788 women over ten years of age employed in the cotton mills, while the "Census of Manufactures" reported 126,882 women over sixteen years of age in the same industry. In general, the statistics in the "Occupations" tables should represent the maximum number of persons employed, since the data for these tables are, as has been said, from the population schedules and in taking the population census, everyone is asked for his occupation, trade, or profession, and many unemployed are inevitably reported as having occupations. The numbers in the "occupations" tables would therefore, in most cases, be larger than those in the "manufactures" tables, which report only the average number of persons actually employed during the year. (See on this point General Walker's note accompanying the tables in the "Industry and Wealth" volume of the "Ninth Census," p. 801.)

But there are two reasons which seem to make the manufactures returns more reliable than those in the occupations tables in an attempt to show the change in the proportion of men and women employed in any of the industries studied.

(1) The first of these is the more general reason. It is well known that so far as the employment of women and children is concerned, the occupations tables are less complete than the manufactures tables. General Walker, in discussing this point in 1870 ("Ninth Census: Wealth and Industry," p. 375, note) said: "The reasons why the occupations tables may be taken as substantially exact as they respect the adult male labor of the country, but not as they respect the employment of women and children, are plain and simple. It is taken for granted that every man has an occupation, and the examination of tens of thousands of pages of schedules returned in the present census has satisfied the superintendent that only in rare cases, too inconsiderable to be taken into account in such a discussion, have assistant marshals failed to ask and obtain the occupation of men, or boys old enough to work with effect. It is precisely the other way with women and young children. The assumption is, as the fact generally is, that they are not engaged in remunerative employments. Those who are so engaged constitute the exception, and it follows from a plain principle of human nature, that assistant marshals will not infrequently forget or neglect to ask the question." And again in the same volume, General Walker makes the further comment (p. 876): "The Tables of Occupations have been assumed to be authentic and to present the true standard by which to criticise the statistics of manufactures; and, in respect to the adult male labor

228

of the country, they are substantially complete and exact. But in respect to the number of women and children employed in manufacturing industry, particularly in large mills and factories, the return of occupations is, for reasons to which attention was called in the remark prefacing the occupations tables, decidedly deficient."

(2) The second reason which applies rather to the specific industries studied than to the totals for all industries, is as follows: The manufactures returns include persons in every occupation in an industry while, e.g., for the cotton mills, the occupations returns report a great many employees whose occupation is not peculiar to the mills, e. g., painters, carpenters, machinists, general laborers, in other occupational groups. That is, in the occupations returns, a machinist employed in the cotton mills would be returned as a machinist, in the manufactures schedule he would be a cotton-mill employee. The manufactures statistics, therefore, represent more complete returns of the number of persons actually employed in the cotton manufacture. Moreover, in the occupations returns of the population census, many occupations are vaguely reported so that in the 1900 occupations tables a large group called "Textiles not otherwise specified" contained 78,312 operatives, many of whom must have been cotton-mill employees.

Owing, therefore, to the fact that the "Census of Manufactures" is in general more complete so far as the employment of women is concerned, and that, for the special industries studied, the "Census of Manufactures" is more complete for both men and women, the statistics from the manufactures returns have seemed more useful for the purpose in hand, and they have, therefore, been used whenever possible.

Another point of importance is that the manufactures schedules for each census (beginning with 1850) report both the number of men and women employed; while the occupations returns for 1850 report only the occupations of men and those of 1860 only the total number of persons engaged in various occupations without distinguishing the sex of those employed. We have then the number of women operatives reported from the manufactures returns for each decade from 1850 to 1900; from the occupations returns only from 1870 to 1900.

When an attempt is made, however, to use these statistics of manufactures, it is discovered that the same schedules were not used for each census and that the returns therefore are not fairly comparable. When the census of 1850 was taken, schedule No. 5, relating to the products of industry, called for "the average number of male and female hands"; and this same schedule was used in 1860. No specification was made as to age, so it may be assumed that the terms "male and female hands" included boys and girls.[364] But in 1870 the schedule was so arranged as to call for the number of employees under a new classification — men over sixteen, women over fifteen, and children; instead of the "average number of male and female hands" that had formerly been required. The classification of 1870 has been used in each succeeding census except that in 1900 "women over sixteen" was substituted for "women over fifteen." The result is that the data we have to compare are statistics for 1850-60 of the number of men and women employed; and for 1870- 1900 the number of men over sixteen, and women over fifteen (or sixteen).

To summarize briefly this information as to available statistics: for 1850 and 1860 we have the number of women reported only from the manufactures schedules, and the age of the women is not given; for 1870-1900 we have the number of women reported both from the population (occupations) schedules and from the manufactures schedules, the former giving the number of men and women over ten and the manufactures returns having been changed in 1870 to give the number of men and women over sixteen and the number of children, boys and girls not distinguished, under sixteen. The number of children was unimportant except in the cotton industry in which 40,258 children were employed in 1900; and in the total for all industries, in which 168,583 children were reported in 1900; and in the latter, although the absolute number of children was large, it was small compared with the total number of persons employed.

In general, three possible methods of using these statistics suggest themselves:

---

[364]See Carroll D. Wright, "History and Growth of the Census" pp. 45, 46, 50, 51, for the early schedules. Professor Levasseur in his "L'ouvrier américain," Vol. i, p. 390, has designated these statistics for 1850 and 1860 as "men over fifteen" and "women over fifteen"; but his so designating them seems to be quite unwarranted. Curiously enough, the population schedule during these years did call only for the occupations of "men over fifteen" and in 1860 "men and women over fifteen" and it would seem as if Professor Levasseur had confused the schedules used for manufactures and occupations during these years. In the "Manufactures Census of 1870" (volume on "Industry and Wealth," pp. 392, 393 f.) the returns for 1850 and 1860 are carefully distinguished as to this point from those for 1870; the latter are marked "men over fifteen" and "women over fifteen," the former only "men" and "women."

230

Table 53: TABLE A, I: OPERATIVES IN COTTON INDUSTRY

Year.	Men: After 1870. "Men over 16."	Women: After 1870. "Women over 16"	Children under 16.* No Data for 1850-60	Percentage of Women Employed
1850	33,150	59,136	Not given	64
1860	46,859	75,169	Not given	62
1870	42,790	68,637	22,942	51
1880	61,760	84,558	28,341	49
1890	88,837	106,607	23,432	49
1900	135,721	126,882	40,258	42

*As pointed out before, "women above fifteen"
is the correct designation until 1900.

1. The manufactures returns for 1860 and 1860 may be compared with those for 1870-1900 (Table A[365][366] below). This would be the logical thing to do if the manufactures schedules had been the same throughout the period; but it has been pointed out that the schedules were not the same and the result is an attempt to compare the number of men and women for 1850-60 with the number of men and women over sixteen for the later decades. In the case of industries in which a relatively small number of

children under sixteen were employed, "boots and shoes," cigar-making, clothing, and printing, this method was extremely satisfactory. But in the cotton industry and in the total for all industries in which the number of girls under sixteen was large, the number of women and therefore the percentage of women employed was reduced. The tables given below show what the results of such a comparison would be for the cotton industry and for the totals for "all industries."

2. Another table has been prepared comparing the manufac-

---

[365]Data for 1850-1900 from "Census of Manufactures." Comparative summary of all industries (Factory, Mechanical and Neighborhood) from 1905 "Census of Manufactures,", i:xxxvi.

[366]The percentage which women formed of the total number of men and women over sixteen, instead of the total number of employees, if substituted for the above percentages 1870-1900, would give the following result:

1850	1860	1870	1880	1890	1900
64	62	62	58	55	48

Table 54: TABLE A, II: ALL INDUSTRIES, 1850-1900

Year.	Men: After 1870. "Men over 16."	Women: After 1870. "Women over 16"	Children under 16.* No Data for 1850-60	Percentage of Women Employed
1850	731,137	225,922	Not given	24
1860	1,040,349	270,897	Not given	21
1870	1,615,598	323,770	114,628	16
1880	2,019,035	531,639	181,921	19
1890	3,327,042	803,606	120,885	19
1900	4,110,527	1,029,296	168,583	19

Table 55: TABLE B, I.: OPERATIVES IN COTTON INDUSTRY, 1850-1900

YEAR	NUMBER OF EMPLOYEES		Percentage of Women Employed
	Men	Women	
1850	33,150	59,136	64
1860	46,859	75,169	62
1870	47,208	64,398	58
1880	78,292	91,479	54
1890	80,177	92,965	52
1900	125,788	120,603	49

232

Table 56: TABLE B, II. ALL INDUSTRIES, 1850-1900

YEAR	NUMBER OF EMPLOYEES		Percentage of Women Employed
	Men	Women	
1850	731,137	225,922	24
1860	1,040,349	270,897	21
1870	2,353,471	353,950	13
1880	3,153,692	631,034	17
1890	4,650,540	1,027,928	18
1900	5,772,641	1,312,688	19

tures returns for 1850-60 with the occupations returns for 1870-1900 (Table B below).

In this table, since the occupations returns for 1870-1900, like the manufactures returns for 1850-60 used the classification into two groups instead of three, the terms "men" and "women" are correct designations throughout the period. There is, however, the objection to any comparison of manufactures and occupations returns that there are differences in the method of obtaining them.

3. A third method — a method of overcoming the difficulty pointed out in regard to Table A, was adopted in preparing Table I, used in the article (*supra*, p. 356). What was needed for Table A was a reclassification to make the threefold division of 1870-1900 into "men, women, and children" correspond with the twofold division of 1850-60 into "men and women." To do this, it is necessary to ascertain in what proportion "children" in column three are divided into girls and boys. This is, unfortunately, not reported in the manufactures census but in turning to the occupations returns in which "girls" and "boys" are reported separately, it is possible to obtain there the percentage of girls in the total number of children. For example, the occupations tables for 1900 report 21,006 boys and 23,442 girls in the industry, and according to these data, therefore, 53 per cent of the children in the cotton mills in 1900 were girls. Therefore, using only this percentage and not the occupations totals, 53 per cent of the number of children employed in 1900 as given in Table A were added to the column "women" and the remaining 47 per cent to the "men" column. For each of the other census years, 1870, 1880, 1890, the proportion of girls to boys was ascertained in the same way from the occupations tables for each census year,

Table 57: TABLE C, I. OPERATIVES IN THE COTTON INDUSTRY, 1850-1900

YEAR	NUMBER OF EMPLOYEES		Percentage of Women Employed
	Men	Women	
1850	33,150	59,136	64
1860	46,859	75,169	62
1870	54,031	81,337	60
1880	75,081	99,579	57
1890	100,319	118,557	54
1900	154,642	148,219	49

Table 58: TABLE C, II. ALL INDUSTRIES, 1850-1900

YEAR	NUMBER OF EMPLOYEES		Percentage of Women Employed
	Men	Women	
1850	731,137	225,922	24
1860	1,040,349	270,897	21
1870	1,691,252	362,744	18
1880	2,137,284	595,311	22
1890	3,400,782	850,831	20
1900	4,213,363	1,095,043	21

and the resulting percentages of the total number of children given in Table A were added to the "men" and "women" columns. The result. Tables C, I and C, II, were used in the text of the article, for it is believed that the statistics in these tables furnish a more correct basis of comparison than those in Tables A or B.

It is of the utmost importance, however, to note that all of these tables point to the same conclusion, viz., a constant decrease in the proportion of women operatives in the last half century. It has already been pointed out that in this, as in most attempts to make comparisons over a long period of years, statistics that are accurately comparable are not available. The census frankly says, in discussing the data for employees and wages: "It is obvious that comparisons between the results of any of the censuses under these heads cannot be exact." ("1900 Census Manufactures," i, p. lxii.)

It has seemed unnecessary to attempt here critically to analyze the census returns of employment decade by decade or to point out how far changes in the population or the manufactures schedules or in the methods of census taking may have affected the comparability of the returns for the different years.

In conclusion, it should be said that this note has seemed necessary lest there be any doubt as to the value placed upon these tables; for while they are believed to be of very great interest and significance, it has not been claimed that any table constructed from them can furnish an accurate measure of the change in the number of women operatives. The essential fact is that, whichever table is used, a decrease in the proportion of women employees is indicated.

It need, moreover, scarcely be repeated, that an attempt has been made in this volume, to study the subject of the employment of women not merely as a statistical problem, but as a chapter in our economic history in order that such material as the census offers may be correctly interpreted and understood. The conclusions drawn therefore, do not rest alone on census statistics, but on statistics explained and confirmed by the facts in our industrial history.

Appendix C - Tables of Women's Wages in the Cotton Mills

The following are the tables[367] of the actual rates of wages taken from an old Waltham (Massachusetts) pay roll of 1821, from which the tables of classified wage groups in Chapter XI were constructed.

Aldrich Report Tables

The tables of average money wages, 1840-90, used in Chapter XI are taken from the more detailed tables given below. The tables of money wages here given were prepared from the original data in the Aldrich Report. A description of these data and an account of the method used here in obtaining these tables, are given in detail in an article accompanying some tables which I prepared four years ago for the wages of unskilled labor (*Journal of Political Economy*, June, 1905). The difference between the method used there and here is that in the former tables, the two quotations given for each year were averaged, while here the January quotation alone is used. The use of the two quotations for each year is more laborious and since, in the cotton industry, there is no substantial difference between the winter and summer rates, the January quotations alone have been used.

A word must be added here as to the establishments and occupations chosen. In the Aldrich Report, reports are given for five "cotton

---

[367] A copy of what is believed to be a complete pay roll from an old wages book preserved in the mill.

Table 59: WAGES IN THE WALTHAM COTTON MILLS IN 1821: CARDING.

Men	Women	
1 at $2.00	3 at $1.50	1 at 2.82
2 at 2.25	1 at 1.75	2 at 2.94
1 at 2.50	9 at 2.00	1 at 3.16
5 at 3.00	12 at 2.08	1 at 3.18
1 at 3.50	24 at 2.25	1 at 3.20
1 at 4.20	1 at 2.58	1 at 3.24
3 at 4.80	1 at 2.64	1 at 3.28
1 at 5.28	1 at 2.70	1 at 3.66
5 at 6.00	1 at 2.75	
1 at 12.00		
21 men.	Total number of women...62.	

Table 60: WAGES IN THE WALTHAM COTTON MILLS IN 1821: SPINNING.

Men.	Women.		
1 at $7.50	3 at $2.00	2 at $2.72	1 at $3.03
1 at 10.00	2 at 2.17	1 at 2.82	1 at 3.06
1 at 10.50	20 at 2.25	2 at 2.88	1 at 3.10
	1 at 2.30	1 at 2.89	1 at 3.14
	1 at 2.37	1 at 2.90	1 at 3.18
	4 at 2.42	2 at 2.91	1 at 3.22
	1 at 2.46	4 at 2.94	1 at 3.24
	1 at 2.56	1 at 2.95	1 at 3.30
	1 at 2.58	1 at 2.97	2 at 3.53
	1 at 2.64	4 at 3.00	1 at 4.00
	1 at 2.68	1 at 3.02	
3 men.	Total number of women...67.		

Table 61: WAGES IN THE WALTHAM COTTON MILLS IN 1821: WEAVERS.

Men.	Women.		
2 at $12.00	3 at $1.75	1 at $2.76	1 at $2.98
2 at 6.60	4 at 2.00	1 at 2.77	5 at 3.00
	1 at 2.10	8 at 2.78	1 at 3.02
	29 at 2.25	1 at 2.80	1 at 3.04
	1 at 2.38	1 at 2.81	3 at 3.05
	1 at 2.40	4 at 2.82	6 at 3.10
	1 at 2.50	6 at 2.83	1 at 3.12
	2 at 2.57	1 at 2.85	1 at 3.16
	1 at 2.60	1 at 2.86	4 at 3.18
	1 at 2.62	2 at 2.88	4 at 3.20
	1 at 2.65	1 at 2.89	2 at 3.25
	2 at 2.68	5 at 2.90	1 at 3.26
	4 at 2.70	2 at 2.93	1 at 3.30
	1 at 2.71	4 at 2.94	1 at 3.37
	1 at 2.75	1 at 2.97	1 at 3.80
			1 at 3.92
4 men.	Total number of women...126.		

Table 62: WAGES IN THE WALTHAM COTTON MILLS IN 1821: DRESSING ROOM.

Men.	Women.	
1 at $10.00 a week	5* at $2.25	1 at $3.24
1 at 9.00 a week	1 at 2.23	1 at 3.25
1 at 7.00 a week	1 at 2.46	2 at 3.30
	1 at 2.88	1 at 3.42
	1 at 2.91	1 at 3.48
	1 at 3.05	1 at 3.60
	1 at 3.12	1 at 3.90
	1 at 3.15	
4 men.	Total number of women...126.	

* Learners.

Table 63: WAGES IN THE WALTHAM COTTON MILLS IN 1821: CLOTH ROOM.

1 man at $7.50	9 women at $2.25

Table 64: WAGES IN THE WALTHAM COTTON MILLS IN 1821: OTHER MEN EMPLOYED.

4 watchmen at	$6.60
1 repairer at	4.80
1 maker of sizing at	7.50
1 card coverer at	10.00
1 machinist at	6.00
1 teamster at	6.00
1 teamster at	7.50
Laborers, 4 at	4.80
” , 1 at	6.00
” , 1 at	7.50
Painters, 2 at	6.60
” , 1 at	7.00
” , 1 at	7.50

goods" establishments including one "ginghams." Tables have been prepared from the data for each of these establishments, for those occupations in which the record begins as early as 1860. Whenever men and women were both reported in an occupation, separate tables were prepared for men in order that the rates for men and for women might be compared.

The value of these tables, it is scarcely necessary to say, is that they present a continuous record of the money wages paid women in certain occupations in the same establishments for a period of approximately fifty years.[368]

---

[368]It should be added that these tables and those in Chapter XI have all been prepared by students under my direction. They were begun by some of my students in Wellesley College and completed with the assistance of some research students in the Chicago School of Civics and Philanthropy. Although the tables are the work of students, every effort has been made to have them made exact through verification.

Table 65: ESTABLISHMENT 38. COTTON GOODS. MAS-SACHUSETTS.

	CARD STRIPPERS WOMEN		SPOOLERS WOMEN		SCRUB-BERS WOMEN		SWEEPERS WOMEN		DOFFERS Women		DOFFERS Men	
	No.	Wage	No.	Wage	No.	Wage	No.	Wage	No.	Wage	No.	Wage
1840	..	..	..	..	..	..	..	..	..	..	..	..
1841	..	..	..	..	..	..	..	..	..	..	..	..
1842	..	..	..	..	..	..	..	..	..	..	..	..
1843	..	..	..	..	..	..	..	..	..	..	..	..
1844	..	..	..	..	..	..	..	..	..	..	..	..
1845	..	..	..	..	..	..	..	..	..	..	..	..
1846	..	..	..	..	..	..	..	..	..	..	..	..
1847	..	..	..	..	..	..	..	..	..	..	..	..
1848	..	..	..	..	..	..	..	..	..	..	..	..
1849	..	..	..	..	..	..	..	..	..	..	..	..
1850	..	..	..	..	..	..	..	..	..	..	..	..
1851	19	$3.27	46	$3.60	..	..	..	..	16	$1.08	23	$1.62
1852	14	3.48	44	3.60	..	..	..	..	18	1.02	27	1.71
1853	19	4.17	42.	3.60	..	..	2	$6.00	13	1.08	29	1.44
1854	19	4.17	42	3.60	..	..	2	6.00	13	1.08	29	1.44
1855	20	4.26	43	3.60	..	..	..	..	2	1.02	36	1.65
1856	7	4.26	45	3.60	..	..	1	4.26	10	1.02	21	1.74
1857	7	4.26	47	3.00	..	..	1	4.26	9	1.02	22	1.71
1858	7	4.02	45	2.76	4	2.70	2	4.26	..	..	32	1.62
1859	6	4.26	49	3.00	4	2.70	2	4.26	..	..	31	1.89
1860	6	4.26	49	3.00	4	2.70	2	4.26	..	..	33	1.89
1861	6	4.08	45	2.52	4	2.25	1	3.00	..	..	33	1.74
1862	6	4.80	45	2.40	4	2.25	1	3.60	..	..	33	1.83
1863	6	6.00	45	3.15	4	3.00	3	4.14	3	1.50	27	2.34
1864	5	6.90	44	2.85	4	3.48	3	4.35	4	1.50	26	2.58
1865	5	8.10	..	..	4	4.02	3	4.35	5	3.60	26	3.51

Table 66: ESTABLISHMENT 38. - CONTINUED.

	CARD STRIPPERS WOMEN		SPOOLERS WOMEN		SCRUB- BERS WOMEN		SWEEPERS WOMEN		DOFFERS Women		DOFFERS Men	
	No.	Wage	No.	Wage	No.	Wage	No.	Wage	No.	Wage	No.	Wage
1866	5	7.10	37	6.00.	7	4.44	14	4.41	6	3.00	27	3.45
1867	5	7.10	37	6.00	7	4.44	14	3.69	..	..	27	4.14
1868	6	7.74	36	5.76	7	4.32	14	3.63	..	..	31	4.32
1869	7	7.71	35	6.24	7	4.11	16	3.75	3	3.24	31	4.20
1870	12	6.99	34	5.52	7	4.23	18	3.30	2	3.24	33	4.08
1871	10	8.13	40	6.00	7	4.56	19	3.33	4	3.51	32	4.08
1872	12	8.01	37	6.00	7	4.56	17	3.48	5	4.26	32	5.55
1873	12	7.98	34	6.00	7	4.56	16	3.51	5	4.26	31	5.55
1874	12	7.29	34	5.16	7	3.93	18	3.15	2	4.98	19	3.65
1875	12	5.70	33	4.83	7	3.42	20	2.73	2	3.24	20	3.75
1876	13	5.28	24	4.14	7	3.33	19	2.43	2	3.18	16	3.18
1877	3	4.41	23	3.90	7	2.67	17	2.40	2	2.46	15	3.21
1878	4	4.65	23	3.90	8	3.12	17	2.46	4	2.91	15	3.15
1879	1	5.10	23	3.90	8	3.12	13	2.40	3	2.46	9	3.12
1880	1	5.70	23	4.14	8	3.24	11	2.43	8	2.70	11	3.81
1881	1	5.70	23	4.56	8	3.45	11	2.55	8	2.70	11	3.81
1882	1	5.70	23	4.56	..	..	11	2.55	8	2.70	11	3.81
1883	9	5.70	23	4.56	..	..	12	2.64	8	2.46	11	3.45
1884	9	5.70	30	4.35	..	..	12	2.55	8	2.46	11	3.45
1885	9	5.70	30	4.35	..	..	12	2.61	6	2.52	13	3.60
1886	9	6.69	25	4.17	..	..	11	2.25	6	2.76	11	3.78
1887	9	9.27	25	4.47	..	..	11	2.34	6	2.76	11	4.93
1888	9	9.27	25	4.65	..	..	11	2.49	6	4.02	10	4.41
1889	9	9.27	24	4.26	..	..	11	2.43	6	4.02	10	4.41
1890	9	9.27	24	4.26	..	..	11	2.43	6	4.02	10	5.13
1891	5	7.86	49	4.38	..	..	18	3.96	6	4.50	10	5.31

Table 67: ESTABLISHMENT 39. COTTON GOODS. MASSACHUSETTS.

	DRAWING-HANDS WOMEN		DRAWERS-IN WOMEN		SPEEDERS WOMEN		SPINNERS WOMEN		WARPERS WOMEN		WEAVERS WOMEN	
	No.	Wage	No.	Wage	No.	Wage	No.	Wage	No.	Wage	No.	Wage
1840	..	..	..	..	..	..	..	..	..	..	..	..
1841	..	..	..	..	..	..	..	..	..	..	..	..
1842	21	$2.61	..	..	7	$2.91	18	$2.73	7	$3.06	41	$3.66.
1843*	10	2.52	..	..	3	2.64	25	2.67	..	..	37	3.12
1843*	9	2.55	..	..	12	2.73	24	2.70	..	..	38	3.81
1844	7	2.52	..	..	10	2.73	28	2.55	..	..	21	2.31
1845	7	2.52	1	$2.76	..	...	29	2.64	1	3.00	18	2.67
1846	5	2.52	4	2.85	1	2.76	28	2.64	3	3.00	21	2.40
1847	8	2.52	4	2.67	4	2.73	22	2.67	4	3.18	14	2.55
1848	6	2.52	8	2.76	4	2.85	28	2.64	3	3.45	23	2.67
1849	6	2.52	3	2.67	1	2.64	26	2.70	3	3.45	25	2.52
1850	6	2.52	3	2.67	2	2.76	24	2.61	5	3.51	26	2.58
1851	3	2.52	2	2.76	3	2.88	23	2.49	3	3.15	21	2.79
1852	4	2.52	3	2.43	3	2.70	27	2.58	4	2.79	25	2.43
1853	3	2.49	8	2.67	7	3.12	27	2.46	6	2.88	20	2.76
1854	5	2.58	6	2.82	6	3.21	18	2.82	7	3.09	26	2.79
1855	5	2.52	10	3.00	4	3.36	19	2.55	6	3.36	27	2.76
1856	..	..	..	..	..	..	..	..	..	..	..	..
1857	..	..	..	..	..	..	..	..	..	..	..	..
1858	3	2.52	4	3.15	5	2.88	7	2.94	7	3.12	15	3.66.
1859	3	2.52	4	2.76	5	2.88	24	2.70	7	3.48	25	3.06
1860	4	2.52	5	2.85	4	3.12	28	2.85	6	3.57	19	2.76
1861	3	3.00	4	2.40	4	3.24	26	2.76	7	3.87	25	3.03
1862	3	3.00	4	3.24	4	3.24	30	2.91	7	2.82	18	3.09
1863	2	2.40	2	3.24	1	2.88	23	2.76	1	2.40	21	3.24
1864	3	3.00	5	3.51	2	3.30	24	3.24	2	3.36	20	3.54
1865	2	3.00	2	4.02	2	3.42	28	3.30	1	3.48	24	3.87

* *Editor's note*: The original 1909 edition of *Women in Industry* reports two distinct figures for 1843.

Table 68: ESTABLISHMENT 39. - CONTINUED.

	DRAWING- HANDS WOMEN		DRAWERS- IN WOMEN		SPEEDERS WOMEN		SPINNERS WOMEN		WARPERS WOMEN		WEAVERS WOMEN	
	No.	Wage	No.	Wage	No.	Wage	No.	Wage	No.	Wage	No.	Wage
1866	4	$4.02	6	5.40	4	5.01	34	5.43	4	4.71	24	5.13
1867	4	4.02	5	6.06	4	5.01	35	5.46	2	6.00	25	5.22
1868	4	4.02	4	5.76	4	5.01	34	4.83	2	6.72	25	5.58
1869	4	4.02	5	5.88	6	5.01	48	5.10	2	5.46	26	4.83
1870	5	4.02	3	5.49	5	5.01	38	6.42	2	5.49	44	5.91
1871	8	4.02	12	4.92	20	6.39	32	6.18	3	6.48	81	6.54
1872	4	4.02	11	5.31	16	6.63	34	6.63	2	6.72	76	7.44
1873	4	3.75	13	5.49	16	7.02	42	5.55	6	6.18	43	7.05
1874	3	3.72	10	5.58	10	5.76	54	6.21	5	5.28	29	5.55
1875	7	3.75	2	5.79	10	5.40	45	5.43	6	5.22	28	3.96
1876	7	3.69	4	5.25	15	5.61	28	5.07	2	5.25	41	4.17
1877	7	3.18	4	5.25	12	4.53	24	5.25	2	5.10	34	4.71
1878	8	3.30	5	4.59	13	5.04	31	5.55	2	5.10	38	6.30
1879	9	2.88	12	5.16	11	5.22	31	6.03	4	4.77	43	6.00
1880	7	2.91	17	5.73	18	5.19	44	6.06	4	5.25	40	6.39
1881	8	2.79	21	6.09	20	5.13	47	6.09	4	5.49	53	6.24
1882	10	3.06	10	5.82	22	5.40	44	6.48	5	5.58	62	5.94
1883	11	2.82	13	5.61	22	5.43	45	6.24	6	5.40	49	5.88
1884	7	3.03	12	5.55	18	5.37	48	6.30	3	5.01	47	5.97
1885	6	3.00	11	5.70	20	5.28	43	6.21	4	4.95	58	6.30
1886	12	4.41	8	6.39	20	5.37	66	6.30	5	5.16	51	5.70
1887	10	3.36	11	5.61	30	5.61	57	6.96	5	5.16	55	6.03
1888	10	3.36	12	5.70	33	5.58	62	7.02	5	5.16	64	5.70
1889	9	3.39	10	5.88	17	6.57	60	6.99	6	5.61	40	6.51
1890	10	3.36	12	5.94	20	6.45	55	7.05	6	6.39	39	6.36
1891	10	3.36	17	5.64	19	6.72	53	7.32	11	6.27	48	6.33

Table 69: ESTABLISHMENT 40. COTTON GOODS. MASSACHUSETTS

| | BACK HANDS | | | | CLOTH ROOM HANDS | | | | DOFFERS | | | | HARNESS HANDS | | | |
| | WOMEN | | MEN | | WOMEN | | MEN | | WOMEN | | MEN | | WOMEN | | MEN | |
	N.	W.	N.	W.	N.	W.	N.	W.	N.	W.	N.	W.	N.	W.	N.	W.
'40	2	2.6	3	2.3	3	2.4	..	..	..	..	..	..	..	..	..	..
'41	..	..	..	..	3	2.4	..	..	..	..	..	..	..	..	..	..
'42	1	2.6	1	2.4	3	2.4	..	..	..	..	..	..	..	..	..	..
'43	2	2.5	1	2.3	4	2.4	..	..	..	..	..	..	1	2.4	..	..
'44	1	2.3	3	1.8	4	2.3	..	..	..	..	..	..	4	2.3	..	..
'45	3	2.4	3	1.8	3	2.4	..	..	..	..	..	..	1	2.3	..	..
'46	2	2.3	3	2.3	..	..	1	2.4	..	..	..	..	7	2.4	..	..
'47	..	..	..	..	..	..	1	2.7	..	..	..	..	5	2.4	1	2.0
'48	..	..	1	2.5	5	2.9	1	2.7	..	..	..	..	5	2.6	..	..
'49	..	..	..	..	5	3.0	2	2.5	..	..	..	..	3	3.1	..	..
'50	..	..	..	..	4	2.8	2	2.5	..	..	..	..	5	2.4	1	2.3
'51	..	..	..	..	2	3.0	1	2.7	..	..	..	..	3	2.6	2	2.4
'52	..	..	..	..	5	2.8	..	.....	..	..	..	..	6	2.5	2	1.8
'53	1	1.8	..	..	6	2.9	2	2.7	..	..	..	..	8	3.0	2	2.5
'54	1	1.8	..	..	7	2.9	2	2.7	..	..	..	..	9	2.5	1	2.4
'55	1	1.8	..	..	6	2.9	2	2.7	..	..	..	..	5	2.6	4	2.3
'56	5	2.8	2	2.6	7	2.9	2	5.5	..	..	24	1.9	..	..	..	..
'57	1	2.7	6	2.7	4	3.1	1	3.0	..	..	25	2.0	..	..	..	..
'58	..	..	..	..	4	3.4	1	3.0	2	2.0	22	1.9	..	..	..	..
'59	1	2.4	..	..	6	3.3	1	3.0	1	2.0	12	1.6	4	2.5	..	..
'60	..	..	..	..	6	3.7	2	3.0	2	1.9	27	1.8	5	3.3	2	2.2
'61	..	..	..	..	4	3.2	2	3.2	5	2.1	25	1.9	1	3.5	2	2.8
'62	..	..	..	..	1	3.0	1	3.5	2	2.0	14	1.9	1	3.9	2	2.9
'63	..	..	..	..	..	..	1	3.5	4	1.9	9	1.7	1	4.2	..	..
'64	6	2.4	2	2.3	3	3.7	..	..	..	..	15	2.3	2	4.5	1	4.5
'65	..	..	1	3.00	3	4.74	..	..	6	2.40	15	2.4	1	4.5	..	..

244

Table 70: ESTABLISHMENT 40. - CONTINUED.

| | BACK HANDS | | | CLOTH ROOM HANDS | | | | DOFFERS | | | | HARNESS HANDS | | | |
| | WOMEN | | MEN | | WOMEN | | MEN | | WOMEN | | MEN | | WOMEN | | MEN | |
	No.	Wg.	No.	Wg.	No.	Wg.	No.	Wg.	No.	Wg.	No.	Wg.	No.	Wg.	No.	Wg.
'66	..	..	2	3.0	8	4.9	2	5.0	6	3.0	10	3.0	3	5.1	2	4.9
'67	..	..	3	3.8	4	5.2	3	5.1	14	3.1	12	3.8	5	5.0	3	5.2
'68	..	..	2	3.0	4	5.3	3	5.1	9	3.6	4	3.4	7	4.9	4	3.3
'69	..	..	1	3.2	3	5.4	4	5.2	9	3.6	4	3.5	8	3.6	5	5.2
'70	..	..	..	..	5	5.8	2	5.1	5	3.2	4	3.3	4	4.6	2	5.2
'71	..	..	..	..	4	5.3	3	5.4	2	3.0	12	3.0	5	5.6	2	5.7
'72	..	..	..	..	3	6.0	3	6.8	5	3.0	15	3.0	6	5.9	2	5.5
'73	..	..	..	..	7	5.7	3	5.6	5	3.0	9	2.8	6	5.9	2	5.5
'74	..	..	..	..	7	5.0	3	5.1	1	3.0	10	2.7	5	6.0	2	5.4
'75	..	..	3	2.4	9	4.8	4	5.4	..	..	17	2.3	6	5.7	2	5.1
'76	..	..	1	2.1	10	4.4	3	4.8	..	..	12	2.7	6	5.7	2	5.2
'77	..	..	3	2.3	11	4.3	6	4.3	..	..	9	2.7	4	5.9	1	5.4
'78	..	..	3	2.6	12	4.3	5	4.3	..	..	10	2.7	4	5.9	1	5.4
'79	..	..	4	2.7	11	4.1	5	4.1	3	3.3	11	2.0	5	5.9	..	..
'80	..	..	3	2.7	12	4.4	5	4.4	3	2.0	13	2.1	5	5.9	..	..
'81	..	..	4	2.7	12	4.3	4	4.5	7	2.0	10	2.2	5	5.9	..	..
'82	..	..	4	2.7	15	4.3	5	4.9	6	2.0	9	2.3	6	5.8	..	..
'83	1	2.4	4	2.5	10	4.5	3	4.4	9	2.1	5	2.1	5	5.9	..	..
'84	4	2.4	4	2.7	12	4.5	3	4.4	6	2.3	12	2.2	2	6.7	1	5.4
'85	5	2.4	..	..	8	4.5	3	4.4	4	2.7	8	2.5	3	5.7	1	5.4
'86	2	2.2	6	3.0	11	4.5	4	4.8	5	2.8	3	3.3	1	8.1	1	5.4
'87	2	2.7	..	..	13	4.5	6	5.8	5	3.4	4	4.8	1	8.1	1	5.4
'88	6	3.0	..	..	..	..	7	5.7	4	4.1	5	4.9	1	8.1	1	5.4
'89	3	2.9	..	..	15	4.70	5	6.6	2	3.1	2	4.8	4	5.9	..	..
'90	4	3.1	..	..	..	..	..	..	10	3.9	8	4.5	5	5.4	..	..
'91	2	3.3	20	3.4	23	4.8	8	6.6	12	4.0	11	3.9	6	5.4	..	..

Table 71: ESTABLISHMENT 40. - CONTINUED #2.

	SPINNERS				SPOOLERS				STRETCHERS				WARPERS			
	WOMEN		MEN		WOMEN		MEN		WOMEN		MEN		WOMEN		MEN	
	No.	Wage	No.	Wage	No.	Wage	No.	Wage	No.	Wage	No.	Wage	No.	Wage	No.	Wage
'40	..	..	..	..	..	..	..	..	7	3.0	3	3.1	..	..	..	..
'41	..	..	..	..	..	..	..	..	..	..	..	..	..	..	..	..
'42	..	..	..	..	..	..	..	..	17	2.9	1	3.3	..	..	..	..
'43	..	..	..	..	..	..	..	..	7	2.7	2	3.1	..	..	..	..
'44	..	..	..	..	..	..	..	..	9	2.7	1	2.2	1	2.5	..	..
'45	..	..	..	..	..	..	..	..	11	2.7	1	2.6	2	2.4	..	
'46	..	..	..	..	..	..	..	..	13	3.0	2	2.8	1	2.2	..	
'47	..	..	..	..	..	..	..	..	27	3.0	3	3.0	1	2.7	..	
'48	..	..	..	..	..	..	..	..	18	3.2	4	3.1	..	..	..	..
'49	..	..	..	..	..	..	..	..	12	3.2	4	3.1	..	..	..	..
'50	..	..	..	..	..	..	..	..	15	3.2	6	3.4	..	..	..	..
'51	..	..	..	..	..	..	..	..	11	3.0	3	3.8	..	..	..	..
'52	..	..	..	..	..	..	..	..	5	3.0	1	3.0	..	..	..	..
'53	..	..	..	..	..	..	..	..	3	3.2	3	3.3	..	..	..	..
'54	..	..	..	..	..	..	..	..	5	3.2	3	3.3	..	..	..	..
'55	..	..	..	..	..	..	..	..	3	3.2	2	3.4	..	..	..	..
'56	..	..	..	..	1	3.9	..	..	6	3.1	4	3.3	..	..	..	..
'57	..	..	..	..	13	2.2	14	1.9	5	3.2	2	3.2	7	3.7	1	3.1
'58	..	..	..	..	13	2.9	11	2.1	3	3.2	3	3.4	7	4.0	2	3.6
'59	..	..	1	5.7	7	2.7	9	2.2	6	3.2	4	3.3	6	3.7	2	3.9
'60	..	..	..	..	9	2.4	4	2.6	3	3.1	4	3.4	7	4.1	..	..
'61	..	..	..	..	15	2.0	2	3.0	6	3.5	1	3.9	11	3.5	..	..
'62	..	..	..	..	13	2.1	2	4.8	8	3.6	2	3.9	6	3.5	..	..
'63	..	..	..	..	7	2.1	1	1.6	8	3.8	..	..	1	3.6	..	..
'64	9	4.5	1	2.4	10	2.9	3	2.4	6	3.7	..	..	3	4.8	..	..
'65	13	4.6	..	..	15	2.8	7	3.74	6	3.9	..	..	2	4.5	..	..

Table 72: ESTABLISHMENT 40. - CONTINUED #3.

| | SPINNERS | | | | SPOOLERS | | | | STRETCHERS | | | | WARPERS | | | |
| | WOMEN | | MEN | | WOMEN | | MEN | | WOMEN | | MEN | | WOMEN | | MEN | |
	No.	Wage	No.	Wage	No.	Wage	No.	Wage	No.	Wage	No.	Wage	No.	Wage	No.	Wage
'66	15	4.2	1	6.0	19	4.1	8	3.1	6	4.2	..	..	6	5.7	1	6.0
'67	19	3.7	1	3.3	22	4.2	5	5.5	6	4.6	..	..	3	6.7	1	6.0
'68	7	3.5	..	..	15	3.7	3	4.2	9	4.9	..	..	3	6.0	1	6.7
'69	14	4.1	3	5.1	11	4.5	2	6.1	9	4.9	..	..	4	5.9	1	6.7
'70	32	4.9	2	5.4	9	5.0	3	4.4	9	5.1	..	..	8	5.9	..	..
'71	21	4.7	..	..	15	4.8	1	2.2	9	5.3	..	..	4	6.6	..	..
'72	32	4.9	..	..	12	4.5	..	..	9	5.3	..	..	4	6.8	..	..
'73	19	6.0	..	..	14	4.3	..	..	6	4.7	..	..	3	6.0	..	..
'74	20	4.9	1	4.8	21	3.9	..	..	6	3.9	..	..	3	6.4	..	..
'75	21	4.9	1	4.8	18	3.9	..	..	7	3.8	..	..	3	8.1	..	..
'76	22	3.6	1	3.9	17	4.2	..	..	6	3.9	..	..	3	6.5	..	..
'77	26	3.6	1	3.6	17	4.3	..	..	3	3.6	..	..	3	5.9	..	..
'78	27	3.8	1	3.9	22	3.6	..	..	2	3.3	..	..	3	6.2	..	..
'79	29	4.2	1	4.2	27	3.4	..	..	1	4.5	8	4.5	6	5.1	..	..
'80	22	4.2	1	4.2	26	4.1	..	..	1	4.5	8	4.3	5	5.7	..	..
'81	24	4.8	..	..	31	4.5	1	6.0	2	4.5	8	4.9	9	5.4	..	..
'82	29	4.8	..	..	38	4.6	1	6.0	2	4.2	8	4.1	9	5.3	1	5.4
'83	25	4.7	..	..	25	4.6	..	..	3	5.4	..	..	8	5.8	..	..
'84	32	4.6	..	..	16	4.5	..	..	2	5.1	..	..	9	6.3	..	..
'85	31	4.5	..	..	13	4.7	..	..	8	4.2	1	3.9	8	6.5	..	..
'86	16	4.4	..	..	10	5.0	1	4.5	8	4.2	..	..	7	6.1	..	..
'87	15	4.4	..	..	9	5.0	1	5.1	8	4.1	..	..	3	6.6	..	..
'88	17	4.5	..	..	18	4.8	..	..	11	4.3	..	..	3	6.9	..	..
'89	17	4.7	2	4.5	22	5.0	4	4.3	10	4.4	..	..	2	6.6	..	..
'90	18	4.6	7	4.8	19	5.1	10	4.8	9	4.3	..	..	1	6.0	4	6.7
'91	18	4.9	7	5.1	12	5.0	7	5.0	5	5.8	..	..	2	6.0	5	6.8

247

Table 73: ESTABLISHMENT 41. COTTON GOODS. NEW YORK

	SPOILERS WOMEN		WARPERS WOMEN		WEAVERS 3 AND 4 LOOM WOMEN		WEAVERS 5 LOOM WOMEN		WEAVERS 6, 7 AND 8 LOOM WOMEN		WEAVERS 6, 7 AND 8 LOOM MEN		WEAVERS SPARE WOMEN	
	No.	Wage	No.	Wage	No.	Wage	No.	Wage	No.	Wage	No.	Wage	No.	Wage
1840	..	..	..	..	..	..	..	..	..	..	..	..	..	..
1841	..	..	..	..	..	..	..	..	..	..	..	..	..	..
1842	..	..	..	..	..	..	..	..	..	..	..	..	..	..
1843	..	..	..	..	..	..	..	..	..	..	..	..	..	..
1844	..	..	..	..	..	..	..	..	..	..	..	..	..	..
1845	..	..	..	..	..	..	..	..	..	..	..	..	..	..
1846	..	..	..	..	..	..	..	..	..	..	..	..	..	..
1847	..	..	..	..	..	..	..	..	..	..	..	..	..	..
1848	..	..	..	..	..	..	..	..	..	..	..	..	..	..
1849	..	..	..	..	..	..	..	..	..	..	..	..	..	..
1850	..	..	..	..	..	..	..	..	..	..	..	..	..	..
1851	..	..	..	..	..	..	..	..	..	..	..	..	..	..
1852	..	..	..	..	..	..	..	..	..	..	..	..	..	..
1853	8	$2.13	2	$3.00	8	$1.80	9	$3.00	8	$4.20	..	..	2	$2.49
1854	10	2.49	2	3.75	6	1.80	18	3.00	20	5.04	..	..	3	2.76
1855	10	2.49	3	3.12	20	3.00	20	3.60	6	4.80	6	$5.04	4	3.00
1856	10	2.55	3	4.11	9	3.00	22	3.60	5	5.10	6	5.16	8	3.00
1857	10	2.76	3	4.56	8	3.00	22	4.32	6	6.00	6	6.30	11	3.00
1858	11	2.13	3	3.60	3	2.40	25	3.30	7	4.50	14	4.80	11	3.00
1859	12	2.37	3	4.20	8	2.40	18	3.60	13	4.68	11	5.40	12	3.00
1860	12	2.37	4	4.35	3	2.40	11	3.72	23	4.92	12	6.00	12	3.00
1861	10	2.37	3	4.68	5	2.40	12	3.66	21	5.40	11	6.30	13	3.00
1862	7	2.37	2	4.20	..	..	4	3.60	15	4.80	9	4.62	..	..
1863	..	..	..	..	..	..	..	..	..	..	..	..	..	..
1864	..	..	..	..	..	..	..	..	..	..	..	..	..	..
1865	12	3.99	3	5.01	9	3.00	8	4.80	9	6.30	3	6.00	6	3.51

248

Table 74: ESTABLISHMENT 41. - CONTINUED

| | SPOILERS | | WARPERS | | WEAVERS 3 AND 4 LOOM | | WEAVERS 5 LOOM | | WEAVERS 6, 7 AND 8 LOOM | | | | WEAVERS SPARE | |
| | WOMEN | | WOMEN | | WOMEN | | WOMEN | | WOMEN | | MEN | | WOMEN | |
	No.	Wage	No.	Wage	No.	Wage	No.	Wage	No.	Wage	No.	Wage	No.	Wage
1866	12	3.99	3	6.03	14	3.00	21	4.80	13	6.00	4	6.00	6	4.50
1867	13	3.12	3	6.00	11	3.18	16	4.92	19	7.08	5	7.74	10	5.01
1868	14	3.63	3	6.99	8	3.36	20	5.40	18	7.68	3	8.04	6	6.00
1869	14	3.63	3	6.30	7	4.20	14	5.52	26	7.50	3	7.50	5	5.49
1870	13	3.63	3	6.30	7	3.78	23	5.16	16	7.02	2	7.56	6	6.00
1871	12	3.63	3	6.99	5	3.72	21	5.28	20	6.96	1	7.56	7	5.01
1872	12	3.99	3	7.20	6	3.84	16	4.86	27	7.20	1	8.28	7	5.01
1873	12	3.99	3	7.29	7	3.78	10	4.80	27	6.90	1	6.18	3	6.00
1874	12	3.75	2	6.09	5	3.00	20	4.56	24	6.60	1	7.02	6	5.25
1875	8	3.87	2	6.30	6	3.78	19	4.92	22	6.90	1	7.14	5	5.61
1876	8	3.87	2	5.88	9	3.60	22	4.86	17	6.24	1	7.08	3	4.89
1877	8	3.63	2	5.25	10	3.42	27	4.86	7	6.12	1	6.00	6	4.38
1878	8	3.63	2	5.25	18	3.78	26	4.80	4	6.24	..	..	6	4.38
1879	8	3.63	2	5.25	15	3.60	23	5.46	6	7.02	..	..	6	3.51
1880	8	3.63	2	5.25	9	3.60	29	4.98	4	6.24	..	..	9	4.38
1881	8	4.20	2	5.76	6	3.72	22	5.46	17	6.96	..	..	9	5.01
1882	8	4.50	2	5.76	3	3.60	10	5.22	30	6.48	..	..	8	6.00
1883	8	4.50	2	5.01	6	3.00	27	5.22	7	6.00	..	..	15	3.51
1884	8	4.50	2	5.01	9	3.66	18	5.52	14	7.32	..	..	6	3.99
1885	8	4.26	2	4.89	22	4.02	8	4.92	1	6.24	..	..	7	4.50
1886	8	3.99	2	4.95	8	3.60	24	5.22	12	6.30	..	..	11	3.51
1887	8	4.50	2	4.95	20	3.42	15	5.10	3	6.00	..	..	8	3.51
1888	6	5.37	2	5.49	8	3.24	21	5.34	8	6.00	..	..	7	3.51
1889	6	4.74	2	5.49	6	3.72	15	5.04	19	6.72	..	..	7	5.01
1890	6	5.25	2	5.49	6	3.84	13	5.20	21	7.20	..	..	7	6.00
1891	6	6.00	2	5.49	7	4.20	12	5.58	22	7.02	..	..	7	6.00

Table 75: ESTABLISHMENT 41. - CONTINUED #2

	DOFFERS WOMEN		DRAWERS-IN WOMEN		DRAWING FRAME TENDERS WOMEN		SLUBBER TENDERS WOMEN		SEEDER TENDERS WOMEN		SPINNERS FRAME WOMEN	
	No.	Wage	No.	Wage	No.	Wage	No.	Wage	No.	Wage	No.	Wage
1840	..	..	..	..	..	..	..	..	..	..	..	..
1841	..	..	..	..	..	..	..	..	..	..	..	..
1842	..	..	..	..	..	..	..	..	..	..	..	..
1843	..	..	..	..	..	..	..	..	..	..	..	..
1844	..	..	..	..	..	..	..	..	..	..	..	..
1845	..	..	..	..	..	..	..	..	..	..	..	..
1846	..	..	..	..	..	..	..	..	..	..	..	..
1847	..	..	..	..	..	..	..	..	..	..	..	..
1848	..	..	..	..	..	..	..	..	..	..	..	..
1849	..	..	..	..	..	..	..	..	..	..	..	..
1850	..	..	..	..	..	..	..	..	..	..	..	..
1851	..	..	..	..	..	..	..	..	..	..	..	..
1852	..	..	..	..	..	..	..	..	..	..	..	..
1853	2	$2.13	2	$3.00	4	$2.49	2	$4.20	6	$4.20	8	$2.34
1854	2	3.00	2	4.80	4	2.49	2	4.80	6	4.20	15	2.49
1855	2	2.79	2	4.20	4	2.49	2	4.80	6	4.20	15	2.49
1856	3	3.24	2	3.90	4	2.49	2	4.32	6	4.20	15	2.49
1857	3	3.75	2	3.90	4	2.49	2	5.40	6	4.56	15	2.49
1858	3	2.34	2	3.60	4	2.49	2	4.32	6	3.60	15	2.01
1859	3	3.00	2	3.90	4	2.49	2	4.26	6	3.90	15	2.28
1860	3	2.76	2	3.72	4	2.49	2	4.56	6	4.20	15	2.19
1861	3	2.76	2	3.60	4	2.49	2	4.68	6	4.38	15	2.19
1862	3	3.21	2	3.00	4	2.49	2	4.26	6	3.96	15	2.91
1863	..	..	..	..	..	..	..	..	..	..	..	..
1864	..	..	..	..	..	..	..	..	..	..	..	..
1865	3	3.99	2	6.00	4	3.51	2	6.36	6	5.40	15	3.00

Table 76: ESTABLISHMENT 41. - CONTINUED #3

	DOFFERS WOMEN		DRAWERS-IN WOMEN		DRAWING FRAME TENDERS WOMEN		SLUBBER TENDERS WOMEN		SEEDER TENDERS WOMEN		SPINNERS FRAME WOMEN	
	No.	Wage	No.	Wage	No.	Wage	No.	Wage	No.	Wage	No.	Wage
1866	3	3.99	2	6.60	4	3.51	2	6.12	6	4.86	15	3.00
1867	3	4.62	2	7.20	4	3.99	3	7.20	7	6.24	15	3.12
1868	3	4.62	2	7.50	4	3.99	3	7.44	7	6.84	15	3.12
1869	3	4.62	2	7.80	4	3.99	2	7.92	7	7.20	15	3.12
1870	3	4.62	2	7.20	4	4.50	2	7.14	7	6.12	15	3.24
1871	3	5.01	2	6.60	4	4.50	2	7.02	7	6.48	15	3.99
1872	3	5.01	2	7.20	4	4.26	2	7.32	6	6.30	15	3.99
1873	3	5.01	2	7.80	4	4.50	2	7.44	6	6.84	15	3.99
1874	3	5.25	2	6.48	4	3.99	2	6.78	6	5.04	15	4.26
1875	3	5.01	2	7.20	4	3.99	2	5.70	6	4.32	15	4.50
1876	3	4.11	2	6.30	4	3.51	2	5.64	6	5.10	15	3.87
1877	3	3.99	2	4.80	4	3.24	2	5.16	6	4.62	15	3.63
1878	3	3.99	2	5.10	4	3.24	2	4.64	6	4.44	15	3.63
1879	3	4.11	2	5.16	4	3.24	2	5.22	6	4.38	15	3.99
1880	3	4.50	2	5.40	2	3.99	2	4.80	6	4.32	15	3.99
1881	3	4.38	2	6.30	2	4.38	2	5.88	6	4.80	15	3.99
1882	3	4.50	2	7.02	2	4.38	2	5.70	6	4.74	15	3.99
1883	3	4.26	2	5.40	2	3.99	2	4.80	6	4.32	15	3.99
1884	3	3.99	2	5.64	2	3.99	2	5.34	6	4.74	15	4.26
1885	2	3.63	2	4.80	2	3.63	2	4.26	6	4.08	15	3.99
1886	2	3.63	3	5.04	2	3.63	2	4.50	6	3.96	15	3.99
1887	2	4.50	3	4.80	2	3.63	2	4.62	6	4.08	15	4.74
1888	2	4.50	3	4.80	2	3.63	2	4.56	6	4.20	13	5.01
1889	2	5.01	3	5.10	2	3.99	2	4.92	6	4.20	10	5.37
1890	2	5.01	2	5.58	2	3.99	2	4.92	6	4.44	8	5.37
1891	2	5.37	2	5.58	2	4.26	2	5.16	6	4.80	8	6.00

Table 77: ESTABLISHMENT 43. GINGHAMS. MASSACHUSETTS.

	DRAWING FRAME TENDERS WOMEN		DRAWERS-IN WOMEN		QUILLERS WOMEN		REELERS WOMEN		SPEEDERS WOMEN	
	No.	Wage	No.	Wage	No.	Wage	No.	Wage	No.	Wage
1840	..	..	..	..	..	..	..	..	..	..
1841	..	..	..	..	..	..	..	..	..	..
1842	..	..	..	..	..	..	..	..	..	..
1843	..	..	..	..	..	..	..	..	..	..
1844	..	..	..	..	..	..	..	..	..	..
1845	..	..	..	..	..	..	..	..	..	..
1846	..	..	..	..	..	..	..	..	..	..
1847	..	..	..	..	..	..	..	..	..	..
1848	..	..	3	4.92	21	$2.70	17	$4.50	..	..
1849	3	$2.82	3	4.98	26	2.70	13	4.20	4	$3.42
1850	8	2.82	6	5.10	61	2.70	28	3.90	12	3.60
1851	8	2.82	7	4.80	66	2.58	27	3.72	14	3.30
1852	7	2.82	6	5.10	32	3.00	24	3.66	9	3.30
1853	9	2.70	5	5.04	34	3.00	21	3.66	11	3.30
1854	10	2.70	5	4.32	31	3.00	22	3.66	14	3.30
1855	10	2.70	5	5.10	34	2.82	33	3.66	14	3.12
1856	10	2.94	4	5.04	30	3.24	28	4.02	14	3.24
1857	10	2.94	4	5.04	35	3.60	33	3.96	11	3.30
1858	10	2.94	5	5.16	35	3.30	29	4.08	12	3.42
1859	10	2.94	5	5.04	36	3.30	37	4.56	10	3.42
1860	10	2.94	5	4.80	36	3.42	34	3.96	12	3.60
1861	10	3.00	4	4.80	37	3.42	33	4.77	10	3.60
1862	10	3.00	4	5.64	34	3.30	26	4.77	12	3.60
1863	8	3.00	5	5.16	23	3.42	14	5.76	6	3.60
1864	11	3.30	5	4.92	25	3.42	21	5.22	12	3.90
1865	12	3.90	5	4.92	29	4.38	26	5.16	11	4.80

Table 78: ESTABLISHMENT 43. - CONTINUED

	DRAWING FRAME TENDERS WOMEN		DRAWERS-IN WOMEN		QUILLERS WOMEN		REELERS WOMEN		SPEEDERS WOMEN	
	No.	Wage	No.	Wage	No.	Wage	No.	Wage	No.	Wage
1866	10	4.80	6	4.92	45	5.22	45	5.70	17	5.70
1867	14	5.10	6	4.92	44	5.64	55	5.88	20	6.00
1868	13	4.92	6	4.92	43	5.70	44	6.36	17	6.00
1869	12	4.92	6	4.92	44	5.88	46	6.36	21	6.00
1870	13	4.92	9	7.38	43	6.30	43	6.00	26	6.00
1871	11	4.92	9	6.90	47	6.30	39	8.22	22	6.00
1872	1	4.92	9	7.86	49	6.36	35	8.22	23	6.00
1873	1	4.92	6	7.44	48	6.36	35	8.52	23	6.90
1874	9	4.92	4	7.74	49	6.54	36	7.71	23	6.90
1875	8	4.50	5	9.33	49	6.15	34	6.78	23	6.30
1876	9	4.50	5	8.58	51	6.36	36	6.78	24	6.30
1877	7	4.02	4	8.22	57	5.76	47	6.12	23	5.70
1878	6	4.02	6	8.17	56	6.00	49	6.30	25	5.70
1879	5	4.02	7	8.52	59	6.06	53	6.06	31	5.70
1880	6	4.02	6	9.00	61	5.82	51	5.91	9	5.70
1881	6	4.80	6	9.10	65	5.76	51	6.12	7	5.40
1882	6	5.10	8	7.32	65	6.60	66	5.88	20	5.70
1883	5	5.10	8	8.58	65	5.70	57	6.00	25	5.70
1884	5	4.50	8	7.98	65	5.40	61	6.24	27	6.00
1885	6	4.02	9	6.90	63	5.40	53	5.88	28	4.80
1886	5	4.56	9	7.44	61	5.34	55	5.67	27	4.80
1887	8	4.80	11	7.20	66	5.58	52	6.60	28	5.10
1888	9	4.80	11	6.72	73	5.64	62	6.42	35	5.10
1889	9	4.80	12	6.90	75	6.12	63	6.78	32	5.70
1890	9	4.80	13	6.72	69	6.96	53	7.02	40	5.70
1891	9	4.80	14	6.30	72	6.30	59	7.20	45	6.30

Table 79: ESTABLISHMENT 43. - CONTINUED #2

	SPINNERS		WARPERS		WINDERS		WEAVERS			
	WOMEN		WOMEN		WOMEN		WOMEN		MEN	
	No.	Wage	No.	Wage	No.	Wage	No.	Wage	No.	Wage
1840	..	..	..	..	..	..	..	..	..	..
1841	..	..	..	..	..	..	..	..	..	..
1842	..	..	..	..	..	..	..	..	..	..
1843	..	..	..	..	..	..	..	..	..	..
1844	..	..	..	..	..	..	..	..	..	..
1845	..	..	..	..	..	..	..	..	..	..
1846	..	..	..	..	..	..	..	..	..	..
1847	..	..	..	..	..	..	..	..	..	..
1848	16	$3.78	12	$4.80	41	$4.20	..	..	..	..
1849	15	3.00	9	5.10	30	3.90	83	$5.40	6	$5.28
1850	18	4.32	33	5.40	83	3.72	199	5.28	11	6.30
1851	21	2.82	31	4.68	85	3.30	221	3.96	6	5.58
1852	10	3.18	27	4.50	75	3.18	232	3.84	8	5.04
1853	16	3.18	35	4.50	84	2.70	240	3.78	17	4.98
1854	15	3.36	24	4.98	69	2.88	196	3.60	23	4.86
1855	17	3.36	30	4.98	85	2.88	200	4.05	30	5.34
1856	17	3.36	34	3.78	105	3.12	164	4.20	65	5.70
1857	17	3.36	37	3.90	97	3.30	144	4.38	73	5.76
1858	17	3.36	29	4.02	90	3.30	110	4.68	69	6.06
1859	17	3.36	32	4.80	104	3.60	118	4.26	90	5.58
1860	19	3.36	26	4.38	103	3.36	115	4.32	85	5.58
1861	10	3.54	27	4.38	99	3.60	98	4.26	108	5.58
1862	10	3.54	20	5.82	61	4.08	120	4.38	82	5.40
1863	6	3.54	11	5.40	43	4.08	88	4.62	23	5.40
1864	16	3.90	18	4.56	44	4.08	115	4.38	35	5.52
1865	20	4.80	20	4.80	49	4.80	140	5.79	40	7.20

Table 80: ESTABLISHMENT 43. - CONTINUED #3

| | SPINNERS | | WARPERS | | WINDERS | | WEAVERS | | | |
| | WOMEN | | WOMEN | | WOMEN | | WOMEN | | MEN | |
	No.	Wage	No.	Wage	No.	Wage	No.	Wage	No.	Wage
1866	26	5.70	35	6.30	82	5.88	196	7.14	85	9.30
1867	26	6.00	37	6.30	83	6.12	171	8.10	106	9.90
1868	22	6.00	30	7.80	77	6.42	137	7.62	139	9.18
1869	26	6.00	35	8.10	85	6.48	152	7.56	121	9.72
1870	37	6.00	37	7.20	86	6.42	138	7.74	36	9.48
1871	21	7.50	36	8.76	85	7.74	148	8.25	154	10.68
1872	22	7.50	36	9.39	86	7.44	151	9.36	142	11.46
1873	22	7.50	36	9.30	86	8.10	150	8.94	159	11.04
1874	23	6.90	20	9.54	92	7.41	144	8.40	164	10.20
1875	22	6.30	16	9.48	98	6.72	143	7.80	190	9.60
1876	22	6.30	18	10.38	104	6.00	148	8.16	199	9.90
1877	28	5.70	24	7.17	137	5.76	183	6.72	255	8.16
1878	27	5.70	25	7.20	143	5.76	172	7.26	272	8.52
1879	24	6.00	25	6.72	137	5.76	175	7.14	298	8.04
1880	28	6.00	27	6.90	141	5.88	172	7.08	303	7.86
1881	22	6.60	32	6.39	149	5.73	196	6.90	296	7.38
1882	28	5.70	38	6.42	163	6.24	245	6.78	351	7.56
1883	25	6.00	35	7.20	153	6.00	240	7.14	320	8.28
1884	28	5.10	35	6.12	147	6.00	246	6.54	316	7.56
1885	29	4.20	35	5.76	148	5.58	258	6.30	303	7.14
1886	40	4.50	37	5.10	147	5.64	291	5.94	296	7.02
1887	43	4.80	36	6.18	149	5.64	287	6.84	330	8.10
1888	75	5.40	39	5.70	171	5.88	357	6.84	346	8.04
1889	83	5.40	36	6.00	168	6.90	393	6.96	388	7.86
1890	70	5.10	31	7.80	158	6.18	359	7.02	372	8.34
1891	74	5.40	36	7.74	169	6.30	384	7.26	372	8.52

Appendix D - Early Corporation Rules and Regulations

I. POIGNAUD AND PLANT BOARDING HOUSE AT LANCASTER[369]

(Decade 1820-30)

Rules and Regulations to be attended to and followed by the Young Persons who come to Board in this House:

Rule first: Each one to enter the house without unnecessary noise or confusion, and hang up their bonnet, shawl, coat, etc., etc., in the entry.

Rule second: Each one to have their place at the table during meals, the two which have worked the greatest length of time in the Factory to sit on each side of the head of the table, so that all new hands will of course take their seats lower down, according to the length of time they have been here.

Rule third: It is expected that order and good manners will be preserved at table during meals — and at all other times either upstairs or down.

---

[369] From the collection of Poignaud and Plant papers in the Lancaster Town Library. There is no date in this paper, but it clearly belongs to the decade 1820-30. For an account of these boarding houses see Chapter VII, "Early Mill Operatives: Conditions of Life and Work."

Rule fourth: There is no unnecessary dirt to be brought into the house by the Boarders, such as apple cores or peels, or nut shells, etc.

Rule fifth: Each boarder is to take her turn in making the bed and sweeping the chamber in which she sleeps.

Rule sixth: Those who have worked the longest in the Factory are to sleep in the North Chamber and the new hands will sleep in the South Chamber.

Rule seventh: As a lamp will be lighted every night upstairs and placed in a lanthorn, it is expected that no boarder will take a light into the chambers.

Rule eighth: The doors will be closed at ten o'clock at night, winter and summer, at which time each boarder will be expected to retire to bed.

Rule ninth: Sunday being appointed by our Creator as a Day of Rest and Religious Exercises, it is expected that all boarders will have sufficient discretion as to pay suitable attention to the day, and if they cannot attend to some place of Public Worship they will keep within doors and improve their time in reading, writing, and in other valuable and harmless employment.

II. THE LOWELL MANUFACTURING COMPANY'S RULES AND REGULATIONS

(Decade 1830-40)[370]

The overseers are to be punctually in their Rooms at the starting of the Mill, and not to be absent unnecessarily during working hours. They are to see that all those employed in their Rooms are in their places in due season; they may grant leave of absence to those employed under them, when there are spare hands in the Room to supply their places; otherwise they are not to grant leave of absence, except in cases of absolute necessity.

All persons in the employ of the Lowell Manufacturing Company are required to observe the Regulations of the overseer of the Room where they are employed; they are not to be absent from work without his consent, except in cases of sickness, and then they are to send him word of the cause of their absence.

---

[370]From the appendix to Seth Luther, "Address to the Working Men of New England" (pamphlet, 3d ed., Philadelphia, 1836).

They are to board in one of the Boarding-Houses belonging to the Company, and to conform to the regulations of the House where they board; they are to give information at the Counting-Room, of the place where they boards when they begin; and also give notice whenever they change their boarding-place.

The Company will not employ any one who is habitually absent from public worship on the Sabbath.

It is considered a part of the engagement that each person remains twelve months if required; and all persons intending to leave the employment of the Company are to give two weeks' notice of their intention to their Overseer, and their engagement is not considered as fulfilled unless they comply with this Regulation.

The Pay Roll will be made up to the last Saturday of every month, and the payment made to the Carpet Mill the following Saturday, and the Cotton Mill the succeeding Tuesday, when every person will be expected to pay their board.

The Company will not continue to employ any person who shall be wanting in proper respect to the females employed by the Company, or who shall smoke within the Company's premises, or be guilty of inebriety, or other improper conduct.

The Tenants of the Boarding-Houses are not to board or permit any part of their houses to be occupied by any person, except those in the employ of the Company.

They will be considered answerable for any improper conduct in their Houses, and are not to permit their Boarders to have company at unseasonable hours.

The doors must be closed at ten o'clock in the evening, and no person admitted after that time without some reasonable excuse.

The keepers of the Boarding-Houses must give an account of the number, names and employment of the Boarders when required, and report the names of such as are guilty of any improper conduct.

The Buildings, and yards about them, must be kept clean and in good order, and if they are injured otherwise than from ordinary use, all necessary repairs will be made and charged to the occupant.

It is desirable that the families of those who live in the Houses, as well as the Boarders, who have not had the Kine Pox, should be vaccinated; which will be done at the expense of the Company for such as wish it.

Some suitable chamber in the House must be reserved, and appropriated for the use of the sick, so that others may not be under the necessity of sleeping in the same room.

No one will be continued as a Tenant who shall suffer ashes to be put into any place other than the place made to receive them, or shall, by any carelessness in the use of fire, or lights, endanger the Company's property.

These regulations are considered a part of the contract with the persons entering into the employment of the Lowell Manufacturing Company.

III. CONDITIONS ON WHICH THE OPERATIVES OR "HELP" WERE HIRED BY THE COCHECO MANUFACTURING COMPANY OF DOVER, NEW HAMPSHIRE.

(Decade 1830-40)[371]

We, the subscribers, do thereby agree to enter the service of the Cocheco Manufacturing Company, and conform, in all respects, to the Regulations which are now, or may hereafter be adopted, for the good government of the Institution.

We further agree to work for such wages per week, and prices by the job, as the Company may see fit to pay, and be subject to the fines as well as entitled to the premiums paid by the Company.

We further agree to allow two cents each week to be deducted from our wages, for the benefit of the sick fund.

We also agree not to leave the service of the Company, without giving two weeks' notice of our intention, without permission of an agent; and if we do, we agree to forfeit to the use of the Company two weeks' pay.

We also agree not to be engaged in any combination, whereby the work may be impeded; if we do, we agree to forfeit to the use of the Company the amount of wages that may be due to us at the time.

We also agree that in case we are discharged from the service of the Company for any fault, we will not consider ourselves entitled to be settled within less than two weeks from the time of such discharge.

Payments for labor performed are to be made monthly.

---

[371] From the appendix to Seth Luther, "Address to the Working Men of New England," 1836.

Appendix E - List of Occupations in Which Women Were Reported to be Employed 1900

The list of occupations in the "Twelfth Census" contained 303 separate employments; in 295 of which women are found. These are as follows:[372]

AGRICULTURAL PURSUITS

Agricultural laborers.
    Farm and plantation laborers.
    Farm laborers (members of family).
    Garden and nursery laborers.
Dairymen and dairywomen.
Farmers, planters and overseers.
    Farmers and planters.
    Farmers (members of family).
    Farm and plantation overseers.
    Milk farmers
Gardeners, florists, nurserymen, etc.
    Gardeners.

---

[372]"Twelfth Census: Occupations," Table I, p. 8.

Florists, nurserymen, and vinegrowers.
Fruit growers.
Lumbermen and raftsmen.
Stock raisers, herders, and drovers.
Stock raisers.
Stock herders and drovers.
Turpentine fanners and laborers.
Woodchoppers.
Other agricultural pursuits.
Apiarists.
Not specified.

PROFESSIONAL SERVICE

Actors, professional showmen, etc.
Actors.
Professional showmen.
Theatrical managers, etc.
Architects, designers, draughtsmen, etc.
Architects.
Designers, draughtsmen, and inventors.
Artists and teachers of art. Clergymen.
Dentists.
Electricians.
Engineers (civil, etc.) and surveyors.
Engineers (civil).
Engineers (mining).
Surveyors.
Journalists.
Lawyers.
Literary and scientific persons.
Authors and scientists.
Librarians and assistants.
Chemists, assayers, and metallurgists.
Musicians and teachers of music
Officials (government).
Officials (National government).
Officials (state government).
Officials (county government).
Officials (city or town government).

Physicians and surgeons.
Teachers and professors in colleges, etc.
    Teachers.
    Professors in colleges and universities.
Other professional service.
    Veterinary surgeons.
    Not specified.

DOMESTIC AND PERSONAL SERVICE

Barbers and hairdressers.
Bartenders.
Boarding and lodging-house keepers.
Hotel keepers.
Housekeepers and stewards.
Janitors and sextons.
    Janitors.
    Sextons.
Laborers (not specified).
    Elevator tenders.
    Laborers (coal yard).
    Laborers (general).
    Longshoremen.
    Stevedores.
Launderers and laundresses.
    Laundry work (hand).
    Laundry work (steam).
Nurses and midwives.
    Nurses (trained).
    Nurses (not specified).
Midwives.
Restaurant keepers.
Saloon keepers.
Servants and waiters.
    Servants.
    Waiters.
Watchmen, policemen, firemen, etc.
    Watchmen, policemen and detectives.
Other domestic and personal service.
    Bootblacks.

Hunters, trappers, guides and scouts.
Not specified.

TRADE AND TRANSPORTATION

Agents.
  Agents (insurance and real estate).
  Agents (not specified).
Bankers and brokers.
  Bankers and brokers (money and stocks).
  Brokers (commercial).
Boatmen and sailors.
  Boatmen and canalmen.
  Pilots.
  Sailors.
Bookkeepers and accountants.
Clerks and copyists.
  Clerks and copyists.
  Clerks (shipping).
  Letter and mail carriers.
Commercial travelers.
Draymen, hackmen, teamsters, etc.
  Draymen, teamsters, and expressmen.
  Carriage and hack drivers.
Foremen and overseers.
  Foremen and overseers (livery stable).
  Foremen and overseers (steam railroad).
  Foremen and overseers (street railway).
  Foremen and overseers (not specified).
Hostlers.
Hucksters and peddlers.
Livery-stable keepers.
Merchants and dealers (except wholesale).
  Boots and shoes.
  Cigars and tobacco.
  Clothing and men's furnishings.
  Coal and wood.
  Drugs and medicines.
  Dry goods, fancy goods and notions.
  General store.

263

Groceries.
Liquors and wines.
Lumber.
Produce and provisions.
Not specified.
Merchants and dealers (wholesale).
Messengers and errand and office boys.
Bundle and cash boys.
Messengers.
Office boys.
Officials of banks and companies.
Bank officials and cashiers.
Officials (insurance and trust companies, etc.).
Officials (trade companies).
Officials (transportation companies).
Packers and shippers.
Porters and helpers (in stores, etc.).
Salesmen and saleswomen.
Steam railroad employees.
Baggagemen.
Brakemen.
Conductors.
Engineers and firemen.
Laborers.
Station agents and employees.
Switchmen, yardmen and flagmen.
Stenographers and typewriters.
Stenographers.
Typewriters.
Street-railway employees.
Conductors.
Laborers.
Motormen.
Station agents and employees.
Telegraph and telephone linemen.
Telegraph and telephone operators.
Telegraph operators.
Telephone operators.
Undertakers.

OTHER PERSONS IN TRADE AND TRANSPORTATION

Auctioneers.
Decorators, drapers, and window dressers.
Newspaper carriers and newsboys.
Weighers, gangers and measurers.
Not specified.

MANUFACTURING AND MECHANICAL PURSUITS

BUILDING TRADES

Carpenters and joiners.
    Carpenters and joiners.
    Ship carpenters.
    Apprentices and helpers.
Masons (brick and stone).
    Masons.
    Masons' laborers.
    Apprentices and helpers.
Painters, glaziers and varnishers.
    Painters, glaziers and varnishers.
    Painters (carriages and wagons).
    Apprentices and helpers.
    Paperhangers.
Plumbers and gas- and steamfitters.
    Plumbers and gas- and steamfitters.
    Apprentices and belpers. Plasterers.
Plasterers.
    Apprentices and belpers.
Roofers and slaters.
    Roofers and slaters.
Mechanics (not otherwise specified).

CHEMICALS AND ALLIED PRODUCTS

Oil-well and oil-works employees
    Oil-well employees.
    Oil-works employees.
Other chemical workers.
    Chemical works employees.
    Fertilizer makers.
    Powder and cartridge makers.
    Salt-works employees.
    Starch makers.

CLAY, GLASS, AND STONE PRODUCTS

Brick- and tilemakers.
    Brickmakers.
    Tilemakers.
    Terra-cotta workers.
Glass workers.
Marble- and stonecutters.
Potters

FISHING AND MINING

Fishermen and oystermen.
Miners and quarrymen.
    Miners (coal).
    Miners (gold and silver).
    Miners (not otherwise specified).
    Quarrymen.

FOOD AND KINDRED PRODUCTS

Bakers.
Butchers.
Butter- and cheesemakers.
Confectioners.
Millers.
Other food preparers.
    Fish curers and packers.
    Meat and fruit canners and preservers.
    Meat packers, curers and picklers.

Sugarmakers and refiners.
Not specified.

IRON AND STEEL AND THEIR PRODUCTS

Blacksmiths.
    Blacksmiths.
    Apprentices and helpers.
Iron and steel workers.
    Iron and steel workers.
    Molders.
Machinists.
    Machinists.
    Apprentices and helpers.
Steam-boiler makers.
    Steam-boiler makers.
Stove-, furnace- and gratemakers.
Tool- and cutlerymakers.
Wheelwrights.
Wireworkers.

LEATHER AND ITS FINISHED PRODUCT

Boot- and shoemakers and repairers.
    Boot and shoe factory operatives.
    Shoemakers (not in shoe factory).
    Apprentices.
Harness- and saddlemakers and repairers.
Leather curriers and tanners.
    Curriers.
    Tanners.
    Apprentices.
Trunk- and leather-case makers, etc.
    Trunkmakers.
    Leather-case and pocketbook makers.

LIQUORS AND BEVERAGES

267

Bottlers and soda-water makers, etc.
 Bottlers.
 Mineral and soda-water makers.
Brewers and maltsters.
Distillers and rectifiers.

LUMBER AND IT MANUFACTURES

Cabinetmakers.
Coopers.
Saw- and planing-mill employees.
 Saw- and planing-mill employees.
 Lumber-yard employees.
Other woodworkers.
 Basketmakers.
 Boxmakers (wood).
 Furniture manufacture employees.
 Piano- and organmakers.
 Not specified.

METAL AND METAL PRODUCTS OTHER THAN IRON AND STEEL

Brass workers.
 Brass workers.
 Molders.
Clock- and watchmakers, and repairers.
 Clock-factory operatives.
 Watch-factory operatives.
 Clock and watch repairers.
Gold and silver workers.
 Gold and silver workers.
 Jewelry manufactory employees.
Tinplate and tinware makers.
 Tinplate makers.
 Tinners and tinware makers.
 Apprentices (tinsmiths).
Other metal workers.
 Copper workers.
 Electroplaters.
Gunsmiths, locksmiths, and bell hangers.

Lead and zinc workers.
Molders (metals).
Not specified.

PAPER AND PRINTING

Bookbinders.
Boxmakers (paper).
Engravers.
Paper and pulp-mill operatives.
Printers, lithographers, and pressmen.
    Printers and pressmen.
    Lithographers.
    Compositors.
    Electrotypers and stereotypers.
    Apprentices (printers).

TEXTILES

Bleachery and dye-works operatives.
    Bleachery operatives.
    Dye-works operatives.
Carpet-factory operatives.
Cotton-mill operatives.
Hosiery and knitting-mill operatives.
Silk-mill operatives.
Woolen-mill operatives.
Other textile-mill operatives.
    Hemp and jute-mill operatives.
    Linen-mill operatives.
    Print-works operatives.
    Rope and cordage-factory operatives.
    Worsted-mill operatives.
    Textile not specified.
Dressmakers.
    Dressmakers.
    Apprentices.
Hat and capmakers.
    Milliners.
    Milliners.

269

Apprentices.
Seamstresses.
Shirt-, collar-, and cuffmakers.
Tailors and tailoresses.
    Tailors and tailoresses.
    Apprentices.
Other textile workers.
    Carpetmakers (rag).
    Lace and embroidery makers.
Sail-, awning-, and tentmakers.
Sewing-machine operators.
Not specified.

MISCELLANEOUS INDUSTRIES

Broom- and Brushmakers.
Charcoaly coke, and lime burners.
Engineers and firemen (not locomotive).
Glovemakers.
Manufacturers and officials, etc.
    Manufacturers and officials, etc.
    Builders and contractors.
    Publishers of books, maps and newspapers.
    Officials of mining and quarrying companies.
Model and pattern makers.
Photographers.
Rubber-factory operatives.
Tobacco- and cigar-factory operatives.
Upholsterers.
Other miscellaneous industries.
    Apprentices and helpers (not specified).
    Artificial flowermakers.
    Buttonmakers.
    Candle-, soap-, and tallowmakers.
    Corsetmakers.
    Cotton ginners.
    Electric light and power company employees.
Gasworks employees.
Piano and organ tuners.
    Straw workers.

Turpentine distillers.
Umbrella- and parasolmakers.
Well borers.
Whitewashers.
Not specified.

EMPLOYMENTS IN WHICH NO WOMEN ARE REPORTED

Soldiers (U.S.)
Sailors (U.S.)
Marines (U.S)
Street-car drivers.
Foremen (fire department).
Apprentices and helpers to roofers and slaters.
Helpers to steam-boiler makers.
Helpers to brass workers.

Appendix F - Trial Bibliography of Books and Magazine Articles relating to the industrial employment of women in England and America

ABRAHAM, MAY E. Report on the Conditions of Women's Work in the Textile Trades for the Royal Commission on Labour, 1893. Lond. (Gt. Brit. Parliament. C.-6894-xxiii.)

ADAMS, T. S., and SUMNER, H. L. *Labor Problems*, Chap, ii: "Woman and Child Labor." 4th ed. N. Y., 1907.

ABBOTT, EDITH. "English Working- Woman and the Franchise" *Atlantic*, cii: 343-6.

— "Municipal Employment of Unemployed Women in London," *Journal Political Economy*, xv: 513-30.

BARMAIDS: *Report of the Joint Committee on the Employment of Barmaids, Lond.*, 1905.

BELL, LADY. *At the Works: A Study of a Manufacturing Town.* Lond., 1907.

BLACK, CLEMENTINA. "London's Tailoresses," *Economic Journal,* xiv: 655-67.

— "Trade Schools for Girls in London," *Economic Journal,* zvi: 449-54.

— AND MRS. CARL MEYER. *Makers of Our Clothes: A Case for Trade Boards.* Lond., 1909.

BOSANQUET, HELEN. "A Study in Women's Wages," *Economic Journal,* xii: 42-49.

— *The Standard of Life,* pp. 157-174, "Industrial Training of Women." Lond., 1898.

BOUCHERETT, JESSIE AND BLACKBURN, HELEN. *The Condition of Working Women and the Factory Acts,* Lond, 1896.

BRANDEIS, LOUIS D. *Curt Miller vs. State of Oregon.* Brief for Defendant. (Supreme Court of the United States, October Term, 1907.) N. Y., 1908.

BRECKINRIDGE, SOPHONISBA P. "Legislative Control of Women's Work," *Journal of Political Economy* , xiv: 107-9.

— SOPHONISBA P., and ABBOTT, EDITH. "Employment of Women in Industries: Twelfth Census," *Journal Political Economy,* xiv: 14-40.

BUTLER, ELIZABETH B. "Working Women of Pittsburgh," *Charities,* xx: 433-49, 649-63, 648-64. xxi: 34-47, 570-80, 1117-42.

CADBURY, E., MATHESON, G., and SHANN, E. *Women's Work and Wages in Birmingham,* Chicago, 1907.

CAMPBELL, HELEN. *Prisoners of Poverty.* Bost, 1889.

— *Prisoners of Poverty Abroad.* Bost., 1890.

— *Women Wage-Earners.* Bost., 1893.

CLARK,   V. S. "Woman and Child Wage-Earners in Great Britain,"
           United States Labor Bulletin, No. 80 : 1-86.

COLLET,   CLARA E. "Women's Work in Leeds," *Economic Jour-
           nal,* i: 460-73.

—   *Report on Changes in the Employment of Women and
           Oirls in Industrial Centres.* Pt. i. *Flax and Jute Mills.*
           Lond., 1898. (Board of Trade, Labour Dept. C. 8794.)

—   Report on Conditions of Women's Labour in London,
           Liverpool, Manchester, and other Provincial Towns for
           the Royal Commission on Labour, 1893. Lond. (Gt.
           Brit. Parliament. C.-6894-xxiiL)

COLLET,   CLARA E. *Report by Miss Collet on the Statistics of Em-
           ployment of Women and Girls.* Lond., 1894. (Board of
           Trade, Labour Department, C 7564.)

—   *Report on the Money Wages of Domestic Servants.* Lond.,
           1899. (Board of Trade, Labour Department.) C. 9346.

—   "Women's Work," in Booth, *Life and Labour in London,*
           iv.

—   "The Collection and Utilization of Official Statistics bear-
           ing on the Extent and Effects of the Industrial Employ-
           ment of Women," *Royal Statistical Society Journal,* Ixi:
           219-60.

—   "The Social Status of Women Occupiers," *Royal Statis-
           tical Society Journal,* Ixxi : 513-515.

—   *Educated Working Women,* Lond., 1902.

DENDY,   H. "The Position of Women in Industry," in B. Bosan-
           quet, *Aspects of the Social Problem,* pp. 82- 103. Lond.,
           1895.

DRAGE,   GEOFFRET. *The Labor Problem,* Chap, v., "The Em-
           ployment of Women." Lond., 1896.

EATON,   ISABEL. "Receipts and Expenditure of Certain Wage-
           Earners in the Garment Trade," *American Statistical So-
           ciety Publications,* iv: 135-80.

GAREAUD, C. H. "Women as Telegraphists," *Economic Journal*, zi: 251-61.

GOLDMARK, J. C., "Workingwomen and the Laws," *American Academy Annals*, xxviii: 261-76.

— "Labor Legrislation for Women," *American Journal of Sociology*, xi: 312-25.

HAMMOND, M. B. "Woman's Wages in Manual Work," *Political Science Quarterly*, xv: 508-35.

HARRISON, AMY. *Women's Work in Liverpool. Liverpool University Pre*

HERRON, BELVA M. *Progress of Labor Organization Among Women, Urbana*, 1908. (Univ. of Illinois studies V. 1, No. 10.)

HOBHOUSE, EMILY. "Dust Women," *Economic Journal*, x: 411-20.

HOBSON, JOHN A. *Evolution of Modern Capitalism*, Chap, xii, "Women in Modern Industry." Lond., 1904.

— *Problems of Poverty*, Chap, viii, "Industrial Condition of Women Workers." Lond., 1906.

HOLYOAKE, EMILIE B. "Need of Organization Among Women," in F. W. Galton, *Workers on their Industries*.

HUTCHINS, B. L. "Salaries and Hours of Work of Typists and Shorthand Writers," *Economic Journal*, xvi: 445-49.

— "Note on The Distribution of Women in Occupations," *Royal Statistical Society Journal*, lxvii: 479-490.

— "Statistics of Women's Life and Employment," *Royal Statistical Society Journal*, lxxii: 205-48.

— "Employment of Women in Paper Mills," *Economic Journal*, xiv: 235-48.

— and HARRISON, A. *A History of Factory Legislation*. Lond., 1903.

IRWIN,   MARGARET H. *Home Work Amongst Women. Report of an Inquiry Conducted for the Glasgow Council for Women's Trades,* Pt. I, "Shirtmaking, Shirt finishing and Kindred Trades," Pt II, "Miscellaneous Minor Trades," Glasgow, 1897.

—   Report on Women's Industries in Scotland, for the Royal Commission on Labour, 1893. Lond. (Gt. Brit. Parliament. C.-6894-xxiii.)

IRWIN,   MARGARET H. *Women's Employment in Shops, Report of an Inquiry Conducted for the National Federated Council for Women's Trades,* Lond, 1894.

JEVONS, W. S. *Methods of Social Reform,* pp. 156-180, "Married Women in Factories." Lond., 1883.

KELLEY   FLORENCE. *Some Ethical Gains through Legislation.* N. Y., 1906.

—   "Women in Trade Unions," *Outlook,* lxxxiv: 926-31.

LAYTON, W. T. "Changes in the Wages of Domestic Servants during Fifty Years," *Royal Statistical Society Journal,* lxxi: 515-24.

LEVASSEUR, E. *The American Workman* (tr. by T. S. Adams), Chap, vii, "Wages of Women and Children." Baltimore, 1900.

MACDONALD, J. RAMSEY. *Women in the Printing Trades.* Lond., 1904.

MACLEAN, ANNIE MARION. "With Oregon Hop Pickers," *American Journal of Sociology,* xv: 83-96.

—   "Life in Pennsylvania Coal Fields, with Particular Reference to Women." *American Journal Sociology,* xiv: 329-61.

METER,   MRS. CARL, and BLACK, CLEMENTINA. *Makers of Our Clothes: a Case for Trade Boards.* Lond., 1909.

MIES, F. P., "Statutory Regulation of Women's Employment — Codification of Statutes," *Journal of Political Economy,* xiv: 109-18.

MITCHELL, JOHN. *Organized Labor,* Chap, xvi, "The Work of Women and Children." Phil, 1903.

NEW YORK ASSEMBLY. *Report and Testimony taken before the Special Committee of the Assembly Appointed to Investigate the Condition of Female Labor in the City of New York.* Albany, 1896.

OAKESHOTT, GRACE. "Women in the Cigar Trade in London," *Economic Journal,* x: 562-72.

ORME, ELIZA. Report on Women's Industries in the Black Country for Eoyal Commission on Labour, 1893. Lond. (Gt. Brit. Parliament. C.-6894-xxiii.)

OSGOOD, IRENE. "Women Workers in Milwaukee Tanneries" in Wisconsin Bureau of Labor and Industrial Statistics. *13th Biennial Report,* Pt. vii. Madison, 1909.

PEARSON, KARL. *The Chances of Death,* ii. Chap, vii, "Woman and Labor." Lond., 1897.

PEIXOTTO, JESSICA B. "Women of California as Trade Unionists," *Association of Collegiate Alumnos,* Dec. '08, pp. 40-49.

RICHARDSON, DOROTHY. *The Long Day,* N. Y., 1905.

— "Report of Committee on the Economic Effect of Legislation Regulating Women's Labour," *British Association for the Advancement of Science,* 1903.

SALMON, LUCY M. *Domestic Service.* New York, 1897.

SHACKLETON, D. J., Editor. *Woman in Industry From Seven Points of View.* Lond., 1908.

SMART, WILLIAM. *Studies in Economics,* Chap, iv, "Women's Wages." Lond., 1895.

SMITH, CONSTANCE. *The Case for Wage Boards.* Lond., 1908.

277

THOMAS, WILLIAM I. "Woman and the Occupations," *American Magazine*, lxviii: 463-70.

TUCKWELL, GERTRUDE M., and SMITH, CONSTANCE. *The Workers Handbook*. Lond., 1908.

UNITED STATES. Bureau of Labor. *Eleventh Annual Report* (1895), "Work and Wages of Men, Women and Children."

UNITED STATES. Bureau of Labor. *Fourth Annual Report* (1888), "Working Women in Large Cities."

— Index of all Reports issued by the Bureaus of Labor Statistics in the United States Prior to March 1, 1902. (Published by the Commissioner of Labor, 1902.)

VAN VORST, B. and M. *The Woman Who Toils*. N. Y., 1903.

WEBB BEATRICE. *The Case for the Factory Acts*. Lond., 1901.

WEBB, SIDNEY AND BEATRICE. *History of Trade-Unionism*. Lond., 1907.

— *Industrial Democracy*. Lond., 1902.

— *Problems of Modern Industry*. Lond., 1898.

WILLET, MABEL HURD. "Employment of Women in the Clothing Trades," *Columbia University Studies*, xvi: 169-257.

WILSON, MONA. *Our Industrial Laws. Working Women in Factories, Workshops and Laundries, and How to Help Them*. Lond., 1899.

— and WALKER, MARY L. *Report on Housing and Industrial Conditions in Dundee*, Chap, iii, "Employment and Wages"; Chap, iv, "Women's Labour and In- fant Mortality." Dundee, 1906.

WOOD, GEORGE H. "An Outline of the History of Women and Children in Lidustry." *Cooperative Wholesale Society Annual*. Manchester, 1904.

—   "Factory Legislation Considered with Kef erence to the Wages of the Operatives Protected Thereby," *Royal Statistical Society Journal*, lxv: 284-320.

WRIGHT, CARROLL D. *Industrial Evolution of the United States*, Chap, xvi, "Women in Industry." N. Y., 1895.

Periodicals and Other Publications of Organizations Concerned with Women's Work.

Annual Reports and Publications of the Women's Cooperative Guild (Kirby Lonsdale, Westmoreland, England.)
Annual Beports of the Women's Trade Union League of America (275 LaSalle Street, Chicago.) Beports of the Conferences, 1890 to date, and other Publications of the National Union of Women Workers. (Parliament Mansions, Victoria St., London, S. W.)
Publications of the Scottish Council of Women's Trades. (68 Benfield Street, Glasgow.)
Reports of Liveripool Women's Industrial Council (8, Sandon Terrace, Liverpool.)
The Englishwoman's Social and Industrial Review. The Women's Industrial News and other Publications of the Women's Industrial Council (7 John Street, Adelphi, London, W. C.)
The Women's Trade Union Review and other Publications of the Women's Trade Union League (Club Union Buildings, Clerkenwell Boad, London, E. C.)

Index

www.ingramcontent.com/pod-product-compliance
Lightning Source LLC
Chambersburg PA
CBHW060418100426
42812CB00030B/3228/J